Professional
iPhone™ and iPod® touch Programming

Professional
iPhone™ and iPod® touch
Programming

Building Applications for Mobile Safari™

Richard Wagner

WILEY

Wiley Publishing, Inc.

Professional iPhone™ and iPod® touch Programming: Building Applications for Mobile Safari™

Published by
Wiley Publishing, Inc.
10475 Crosspoint Boulevard
Indianapolis, IN 46256
www.wiley.com

ISBN: 978-0-470-25155-3

Manufactured in the United States of America

10 9 8 7 6 5 4 3 2 1

Library of Congress Cataloging-in-Publication Data is available from the publisher.

To Kim and the J-boys

About the Author

Richard Wagner is an experienced Web designer and developer as well as author of several Web-related books on the underlying technologies of the Mobile Safari platform. These books include *XSLT For Dummies*, *Creating Web Pages All-In-One Desk Reference For Dummies*, *XML All-In-One Desk Reference For Dummies*, *Web Design Before & After Makeovers*, and *JavaScript Unleashed* (1st, 2nd ed.). Before moving into full-time authoring, Richard was an experienced programmer and head of engineering. He was also inventor and chief architect of the award-winning NetObjects ScriptBuilder. A versatile author with a wide range of interests, he is also author of *The Myth of Happiness*. Richard can be located online at tech.digitalwalk.net.

About the Technical Editor

Ishan Anand is cofounder and developer for AppMarks.com, a Web desktop for iPhone. Prior to AppMarks, he worked at Digidesign, a division of Avid. Ishan has a B.S. in Computer Science, Electrical Engineering and Mathematics from M.I.T. He can be reached through his Web site at http://ishananand.com.

Credits

Executive Editor
Chris Webb

Development Editor
Kenyon Brown

Technical Editor
Ishan Anand

Copy Editor
Mildred Sanchez

Editorial Manager
Mary Beth Wakefield

Production Manager
Tim Tate

Vice President and Executive Group Publisher
Richard Swadley

Vice President and Executive Publisher
Joseph B. Wikert

Project Coordinator, Cover
Lynsey Stanford

Proofreader
Christopher M. Jones

Indexer
Johnna VanHoose Dinse

Contents

Contents

Contents

Contents

Acknowledgments

I extend a heartfelt tip of the hat to Kenyon Brown for his flawless management of this project. Thanks also to Ishan Anand for his technical insights and prowess, which made a strong impact on the accuracy and coverage of the book. Finally, I thank Chris Webb for getting this project off the ground and for his support throughout the process.

Introduction

The amazing success of iPhone and iPod touch is a clear indication that application developers are entering a brave new world of sophisticated, multifunctional mobile applications. No longer do applications and various media need to live in separate silos. Instead, applications on these Apple devices can bring together elements of Web 2.0 apps, traditional desktop apps, multimedia video and audio, and the cell phone.

Professional iPhone™ and iPod touch® Programming: Building Applications for Mobile Safari™ covers the various aspects of developing Web-based applications for the iPhone and iPod touch environments. Specifically, you will discover how to create a mobile application from the ground up, utilize existing open source libraries in your code, emulate the look and feel of built-in Apple applications, capture finger-touch interactions, using AJAX to load external pages, and optimize applications for Wi-Fi and the EDGE network.

Whom This Book Is For

This book is aimed primarily at Web developers already experienced in Web 2.0 technologies who want to build new applications for iPhone and iPod touch or migrate existing Web apps to this new platform. Readers should have a working knowledge of the following technologies:

- ❏ HTML/XHTML
- ❏ CSS
- ❏ JavaScript
- ❏ AJAX

What This Book Covers

Professional iPhone and iPod touch Programming introduces readers to the Web application platform for iPhone and iPod touch. The book guides readers through the process of building new applications from scratch and migrating existing Web 2.0 applications to this new mobile platform. As it does so, it helps readers design a user interface that is optimized for iPhone's touch-screen display and integrates their applications with iPhone services, including Phone, Mail, and Google Maps.

The chapter-level breakdown is as follows:

- ❏ **Chapter 1, "Introducing the iPhone and iPod touch Development Platform":** Explores the Mobile Safari development platform and walks you through the four ways you can develop for iPhone and iPod touch.

- ❏ **Chapter 2, "Designing an iPhone and iPod touch User Interface":** Provides an overview of the key design concepts and principles you need to use when developing a highly usable interface for Mobile Safari.

- ❑ **Chapter 3, "Implementing an iPhone Interface":** Provides a code-level look at developing an iPhone and iPod touch application interface.

- ❑ **Chapter 4, "Styling with CSS":** Discusses WebKit-specific styles that are useful for developing applications for iPhone and iPod touch.

- ❑ **Chapter 5, "Handling Touch Interactions and Events":** The heart of iPhone and iPod touch is its touch-screen interface. This chapter explores how to handle touch interactions and capture JavaScript events.

- ❑ **Chapter 6, "Advanced Programming Topics: Canvas and Video":** Discusses how the Mobile Safari browser provides full support for canvas drawing and painting, therefore opening up opportunities for developers. What's more, the built-in iPod for each mobile device enables tight video integration.

- ❑ **Chapter 7, "Integrating with iPhone Services":** Discusses how a Web application can integrate with core iPhone services, including Phone, Mail, and Google Maps.

- ❑ **Chapter 8, "Enabling and Optimizing Web Sites for iPhone and iPod touch":** Covers how to make an existing Web site compatible with Mobile Safari and how to optimize the site for use as a full-fledged application.

- ❑ **Chapter 9, "Bandwidth and Performance Optimizations":** Deals with the all-important issue of performance of Web-based applications and what techniques developers can use to minimize constraints and maximize bandwidth and app execution performance.

- ❑ **Chapter 10, "Packaging Apps as Bookmarks: Bookmarklets and Data URLs":** iPhone and iPod touch require applications to be based remotely. Well almost. This Chapter explains how you can use two little-used Web technologies to support limited offline support.

- ❑ **Chapter 11, "Case Studies: Beyond Edge-to-Edge Design":** Explores the creation of two applications that go beyond the basic edge-to-edge structure.

- ❑ **Chapter 12, "Testing and Debugging":** Discusses various methods of debugging Mobile Safari applications.

What You Need to Use This Book

In order to work with the examples of the book, you will need the following:

- ❑ iPhone or iPod touch (iPhone is needed for Chapter 7)
- ❑ Mobile Safari for Mac or Windows

The complete source code for the examples is available for download from this book's Web site at www.wrox.com.

Conventions

I have used several conventions throughout this book to help you get the most from the text.

- ❑ New terms are italicized when I introduce them.

- ❑ URLs and code within the text is given a monospaced font, such as `<div class="panel">`.

- ❑ Within blocks of source code, I occasionally want to highlight a specific section of the code. To do so, I use a gray background. For example:

```
addEventListener("load", function(event) {
    convertSrcToImage(0);
    photoEnabled = true;
    showPhoto(1);
    }, false);
```

Source Code

As you work through the examples in the book, you can type all of the code manually or download the source code files from the Wrox Web site (`www.wrox.com`). At the site, locate the book's detail page using Search or by browsing through the title listings. On the page, click the Download Code link and you are ready to go.

You may find it easiest to search by ISBN. This book's ISBN is **978-0-470-25155-3**.

Errata

The editors and I worked hard to ensure that the contents of this book are accurate and there are no errors either in the text or in the code examples. However, because of the fluid "early adaptor" nature of developing applications for iPhone and iPod touch right now, Apple is regularly updating the capabilities of the Mobile Safari browser. As a result, some things that worked at the time of writing might get broken, and some new functionality may be introduced that makes the life of the developer easier.

Therefore, to find the errata page for this book, go to `www.wrox.com` and locate its details page. Once on the book details page, look for the Book Errata link. You will be taken to a page that lists all errata that has been submitted for the book and posted by Wrox editors.

If you discover an issue that is not found on the errata page, I would be grateful for you to let us know about it. To do so, go to `www.wrox.com/contact/techsupport.shtml` and provide this information in the online form. The Wrox team will double-check your information and, as appropriate, post it on the errata page as well as correct the problem in future versions of the book.

Professional
iPhone™ and iPod® touch
Programming

Introducing the iPhone and iPod touch Development Platform

The introduction of the iPhone and subsequent unveiling of the iPod touch revolutionized the way people interacted with handheld devices. No longer did users have to use a keypad for screen navigation or browse the Web through "dumbed down" pages. These Apple devices brought touch screen input, a revolutionary interface design, and a fully functional Web browser right into the palms of people's hands. However, the question in the developer community in the months leading up to the release of the iPhone was: Will Apple allow third-party developers to develop custom applications for this new mobile platform? Apple's response was one that made Web developers happy and Objective-C programmers sad — iPhone and iPod touch applications would be Safari-based apps that are built using standard Web technologies. Apple opted for this solution as a way to provide developers with the freedom to create custom apps, all the while maintaining control of the user experience of these two devices.

Discovering the Mobile Safari Platform

An iPhone and iPod touch application runs inside of the built-in Safari browser that is based on Web standards, including:

- ❑ HTML/XHTML (HTML 4.01 and XHTML 1.9, XHTML mobile profile document types)
- ❑ CSS (CSS 2.1 and partial CSS3)
- ❑ JavaScript (ECMAScript 3, JavaScript 1.4)
- ❑ AJAX (e.g., XMLHTTPRequest)
- ❑ Ancillary technologies (video and audio media, PDF, and so on)

Safari on iPhone and iPod touch (which I refer to throughout the book as *Mobile Safari*) becomes the platform upon which you develop applications and becomes the shell in which your apps must operate (see Figure 1-1).

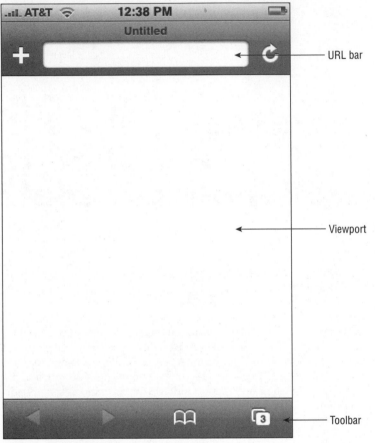

Figure 1-1: Mobile Safari user interface

Mobile Safari is built with the same open source WebKit browser engine as Safari for OS X and Safari for Windows. However, while the Safari family of browsers is built on a common framework, you'll find it helpful to think of Mobile Safari as a close sibling to its Mac and Windows counterparts, not an identical twin to either of them. Mobile Safari, for example, does not provide the full extent of CSS or JavaScript functionality that its desktop counterpart does.

In addition, Mobile Safari provides only a limited number of settings that users can configure. As Figure 1-2 shows, users can turn off and on support for JavaScript, plug-ins, and a pop-up blocker. Users can also choose whether they want to always accept cookies, accept cookies only from sites they visit, or never accept cookies. A user can also manually clear the history, cookies, and cache from this screen.

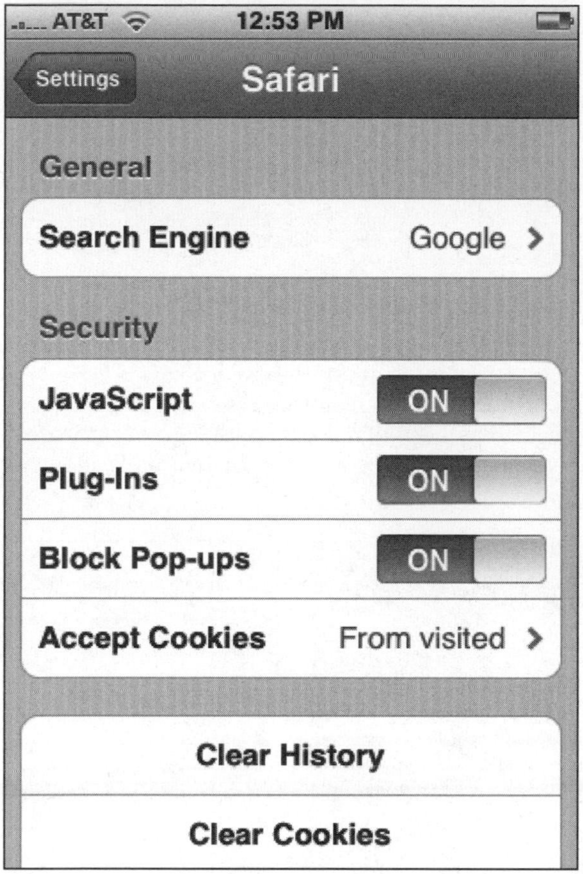

Figure 1-2: Mobile Safari preferences

Quite obviously, there are important differences between an iPhone/iPod touch application running inside of Mobile Safari and a native application. From a developer standpoint, the major difference is the programming language — utilizing Web technologies rather than Objective-C. However, there are also key end-user implications, including:

❑ *Performance:* The performance of a Safari-based application is not going to be as responsive as a native compiled application, both because of the interpretive nature of the programming languages as well as the fact that the application operates over Wi-Fi and EDGE networks. (Remember, iPod touch supports Wi-Fi access only.) However, in spite of the technological constraints, you can perform many optimizations to achieve acceptable performance. (Several of these techniques are covered in Chapter 10.)

Table 1-1 shows the bandwidth performance of Wi-Fi and EDGE networks.

Table 1-1: Network Performance

Network	Bandwidth
Wi-Fi	54 Mbps
EDGE	70–135 Kbps, 200 Kbps burst

❑　*Launching:* While the built-in applications are all launched from the main Springboard screen of the iPhone and iPod touch (see Figure 1-3), Web developers do not have access to this area for their applications. Instead, a user can only access your application by entering its URL or by selecting a bookmark from the Bookmarks list (see Figure 1-4). Unfortunately, there is absolutely nothing a Web developer can do to emulate the native application launch process.

Figure 1-3: Built-in applications launch from the main Springboard.

Figure 1-4: Web applications launch from the Bookmarks list.

❑ *User interface (UI):* The built-in iPhone and iPod touch applications adhere to very specific Apple UI design guidelines. As Chapters 3 and 4 explain in detail, you can closely emulate native application design using a combination of HTML, CSS, and JavaScript. The only constraint to complete emulation is the ever present bottom toolbar in Mobile Safari. Figures 1-5 and 1-6 compare the UI design of a native application and a Safari-based application.

Figure 1-5: Edge-to-edge navigation pane in the iPod app

Figure 1-6: Edge-to-edge navigation pane in a custom application

Four Ways to Develop for iPhone and iPod touch

A Web application that you can run in any browser and an iPhone/iPod touch application are certainly made using the same common ingredients — HTML, CSS, JavaScript, and AJAX — but they are not identical. In fact, there are four approaches to developing for iPhone and iPod touch:

❑ *Level 1: Fully compatible Web site/application:* The ground level approach is to develop a Web site/app that is "iPhone/iPod touch–friendly" and is fully compatible with the Apple mobile devices (see Figure 1-7). These sites avoid using technologies that the Apple mobile devices do not support, including Flash, Java, and other plug-ins. The basic structure of the presentation layer also maximizes use of blocks and columns to make it easy for users to navigate and zoom within the site. This basic approach does not do anything specific for iPhone/iPod touch users, but makes sure that there are no barriers to a satisfactory browsing experience. (See Chapter 8 for converting a Web site to be friendly for iPhone and iPod touch users.)

Figure 1-7: Site is easy to navigate.

❑ *Level 2: Web site/application optimized for Safari:* The second level of support for iPhone and iPod touch is to not only provide a basic level of experience for the Mobile Safari user, but also to provide an optimized user experience for users who use Safari browsers, such as utilizing some of the enhanced WebKit CSS properties supported by Safari.

❑ *Level 3: Dedicated iPhone/iPod touch Web site/application:* A third level of support is to provide a Web site tailored to the viewport dimensions of the iPhone and iPod touch and provide a strong

Web browsing experience for Apple device users (see Figures 1-8 and 1-9). However, while these sites are tailored for iPhone/iPod touch viewing, they do not always seek to emulate Apple UI design. And, in many cases, these are often stripped-down versions of a fuller Web site or application.

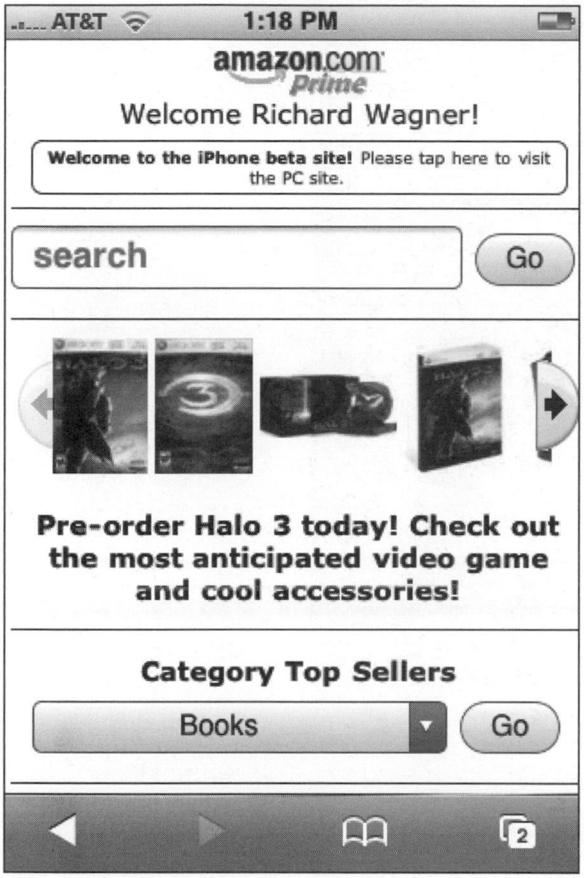

Figure 1-8: Amazon's iPhone site    Figure 1-9: Facebook closely emulates Apple UI design.

❑   *Level 4: Native-looking iPhone/iPod touch application:* The final approach is to provide a Web application that is designed exclusively for iPhone and iPod touch and closely emulates the UI design of native applications (see Figure 1-10). One of the design goals is to minimize user awareness that they are even inside of a browser environment. Moreover, a full-fledged iPhone application will, as is relevant, integrate with iPhone-specific services, including Phone, Mail, and Google Maps.

Therefore, as you consider your application specifications, be sure to identify which level of user experience you wish to provide iPhone and iPod touch users and design your application accordingly. In this book, I'll focus primarily on developing native-looking applications.

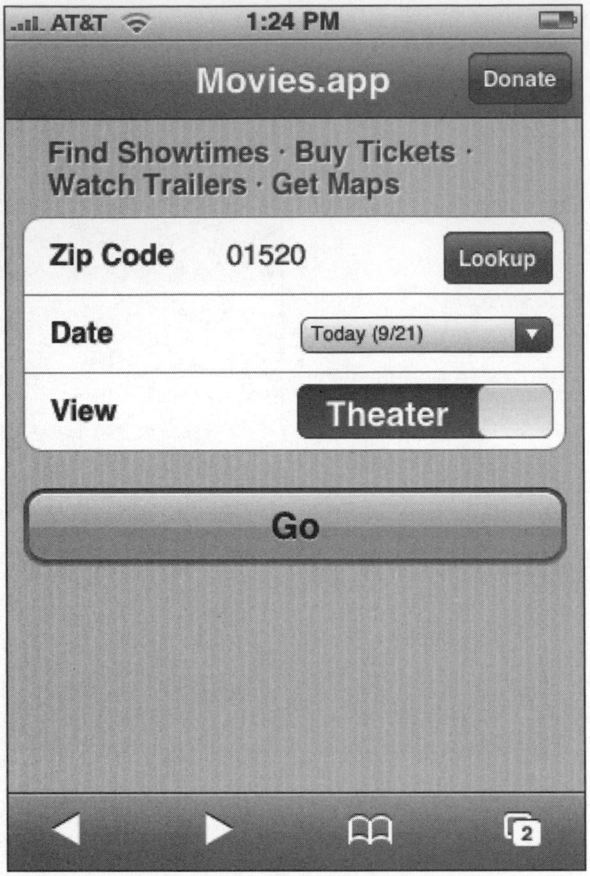

Figure 1-10: Application emulating Apple UI design

The Finger Is Not a Mouse

As you develop applications for iPhone and iPod touch, one key design consideration that you need to drill into your consciousness is that *the finger is not a mouse*. On the desktop, a user can use a variety of input devices — such as an Apple Mighty Mouse, a Logitech trackball, or a laptop touchpad. But, on screen, the mouse pointer for each of these pieces of hardware is always identical in shape, size, and behavior. However, on iPhone and iPod touch, the pointing device is always going to be unique. Ballerinas, for example, will probably input with tiny, thin fingers, while NFL players will use big, fat input devices. Most of the rest of us will fall somewhere in between. Additionally, fingers are also not nearly as precise as mouse pointers are, making interface sizing and positioning issues very important, whether you are creating an iPhone/iPod touch–friendly Web site or a full-fledged iPhone/iPod touch application.

Additionally, finger input does not always correspond to a mouse input. A mouse has a left click, right click, scroll, and mouse move. In contrast, a finger has a tap, flick, drag, and pinch. However, as an application developer, you will want to manage what types of gestures your application supports. Some of the gestures that are used for browsing Web sites (such as the double-tap zoom) are actually not something you want to support inside of an iPhone and iPod touch application. Table 1-2 displays the gestures that are supported on iPhone and iPod touch as well as an indication as to whether this type of gesture should be supported on a Web site or application. (However, as Chapter 5 explains in detail, you will not have programmatic access to managing all of these inputs inside of Mobile Safari.)

Table 1-2: Finger Gestures

Gesture	Result	Web site	App
Tap	Equivalent to a mouse click	Yes	Yes
Drag	Moves around the viewport	Yes	Yes
Flick	Scrolls up and down a page or list	Yes	Yes
Double-tap	Zooms in and centers a block of content	Yes	No
Pinch open	Zooms in on content	Yes	No
Pinch close	Zooms out to display more of a page	Yes	No
Touch and hold	Displays an info bubble	Yes	No
Two-finger scroll	Scrolls up and down an `iframe` or element with CSS `overflow:auto` property	Yes	Yes

Finally, several mouse actions have no finger touch equivalents on iPhone and iPod touch. These include:

❑ No right-click

❑ No text selection

❑ No cut, copy, and paste

❑ No hover

❑ No drag-and-drop (though I offer a technique to roughly emulate it in Chapter 5)

Limitations and Constraints

Since iPhone and iPod touch are mobile devices, they are obviously going to have resource constraints that you need to be fully aware of as you develop applications. Table 1-3 lists the resource limitations and technical constraints. What's more, certain technologies (listed in Table 1-4) are unsupported, and you will need to steer away from them when you develop for iPhone and iPod touch.

Table 1-3: Resource Constraints

Resource	Limitation
Downloaded text resource (HTML, CSS, JavaScript files)	10MB
JPEG images	128MB (all JPEG images over 2MB are subsampled—decoding the image to 16x fewer pixels)
PNG, GIF, and TIFF images	8MB (in other words, `width*height*4<8MB`)
Animated GIFs	Less than 2MB ensures that frame rate is maintained (over 2MB, only first frame is displayed)
Non-streamed media files	10MB
PDF, Word, Excel documents	30MB and up (very slow)
JavaScript stack and object allocation	10MB
JavaScript execution limit	5 seconds for each top-level entry point (`catch` is called after 5 seconds in a `try/catch` block)
Open pages in Mobile Safari	8 pages

Table 1-4: Technologies not Supported by iPhone and iPod touch

Area	Technologies not supported
Web technologies	Flash media, Java applets, SOAP, XSLT, SVG, and Plug-in installation
Mobile technologies	WML
File access	Local file system access
Text interaction	Text selection, Cut/Copy/Paste
Embedded video	In-place video (tapping an embedded element will put iPhone/iPod touch into video playback mode)
Security	Diffie-Hellman protocol, DSA keys, self-signed certificates, and custom x.509 certificates
JavaScript events	Several mouse-related events (see Chapter 5)
JavaScript commands	`showModalDialog()`, `print()`
Bookmark icons	`.ico` files
HTML	`input type="file"`, tool tips
CSS	Hover styles, `position:fixed`

Accessing Files on a Local Wi-Fi Network

Since iPhone and iPod touch do not allow you to access the local file system, you cannot place your application directly onto the device itself. As a result, you need to access your Web application through another computer. On a live application, you will obviously want to place your application on a publicly accessible Web server. However, testing is another matter. If you have a Wi-Fi network at your office or home, I recommend running a Web server on your main desktop computer to use as your test server during deployment.

If you are running Mac OS X, you already have Apache Web server installed on your system. To enable iPhone and iPod touch access, go to System Preferences ➪ Sharing ➪ Services and turn the Personal Web Sharing option on (see Figure 1-11). When this feature is enabled, the URL for the Web site is shown at the bottom of the window. You'll use this base URL to access your Web files from iPhone or iPod touch.

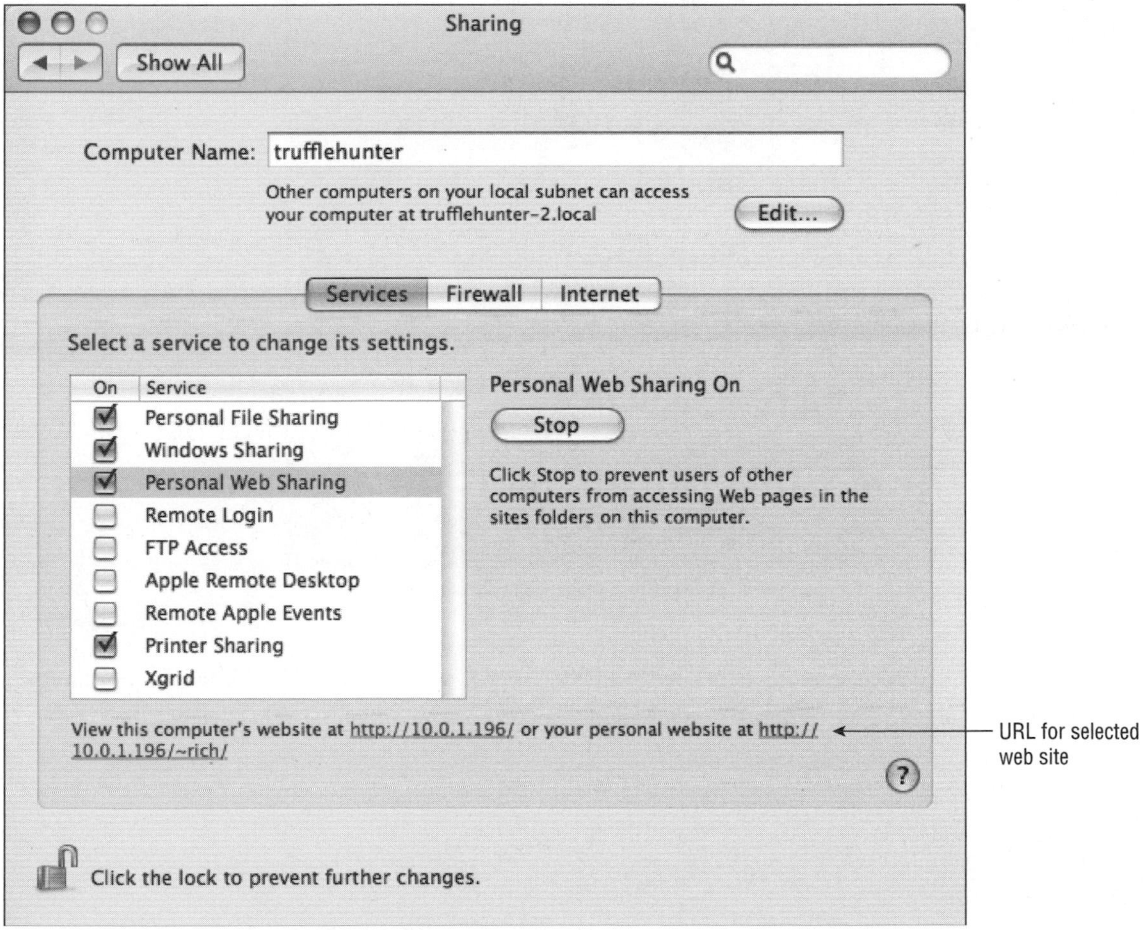

Figure 1-11: Turn on Personal Web Sharing.

You can add files either in the computer's Web site directory (`/Library/WebServer/Documents`) or your personal Web site directory (`/Users/`*YourName*`/Sites`) and then access them from the URL bar on your iPhone or iPod touch (see Figure 1-12).

Figure 1-12: Accessing desktop files from iPhone

If your users experience crashing or instability inside Mobile Safari, direct them to clear the cache by tapping the Clear Cache button in the Safari Settings pane.

Designing a User Interface

2

User interface design has been evolutionary rather than revolutionary over the past decade. Most would argue that Mac OS X and Windows Vista both have much more refined UIs than their predecessors. As true as that may be, their changes improve upon existing ideas rather than offer groundbreaking new ways of interacting with the computer. Web design is no different. All of the innovations that have transpired — such as AJAX and XHTML — have revolutionized the structure and composition of a Web site, but not how users interact with it. Moreover, mobile and handheld devices offered a variety of new platforms to design for, but these were either lightweight versions of a desktop OS or a simplistic character-based menu.

Enter iPhone and iPod touch.

An iPhone/iPod touch interface (I'll refer to it as an "iPhone interface" for short) is not a traditional desktop interface, though it is has a codebase closely based on Mac OS X. It is not a traditional mobile interface, though iPhone and iPod touch are mobile devices. Despite the fact that you build apps using Web technologies, an iPhone interface is not a normal Web application interface either. iPhone is clearly the first groundbreaking UI platform that many developers will have ever worked with.

Because the underlying guts of iPhone applications are based on Web 2.0 technologies, many Web developers will come to the iPhone platform and naturally think they are just creating a Web application that runs on a new device. That's why the biggest mindset change for developers is to grasp that they are creating iPhone applications, not Web applications that run on iPhone. The difference is significant. In many ways, iPhone applications are far more like Mac or Windows desktop applications — users have a certain look and feel and core functionality that they will expect to see in your iPhone application.

On the Web, users expect every interface design to be one-offs. Navigation, controls, and other functionality are unique to each site. However, when working on a platform — be it Windows, Mac OS X, or iPhone — the expectation is much different. Users anticipate a common way to do tasks — from application to application. Operating systems provide application program interfaces (APIs) for applications to call to display a common graphical user interface (GUI). Since the iPhone does not have such a concept, it is up to the application developer to implement such consistency.

This chapter will provide the high-level details and specifications you need to consider when designing a UI for iPhone. Chapter 4 continues on by diving into the actual code needed to implement these user interfaces.

The iPhone Viewport

A *viewport* is a rectangular area of screen space within which an application is displayed. Traditional Windows and Mac desktop applications are contained inside their own windows. Web apps are displayed inside a browser window. A user can manipulate what is seen inside of the viewport by resizing the window, scrolling its contents, and in many cases, changing the zoom level. The actual size of the viewport depends entirely on the user, though an average size for a desktop browser is roughly 1000 × 700 pixels.

The entire iPhone display is 320 × 480 pixels in portrait mode and 480 × 320 in landscape. However, application developers don't have access to all of that real estate. Instead, the viewport in which an iPhone developer is free to work with is a smaller rectangle: 320 × 416 in portrait mode without URL bar displayed (320 × 356 with the URL bar shown), and 480 × 268 in landscape mode (480 × 208 with URL bar). Figures 2-1 and 2-2 show the dimensions of the iPhone viewport in both orientations.

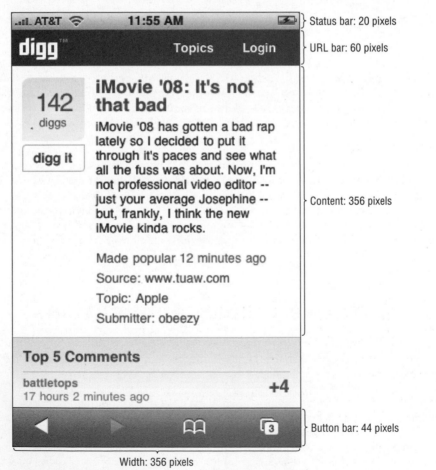

Figure 2-1: Portrait viewport

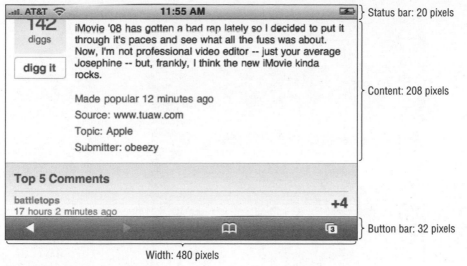

Figure 2-2: Landscape viewport

Users can scroll around the viewport with their fingers. However, they cannot resize it. To use desktop lingo, an iPhone application is always "maximized" and takes up the full available space.

If the on-screen keyboard is displayed, the visibility of the viewport is further restricted with the keyboard overlay, as shown in Figures 2-3 and 2-4.

Because users have a much smaller viewport than they are used to working with on their desktop, the iPhone viewport has a scale property that can be manipulated. When Mobile Safari loads a Web page, it automatically defines the page width as 980 pixels, a common size for most fixed width pages. It then scales the page to fit inside of the 320 or 480 pixel width viewport. While 980 pixels may be acceptable for browsing a scaled down version of ESPN.com or CNN.com, an iPhone application will almost certainly want to avoid this type of scaling by customizing the `meta viewport` element. You learn how this is done in Chapter 4.

Exploring Native iPhone Applications

Before you begin designing your iPhone application, a valuable exercise is exploring the built-in Apple applications that come with the iPhone right out of the box. As you do so, you can consider how Apple designers handled a small viewport as well as how to design an intuitive interface for touch screen input.

However, to fully appreciate the design decisions that went into these applications, you need to understand the differences in the way in which users use iPhone applications compared to their desktop

Figure 2-3: Forms in Portrait viewport

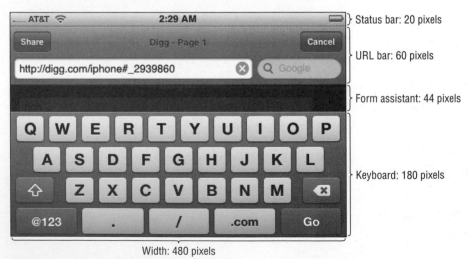

Figure 2-4: Landscape viewport

counterparts. After all, consider the types of applications that you will find installed on your desktop computer. An overly simplistic categorization is as follows:

❑ *Task-based applications:* The typical desktop application, whether it is on Mac, Windows, or Linux, is designed to solve a particular problem or perform a specific task. These applications, (such as Word, Excel, PowerPoint, Photoshop, or iCal) tend to act upon one file or a few files at a time. The UI for these applications is often quite similar, including a top-level menu, toolbar, common dialogs for open/save, main destination window, and side panels.

❑ *Aggregators:* The second category of desktop application is aggregators — those applications that manage considerable amounts of data and you tend to work with many pieces of data at a time rather than just one or two. iTunes manages your songs and videos. iPhoto and Picasa manage your photos, and Outlook and Apple Mail store your emails. The UI for aggregator applications is typically navigation-based, consisting of top-level navigable categories in a left-side panel (playlists in iTunes, folders in Mail, albums in iPhoto) and scrolling listings in the main window.

❑ *Widgets:* A third category is "widget" style applications, which are mini applications that display system or other information (battery status meter, weather, world clock), or perform a very specific task (lyrics grabber, radio tuner). A widget UI typically consists of a single screen and a settings pane.

On the desktop, task-based applications have traditionally been the dominant category, though aggregators have become more and more important over the past decade with the increasing need to manage digital media. While widgets are quite popular now that Apple and Microsoft have added this functionality directly into their OS, they remain far less important.

When you look at built-in iPhone applications, you can see that they generally fall into these three categories as well. However, because of iPhone's viewport and file storage constraints, task-based applications take a back seat role to the aggregators (see Table 2-1).

Table 2-1: Categorizing Apple's iPhone Applications

Aggregators	Task-based	Widgets
Mail	Safari	Stocks
SMS	Phone	Weather
Photos	Camera	Clock
YouTube	Calendar	Calculator
Notes	Maps	
Contacts (Address Book)		
iPod		

While the document is the primary point of focus in a traditional desktop application, a document is often consumable and non-permanent on the iPhone device. Most of the documents that users work with are consumable: Web pages, SMS messages, YouTube videos, quick notes, Google maps. Even Word, Excel, and Acrobat documents are read-only and only accessible as email attachments. What's more, for the more permanent storage pieces of information, you tend to sync with a master copy on your desktop — iPod songs, videos, and photos. In fact, there are only three cases in which you actually create data on the iPhone that you then store permanently — calendar appointments, emailed photos, and contacts.

The focus of iPhone usage is consuming information far more than creating information. If your application conforms to this usage model, your UI design needs to account for that reality.

Navigation List–Based UI Design

Since the focus of the iPhone is to consume various amounts of information, navigation list–based design becomes an essential way to present large amounts of information to users. As I mentioned earlier, desktop applications typically relegate navigation lists to a side panel on the left of the main window, but many iPhone applications use "edge-to-edge" navigation as the primary driver of the UI.

Not all navigation list designs are equal. In fact, the iPhone features at least eight distinct varieties of navigation lists. For example, the Contacts list uses a single line to display the name of a contact in bold letters (see Figure 2-5), whereas Mail uses a 4-line list style to display both message header information and optional text preview (see Figure 2-6). Finally, YouTube sports a wealth of information in its 2-line item (see Figure 2-7). Table 2-2 lists each of the various navigation style lists.

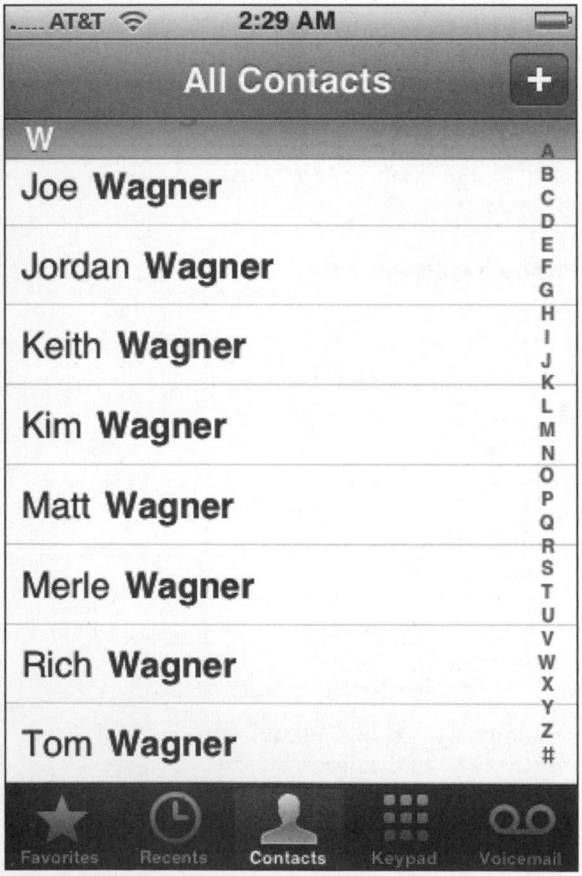

Figure 2-5: Contacts' 1-line navigation list

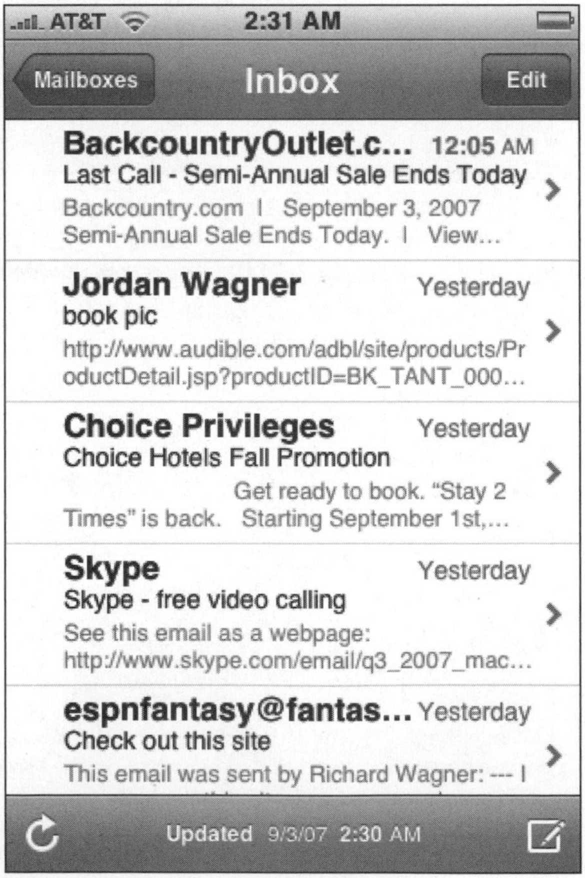

Figure 2-6: Mail's 4-line navigation list

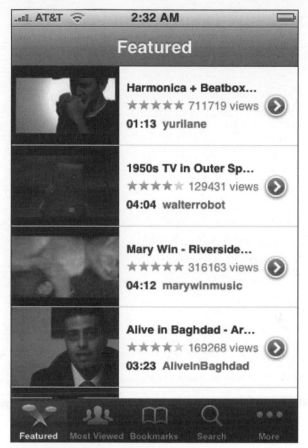

Figure 2-7: YouTube's 2-line navigation list

Table 2-2: Different Types of Navigation Lists

Application	Style	Displays
Contacts	1 line	Name of contact (last name bolded)
Mail	2.7 lines (default 4)	Message title and optional text preview
Google Maps List	2 lines	Location name, address
SMS	3 lines	Message title and text preview

Table continued on following page

Table 2-2 (*continued*)

Application	Style	Displays
Photos	1 line	Album title and thumbnail image
YouTube	3 lines	Thumbnail, title, rating, length, views, and submitter
Notes	1 line	First line of note text
iPod Playlists	1 line	Playlist name
Settings	1 line	Grouped items with icons

However, no matter the style of the navigation lists, they are each designed to quickly take you to a destination page in as few interactions as possible.

Application Modes

Built-in iPhone applications also often have modes or views to the information or functionality with which you can work. These modes are usually displayed as icons on the bottom toolbar (see Figure 2-8), although on exception they are displayed on the top toolbar (see Figure 2-9). Table 2-3 details these modes.

Therefore, as you begin to examine how the UI of your application should be designed, look to see what parallels there are with the built-in iPhone application design and emulate its general look and feel.

Screen Layout: Emulating Apple Design

By the time you have studied and evaluated the UI design of the built-in applications, you can then begin to determine what parallels may exist with the type of application in which you are building.

For applications that need to use a navigation list design, you will want to download Joe Hewitt's iUI framework. iUI enables you to easily implement edge-to-edge navigation list–based applications. iUI consists of a .css style sheet, a .js code library, and a set of images that can easily be integrated into your applications. (Chapter 4 discusses iUI in more detail.)

The four common components of a typical iPhone application are a titlebar, a navigation list, a destination page, and a button bar.

Titlebar

Most Safari-based iPhone applications will want to include a titlebar to emulate the look of the standard titlebar available in nearly all built-in iPhone applications. When the URL bar is hidden (and I explain

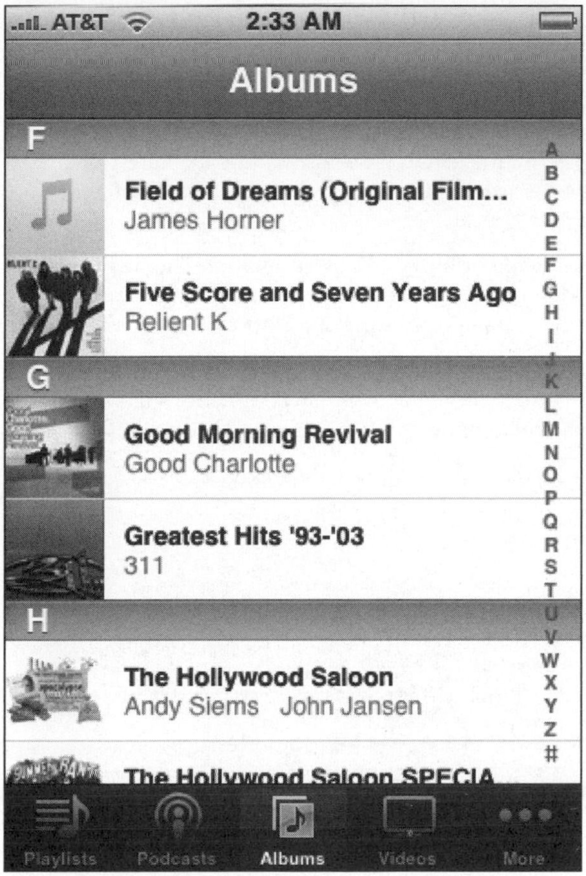

Figure 2-8: Bottom toolbar in iPod provides different views of a digital media library.

Figure 2-9: iCal puts its calendar views up on top.

Table 2-3: Application Modes and UI Access

Application	Modes	UI controls
iCal	List, Day, Month	Top toolbar
Phone	Favorites, Recents, Contacts, Keypad, Voicemail	Bottom toolbar
iPod	Playlists, Podcasts, Albums, Videos, and so on	Bottom toolbar
YouTube	Featured, Most Viewed, Bookmarks, Search	Bottom toolbar
Clock	World Clock, Alarm, Stopwatch, Timer	Bottom toolbar

how to do this in Chapter 4), then the custom titlebar will appear just below the status bar at the top of the viewport (see Figure 2-10). The titlebar includes the following elements:

❑ *Back button:* A back button should be placed on the left-hand side of the toolbar to allow the user to return to the previous page. The name of the button should be the same name as the title of the previous screen. This "bread crumbs" technique lets the user know how they got to the page and how to get back. If the page is at the top level of the application, then remove the back button completely.

❑ *Screen title:* Each screen should have a title displayed in the center of the toolbar. The title of the page should be one word and appropriately describe the content of the current screen. You will not want to include the application name in each screen title of the application, as you will for a standard Web application.

❑ *Command button:* For some screens, you will want to employ a common command, such as Cancel, Edit, Search, or Done. If you need this functionality, place a command button at the top right of the titlebar.

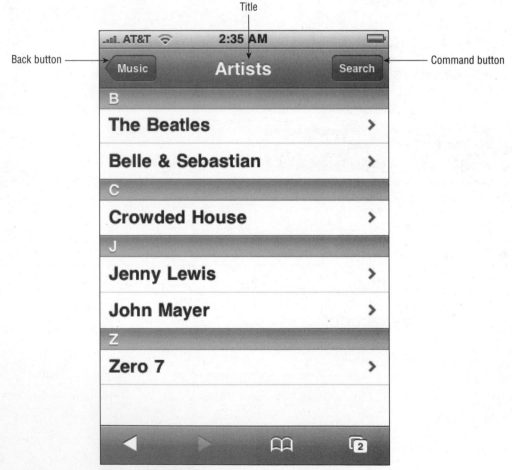

Figure 2-10: Titlebar

As discussed in Chapter 4, you will want to programmatically ensure that the titlebar stays in place whether iPhone is in portrait or landscape orientation.

Edge-to-Edge Navigation Lists

If your application aggregates or organizes lists of information, you will typically want your UI to emulate iPhone's edge-to-edge navigation list design, as shown in Figure 2-11. Each of the cells, or subsections, is extra large to allow for easy touch input. In addition, to ensure that a user never loses context and gets lost, the title shows the current page, while a back button indicates the screen in which the user can return to if they chose to. And, when a list item expands to a destination page or another list, an arrow is placed on the right side indicating a next page is available to the right.

When a list item is selected, the navigation list should emulate Apple's slide-in animation, appearing as if the new page is coming in from the right side of the screen replacing the old.

Table 2-4 lists each of the specific metrics to emulate the same look and feel of the Apple design in edge-to-edge navigation lists. Note that iUI defines navigation lists based on these specifications and also implements the slide-in animation effect.

Figure 2-11: Emulating Apple's edge-to-edge navigation design

Table 2-4: Metrics for Apple's Edge-to-Edge Design

Item	Value
Cell height (including bottom line)	44px
Cell width	320px (portrait), 480px (landscape)
Font	Helvetica, 20pt bold (normal text acceptable for less important text)
Font color	Black
Horizontal lines (between cells)	#d9d9d9 (RGB=217, 217, 217)
Left padding	10px
Bottom padding	14px
Control height	29px
Control alignment	Right, 10px
Control shape	Rounded Rectangle of 7-degree radius
Control text	Helvetica, 12pt
Background color	White

Rounded Rectangle Design Destination Pages

In a navigation list UI design, a user will ultimately wind up at a destination page that provides a full listing of the specific piece of information in which they were looking. Apple implements a rounded rectangle design, as shown in Figure 2-12. Labels are displayed on a blue background, while items are grouped together logically and surrounded by a rounded rectangle box. Table 2-5 describes the specifications you should follow to implement this Apple design.

Button Bar

While you can use a JavaScript technique to hide the URL bar, there is no way to programmatically hide the Mobile Safari bottom button bar (see Figure 2-13). Therefore, your application needs to account for the fact that these 44 pixels of real estate (32px in landscape) are dead weight to your application. Given that reality, emulating a black "mode/view bar" like the iPod application becomes much more challenging unless you want to eat up considerable space to controls.

Designing for Touch

One of the most critical design considerations you need to take into account is that that you are designing an interface that will interact with a finger, not a mouse or other mechanical pointing device. While a mouse pointer has a small point just a couple pixels in height, a finger can touch 40 pixels or

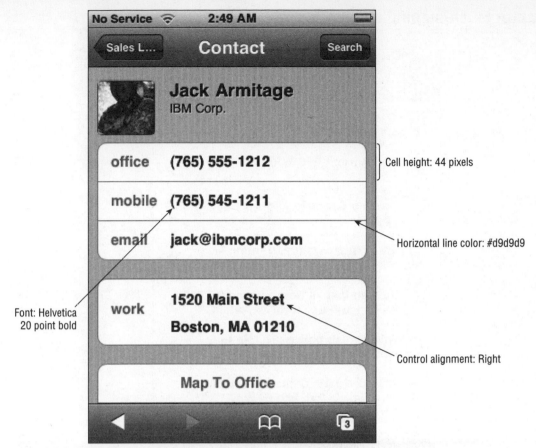

Figure 2-12: Implement rounded rectangle design for destination pages.

Table 2-5: Metrics for Apple's Rounded Rectangle Design

Item	Value
Cell height	44px
Rounded rectangle corner radius	10px × 10px radius (-webkit-border-radius:10px)
Rounded rectangle left and right margins	10px
Rounded rectangle top and bottom margins	17px
Horizontal lines (between cells)	#d9d9d9 (RGB=217, 217, 217)
Label font	Helvetica 17pt, bold
Label font color	#4c566c (RGB=76, 86, 108)
Cell font	Helvetica 17pt, bold
Cell font color	Black
Cell text position	10px from left edge, 14px bottom edge
Background color	#c5ccd3 (RGB= 197, 204, 211)

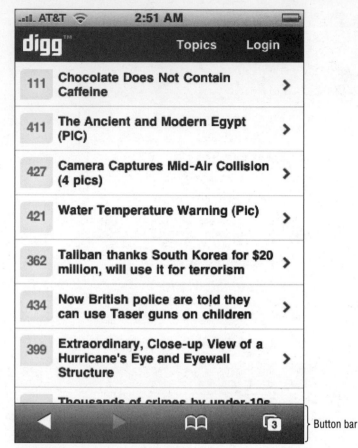

Figure 2-13: Like it or not, you are stuck with the bottom toolbar.

more of the screen during a typical click action. Therefore, when laying out controls in an application, make sure the height of controls and spacing between controls are easy to use even for someone with large fingers.

Since iPhone is a mobile device, keep in mind that users may be on the go when they are interacting with your application. Maybe they are walking down the street, waiting in line at Starbucks, or perhaps even jogging. Therefore, you will want to allow enough space in your UI to account for shaky fingers in those use case scenarios.

Standard navigation list cells should be 44px in height. Buttons should be sized about the size of a finger, typically 40px in height or more and have sufficient space around them to prevent accidental clicks. You can get by with a button of 29–30 pixels in height if no other buttons are around it, but be careful. Table 2-6 lists the recommended sizes of the common elements.

In addition to sizing and spacing issues, another important design decision is to minimize the need for text entry. Use select lists rather than input fields where possible. What's more, use cookies to remember last values entered to prevent constant data reentry.

Table 2-6: Metrics for Touch Input Screen

Element metric	Recommended size
Element height	40px (min. 29px)
Element width	Min. 30px
Select, Input height	30px
Navigation list cell height	44px
Spacing between elements	20px

Working with Fonts

With its 160 pixels-per-inch display and anti-aliasing support, iPhone is an ideal platform to work with typefaces. Quality fonts will render beautifully on the iPhone display, enhancing the overall attractiveness of your application's UI.

Helvetica, Apple's font of choice for iPhone, should generally be the default font of your application. However, iPhone does offer several font choices for the developer. Unlike a typical Web environment in which you must work with font families, iPhone allows you make some assumptions on the exact fonts that users will have when they run your application. Table 2-7 lists the fonts that are supported on iPhone.

Table 2-7: iPhone Fonts

Name	Example
American Typewriter (no italics)	Bold *Italic* and ***Bold Italic***
Arial	Bold *Italic* and ***Bold Italic***
Arial Rounded MT Bold (no italics)	**Bold** *Italic* and ***Bold Italic***
Courier New	Bold *Italic* and ***Bold Italic***
Georgia	Bold *Italic* and ***Bold Italic***

Table continued on following page

Table 2-7 (*continued*)

Name	Example
Helvetica	Bold *Italic* and ***Bold Italic***
Marker Felt	**Bold *Italic* and *Bold Italic***
Times New Roman	Bold *Italic* and ***Bold Italic***
Trebuchet MS	Bold *Italic* and ***Bold Italic***
Verdana	Bold *Italic* and ***Bold Italic***
Zapfino	*Bold Italic and Bold Italic*

Mobile Safari will automatically substitute three unsupported fonts with their built-in counterparts. Courier New is substituted when Courier is specified. Helvetica is substituted for Helvetica Neue, and Times New Roman is used in place of Times.

Best Practices in iPhone UI Design

When you are designing for iPhone, there are several best practices to keep in mind:

❑ *Remember the touch!* Perhaps no tip is more critical in iPhone UI design than always double-checking every design decision you make with the reality of touch input. For example, ESPN's Podcenter, shown in Figure 2-14, uses a UI that roughly simulates the Apple navigation list design. However, the rows are thinner, making it harder to touch the correct podcast item, especially if the user is walking or performing another physical activity.

❑ *Make sure you design your application UI to work equally well in portrait and landscape modes.* Some native applications, such as Mail, optimize their UI for portrait mode and ignore any changes the user makes to orientation. Third-party iPhone developers do not have that same level of control. Therefore, any UI design you create needs to work in both orientation modes.

❑ *Avoid UI designs that require horizontal scrolling.* If your interface design requires the user to scroll from side to side within a single display screen, change it. Horizontal scrolling is confusing to users and leaves them feeling disoriented within your application.

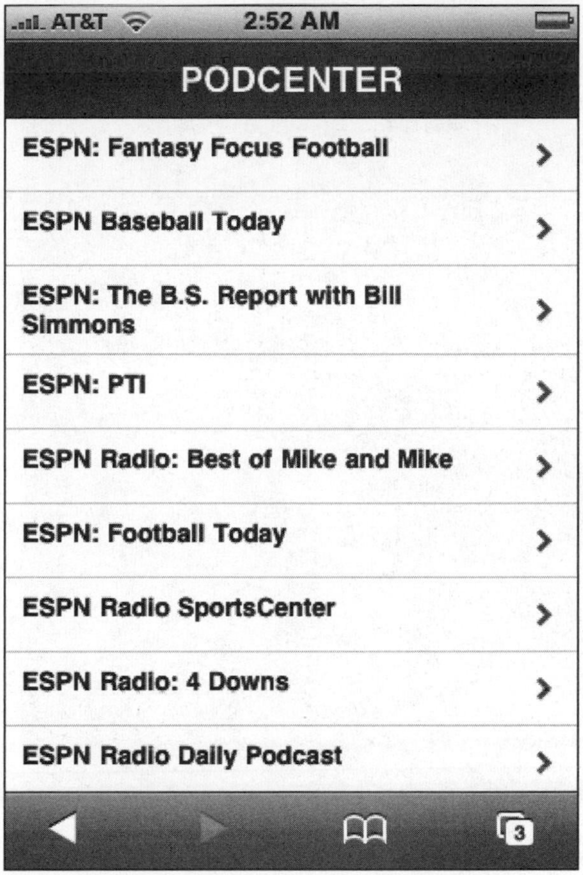

Figure 2-14: The shorter cells make it easy for fat
or shaky fingers to select the wrong choice.

❑ *Keep your design simple.* As attractive as the iPhone interface is, perhaps its most endearing quality is its ease of use and simplicity. Your UI design should follow suit. Avoid adding complexity where you do not need to — either in functionality or design (see Figure 2-15).

❑ *Use standard iPhone terminology.* You know the saying, "When in Rome..." Well, when designing for iPhone, be sure you do not bring along the UI baggage you are used to in the Windows, Mac, or the Web world. For example, "Preferences" are "Settings" and "OK" should be "Done."

❑ *Use iUI and other UI frameworks, but use them wisely.* The iUI framework is a major asset to the iPhone developer community and provides a major head start in developing applications. However, don't automatically assume that an edge-to-edge navigation list design is the best way to go for your application. You may find another approach is better for your specific needs.

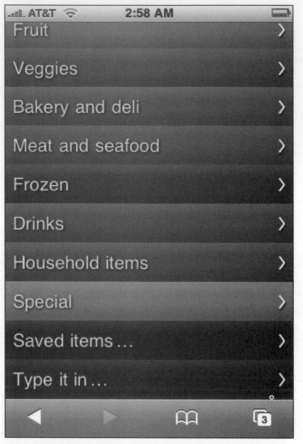

Figure 2-15: Multi-color list makes for hard reading.

❑ *Restrict use of a black button bar.* A translucent black button bar (such as the one used by the iPod app in Figure 2-8) should only be used in your application for displaying modes or views, not for commands. Use the other button types for commands.

❑ *Minimize the rabbit trail.* Because iPhone users are primarily concerned with consuming data, you will want to get them to their destination page as soon as possible. Therefore, make sure you are optimally organizing the information in a way that enables a user to get to the data they need in just a couple of flicks and clicks.

❑ *Place text entry fields at the top of the page.* When your application requires data entry fields, work to place these input fields as near to the top of the page as possible. Top positioning of text entry fields helps minimize the chances of the user losing context when the on-screen keyboard suddenly appears at the bottom of the screen when the user selects the field.

❑ *Communicate status.* Because your application may be running via an EDGE connection, its response may be slow. As a result, be sure to provide status to the user when performing a function that requires server processing. This visual clue helps users feel confident that your application is working as expected and is not in a hung state.

❑ *Label the titlebar appropriately.* Make sure each screen/page has its own title. The Back button should always be named the name of the previous screen.

❑ *Unselect previously selected items.* When a user clicks the Back button in a navigation-list UI, be sure that the previously selected item is unchecked.

❑ *Break the rules — competently.* While you should generally adhere to the Apple UI design guidelines that I've been discussing in this chapter, not every iPhone application UI needs to rigidly conform to a design implemented already by Apple. You may have an application in which a different look-and-feel works best for its target users. However, if you decide to employ a unique design, be sure it complements overall iPhone design, not clashes with it.

3

Implementing the Interface

The previous chapter surveyed the UI standards and guidelines that you need to keep in mind as you design an application that works well on iPhone and iPod touch. With these design principles in hand, you are ready to apply them as you develop and program your application.

In order to demonstrate how to implement an iPhone interface, I will walk you through a case study application I am calling iRealtor. The concept of iRealtor is to provide a mobile *house-hunter* application for potential buyers. The current pattern for Internet-based house hunting is to search MLS listings online, print out individual listing addresses, get directions, and then travel to these houses. However, with iRealtor, all of those tasks can be done on the road with an iPhone-based application. The design goals of iRealtor are to provide a way for users to:

❑ Browse and search the MLS listings of a local realtor.

❑ Get a map of an individual listing directly from its listing page.

❑ Access information about the realtor and easily contact the realtor using iPhone phone or mail services.

❑ Browse other helpful tools and tips.

As you look at these overall objectives, an edge-to-edge navigation design looks like an obvious choice given the task-based nature of the application. Joe Hewitt's iUI (`code.google.com/p/iui/`) will serve as the underlying framework for the user interface. iUI is designed to retrieve and format HTML fragments and automatically handle many application events, such as phone rotation. The realtor information will be relatively static, but the MLS listings will need to be database-driven. Therefore, you will take advantage of the AJAX capabilities of iUI to seamlessly integrate listing data into the application.

The initial version of iUI should be used only in iPhone and iPod touch–specific applications. It is not compatible with Internet Explorer, Firefox, and earlier versions of Safari for Mac.

Here's an overview of the technologies that will be used for iRealtor:

❑ XHTML/HTML and CSS for presentation layer

❑ JavaScript for client-side logic

❑ AJAX for loading data into the application

❑ PHP or other server-side technology to serve MLS listing data (not included in case study example)

As I walk you through the application, I'll examine both the custom code I am writing for iRealtor as well as the underlying iUI styles and code that power it. Therefore, even if you decide not to use iUI, then you at least will have a solid grasp on the key design issues you will need to consider.

Top Level of Application

The top level of iRealtor is best presented as an edge-to-edge navigation style list that contains links to the different parts of the application. When assembled, the design will look like what is shown in Figure 3-1.

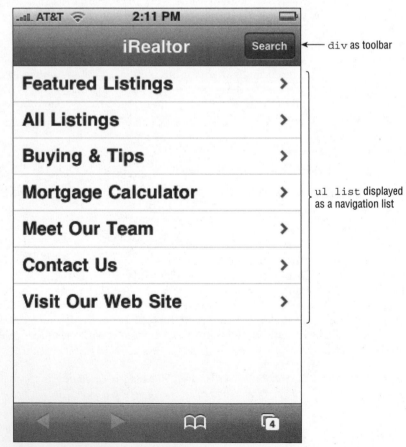

Figure 3-1: iRealtor top-level page

Creating Irealtor.html

To build the initial page, start off with a basic XHTML document, linking the iUI style sheet and scripting library files:

```
<!DOCTYPE html PUBLIC "-//W3C//DTD XHTML 1.0 Strict//EN"
          "http://www.w3.org/TR/xhtml1/DTD/xhtml1-strict.dtd">
<html xmlns="http://www.w3.org/1999/xhtml">
<head>
<title>iRealtor</title>
<meta name="viewport" content="width=device-width; initial-scale=1.0; maximum-
scale=1.0; user-scalable=0;"/>
<style type="text/css" media="screen">@import "../iui/iui.css";</style>
<script type="application/x-javascript" src="../iui/iui.js"></script>
</head>
<body>
</body>
</html>
```

The `viewport meta` tag tells Mobile Safari exactly how to scale the page and sets 1.0 scale and does not change layout on reorientation. It also specifies that the width of the viewport is the size of the device (`device-width` is a constant).

These properties ensure that iRealtor behaves like an application, not a Web page. (Chapters 2 and 8 provide additional details on the viewport.)

Examining Top-Level Styles in iui.css

The iui.css style sheet sets up several top-level styles. The `body` style sets up the default `margin`, `font-family`, and colors. It also uses `-webkit-user-select` and `-webkit-text-size-adjust` to ensure that iRealtor behaves as an application rather than a Web page. (See Chapter 4 for more on these `-webkit` styles.) Here's the definition:

```
body {
    margin: 0;
    font-family: Helvetica;
    background: #FFFFFF;
    color: #000000;
    overflow-x: hidden;
    -webkit-user-select: none;
    -webkit-text-size-adjust: none;
}
```

For iPhone/iPod touch applications, it is important to assign `-webkit-text-size-adjust: none` to override the default behavior.

All elements, except for the `.toolbar` class, are assigned the following properties:

```
body > *:not(.toolbar) {
    display: none;
    position: absolute;
    margin: 0;
    padding: 0;
    left: 0;
    top: 45px;
    width: 100%;
    min-height: 372px;
}
```

In landscape mode, the `min-height` changes for these elements:

```
body[orient="landscape"] > *:not(.toolbar) {
    min-height: 268px;
}
```

The `orient` attribute changes when the orientation of the viewport changes between portrait and landscape. You'll see how this works later in the chapter.

iUI uses a `selected` attribute to denote the current page of the application. From a code standpoint, the page is typically either a `div` or a `ul` list:

```
body > *[selected="true"] {
    display: block;
}
```

Links also are assigned the `selected` attribute:

```
a[selected], a:active {
    background-color: #194fdb !important;
    background-image: url(listArrowSel.png), url(selection.png) !important;
    background-repeat: no-repeat, repeat-x;
    background-position: right center, left top;
    color: #FFFFFF !important;
}
a[selected="progress"] {
    background-image: url(loading.gif), url(selection.png) !important;
}
```

The `a[selected="progress"]` style is used to display an animated GIF showing the standard iPhone loading animation.

Adding the Top Toolbar to irealtor.html

The first UI element to add is the top toolbar, which serves a common UI element throughout the application. To create the toolbar, use a `div` element assigning it the iUI `toolbar` class:

```
<!-- Top iUI toolbar -->
<div class="toolbar">
    <h1 id="pageTitle"></h1>
    <a id="backButton" class="button" href="#"></a>
    <a class="button" href="#searchForm">Search</a>
</div>
```

The h1 element serves as a placeholder for displaying the active page's title. The a backbutton is not shown at the top level of the application, but is used on subsequent pages to go back to the previous page. The Search button allows access to the search form anywhere within the application. Here are the corresponding style definitions in iui.css for each of these elements:

```
body > .toolbar {
        box-sizing: border-box;
    -webkit-box-sizing: border-box;
    -moz-box-sizing: border-box;
    border-bottom: 1px solid #2d3642;
    border-top: 1px solid #6d84a2;
    padding: 10px;
    height: 45px;
    background: url(toolbar.png) #6d84a2 repeat-x;
}
.toolbar > h1 {
    position: absolute;
    overflow: hidden;
    left: 50%;
    margin: 1px 0 0 -75px;
    height: 45px;
    font-size: 20px;
    width: 150px;
    font-weight: bold;
    text-shadow: rgba(0, 0, 0, 0.4) 0px -1px 0;
    text-align: center;
    text-overflow: ellipsis;
    white-space: nowrap;
    color: #FFFFFF;
}
body[orient="landscape"] > .toolbar > h1 {
    margin-left: -125px;
    width: 250px;
}
.button {
    position: absolute;
    overflow: hidden;
    top: 8px;
    right: 6px;
    margin: 0;
    border-width: 0 5px;
    padding: 0 3px;
```

(continued)

(continued)

```
        width: auto;
        height: 30px;
        line-height: 30px;
        font-family: inherit;
        font-size: 12px;
        font-weight: bold;
        color: #FFFFFF;
        text-shadow: rgba(0, 0, 0, 0.6) 0px -1px 0;
        text-overflow: ellipsis;
        text-decoration: none;
        white-space: nowrap;
        background: none;
        -webkit-border-image: url(toolButton.png) 0 5 0 5;
    }
    #backButton {
        display: none;
        left: 6px;
        right: auto;
        padding: 0;
        max-width: 55px;
        border-width: 0 8px 0 14px;
        -webkit-border-image: url(backButton.png) 0 8 0 14;
    }
```

The body > .toolbar class style is set to 45px in height. The .toolbar > h1 header emulates the standard look of an application caption when in portrait mode and body[orient="landscape"] > .toolbar > h1 updates the position for landscape mode. Notice that the limited width of the iPhone and iPod touch viewport dictate use of overflow:hidden and text-overflow:ellipsis.

Notice that the toolbar class includes both box-sizing *and* -webkit-box-sizing *definitions. Mobile Safari under iPhone 1.0 supported* box-sizing, *but 1.1.1 replaced support for that property with* -webkit-box-sizing *instead. For maximum compatibility, I recommend defining both.*

Adding a Top-Level Navigation Menu in irealtor.html

Once the toolbar is created, then the top-level navigation menu needs to be created. Under the iUI framework, use a ul list, such as the following:

```
<ul id="home" title="iRealtor" selected="true">
    <li><a href="featured.html">Featured Listings</a></li>
    <li><a href="listings.html">All Listings</a></li>
    <li><a href="tips.html">Buying & Tips</a></li>
    <li><a href="calc.html">Mortgage Calculator</a></li>
    <li><a href="#meet_our_team">Meet Our Team</a></li>
    <li><a href="contact_us.html">Contact Us</a></li>
    <li><a href="index.html" target="_self">Visit our Web Site</a></li>
</ul>
```

The title attribute is used by iUI to display in the toolbar's h1 header. The selected attribute indicates that this ul element is the active block when the application loads. Each of the menu items is defined as a link inside of li items. The href attribute can point to either another div or ul block inside of the same file (called a *panel*) using an anchor reference (such as #meet_our_team). Alternatively, you can also use AJAX to load a block element from an external URL. Table 3-1 displays the four types of links you can work with inside of iUI.

Table 3-1: iUI Link Types

Link type	Description	Syntax
Internal URL	Loads a panel that is defined inside of the same HTML page	`<a href="#meet_our_team">`
AJAX URL	Loads document fragment via AJAX	`<a href="listings.html">`
AJAX URL Replace	Loads document fragment via AJAX replacing contents of the calling link	`<a href="listings1.html" target="_replace">`
External URL	Loads external Web link	`<a href="index.html" target="_self">`

The styles for the list items and links are as follows:

```
body > ul > li {
    position: relative;
    margin: 0;
    border-bottom: 1px solid #E0E0E0;
    padding: 8px 0 8px 10px;
    font-size: 20px;
    font-weight: bold;
    list-style: none;
}
body > ul > li > a {
    display: block;
    margin: -8px 0 -8px -10px;
    padding: 8px 32px 8px 10px;
    text-decoration: none;
    color: inherit;
    background: url(listArrow.png) no-repeat right center;
}
```

Notice that the listArrow.png is displayed at the right side of the list item's a link.

Displaying a Panel with an Internal URL

If you are linking to another block section inside of the same page, then you simply need to add the code. For example, the Meet Our Team item links to the following `div`:

```
<div id="meet_our_team" class="panel" title="Meet Our Team">
    <h2>J-Team Reality</h2>
    <fieldset>
    <p class="normalText">Lorem ipsum dolor sit amet, consect etuer adipis cing
elit. Suspend isse nisl. Vivamus a ligula vel quam tinci dunt posuere. Integer
venen atis blandit est. Phasel lus ac neque. Quisque at augue. Phasellus purus. Sed
et risus. Suspe ndisse laoreet consequat metus. Nam nec justo vitae tortor
fermentum interdum. Aenean vitae quam eu urna pharetra ornare.</p>
    <p class="normalText">Pellent esque habitant morbi tristique senectus et
netus et malesuada fames ac turpis egestas. Aliquam congue. Pel lentesque pretium
fringilla quam. Integer libero libero, varius ut, faucibus et, facilisis vel, odio.
Donec quis eros eu erat ullamc orper euismod. Nam aliquam turpis. Nunc convallis
massa non sem. Donec non odio. Sed non lacus eget lacus hend rerit sodales.</p>
    </fieldset>
</div>
```

The `id` attribute value of the block element is identical to the `href` value of the source link (except for the # sign). The `div` element is assigned the `panel` class, and the `title` attribute supplies the new page title for the application. Inside of the `div` element, the h2 element provides a header, while the `fieldset` element, which is commonly used as a container inside of iUI destination pages, is used to house the content. Figure 3-2 displays the results (based in part on additional styles that will be described shortly).

The `panel` class and `fieldset` styles are shown in the following code. In addition, the default h2 style is provided (though I will be updating this style in my own irealtor.css file):

```
body > .panel {
    box-sizing: border-box;
    -webkit-box-sizing: border-box;
    padding: 10px;
    background: #c8c8c8 url(pinstripes.png);
}
.panel > fieldset {
    position: relative;
    margin: 0 0 20px 0;
    padding: 0;
    background: #FFFFFF;
    -webkit-border-radius: 10px;
    border: 1px solid #999999;
    text-align: right;
    font-size: 16px;
}
.panel > h2 {
    margin: 0 0 8px 14px;
    font-size: inherit;
    font-weight: bold;
    color: #4d4d70;
    text-shadow: rgba(255, 255, 255, 0.75) 2px 2px 0;
}
```

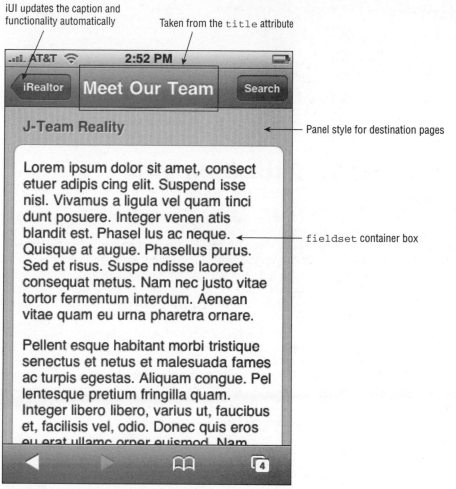

Figure 3-2: Destination page

The panel class property displays the vertical pinstripes, which is a standard background for iPhone and iPod touch applications. The fieldset, used primarily for displaying rows, is used because it provides a white background box around the text content the page will display. However, because the iui.css styles did not display the margin/padding properties of h2 or p text as I needed it to, I linked irealtor.html with a new style sheet by placing the following declaration *below* the iui.css declaration:

```
<style type="text/css" media="screen">@import "irealtor.css";</style>
```

Inside of irealtor.css, the following styles are defined:

```
.panel p.normalText {
    text-align: left;
    padding: 0 10px 0 10px;
}
.panel > h2 {
    margin: 3px 0 10px 10px;
}
```

Displaying AJAX Data from an External URL

You could create an entire iPhone/iPod touch application inside of a single HTML page using internal links. However, this single-page approach breaks down when you begin to deal with large amounts of data. Therefore, iUI enables you to break up your application into chunks, yet still maintain the same integrated look and feel of a single page app. When you use AJAX, iUI allows you to load content into your application on demand by providing an external URL. However, the document that is retrieved needs to be a document fragment, not a complete HTML page.

iUI fully encapsulates XMLHttpRequest() for you. Therefore, when you supply an external URL in a link that does not have target="_self" defined, it will retrieve the document fragment and display it within iUI.

In iRealtor, tapping the Featured Listings menu item (<li><a href="featured.html">Featured Listings</a></li>) should display a list of special homes that are being featured by this fictional local realtor. The contents of the file named featured.html are shown below:

```
<ul id="featuredListings" title="Featured">
<li><a href="406509171.html">30 Bellview Ave, Bolton</a></li>
<li><a href="306488642.html">21 Milford Ave, Brandon</a></li>
<li><a href="326425649.html">10 Main St, Leominster</a></li>
<li><a href="786483624.html">12 Smuggle Lane, Marlboro</a></li>
<li><a href="756883629.html">34 Main Ave, Newbury</a></li>
<li><a href="786476262.html">33 Infinite Loop, Princeton</a></li>
<li><a href="706503711.html">233 Melville Road, Rutland</a></li>
<li><a href="767505714.html">320 Muffly, Sliver</a></li>
<li><a href="706489069.html">1 One Road, Zooly</a></li>
</ul>
```

The result is a basic navigation list, as shown in Figure 3-3. Each list item specifies a unique URL in which iUI will load using AJAX when selected. You'll see this MLS listing destination page shortly.

The All Listings menu item illustrates some additional capabilities that you can add to a navigation list. Figure 3-4 displays the additional details added to the navigation list item, including a thumbnail picture and summary details in a second line.

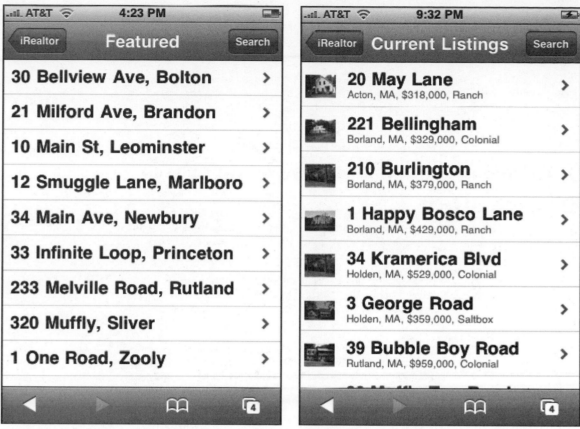

Figure 3-3: Listing data coming from AJAX   Figure 3-4: Enhanced navigational menu items

The document fragment that is loaded via AJAX is as follows:

```
<ul id="listings" title="Current Listings">
<li>
    <img class="listingImg" src="images/406509171-sm.png"/>
    <a class="listing" href="406509171.html">20 May Lane</a>
    <p class="listingDetails">Acton, MA, $318,000, Ranch</p>
</li>
<li>
    <img class="listingImg" src="images/306488642-sm.png"/>
    <a class="listing" href="306488642.html">221 Bellingham</a>
    <p class="listingDetails">Borland, MA, $329,000, Colonial</p>
</li>
<li>
    <img class="listingImg" src="images/326425649-sm.png"/>
    <a class="listing" href="326425649.html">210 Burlington</a>
    <p class="listingDetails">Borland, MA, $379,000, Ranch</p>
</li>
<li>
    <img class="listingImg" src="images/786483623-sm.png"/>
```

(continued)

(continued)

```
            <a class="listing" href="786483624.html">1 Happy Bosco Lane</a>
            <p class="listingDetails">Borland, MA, $429,000, Ranch</p>
    </li>
    <li>
            <img class="listingImg" src="images/756883629-sm.png"/>
            <a class="listing" href="756883629.html">34 Kramerica Blvd</a>
            <p class="listingDetails">Holden, MA, $529,000, Colonial</p>
    </li>
    <li>
            <img class="listingImg" src="images/786476262-sm.png"/>
            <a class="listing" href="786476262.html">3 George Road</a>
            <p class="listingDetails">Holden, MA, $359,000, Saltbox</p>
    </li>
    <li>
            <img class="listingImg" src="images/706503711-sm.png"/>
            <a class="listing" href="706503711.html">39 Bubble Boy Road</a>
            <p class="listingDetails">Rutland, MA, $959,000, Colonial</p>
    </li>
    <li>
            <img class="listingImg" src="images/767505713-sm.png"/>
            <a class="listing" href="767505714.html">98 Muffin Top Road</a>
            <p class="listingDetails">Rutland, MA, $99,000, Ranch</p>
    </li>
    <li>
            <img class="listingImg" src="images/706489069-sm.png"/>
            <a class="listing" href="706489069.html">1291 Blackjack Lane</a>
            <p class="listingDetails">Zambo, MA, $159,000, Saltbox</p>
    </li>
    </ul>
```

Each element inside of the li element has a class style assigned to it. The following CSS styles are located in the irealtor.css file:

```
a.listing {
    padding-left: 54px;
    padding-right: 40px;
    min-height: 34px;
}
img.listingImg {
    display: block;
    position: absolute;
    margin: 0;
    left: 6px;
    top: 7px;
    width: 35px;
    height: 27px;
    padding: 7px 0 10px 0;
}
p.listingDetails {
    display: block;
    position: absolute;
    margin: 0;
    left: 54px;
    top: 27px;
```

```
    text-align: left;
    font-size: 12px;
    font-weight: normal;
    color: #666666;
    text-decoration: none;
    width: 100%;
    height: 13px;
    padding: 3px 0 0 0;
}
```

The `img.listingImg` class positions the thumbnail at the far left side of the item. The `p.listingDetails` class positions the summary text just below the main link.

Designing for Long Navigation Lists

While a document fragment such as the one shown previously works fine for small amounts of data, the performance would quickly drag with long lists. To deal with this issue, iUI allows you to break large lists into manageable chunks by loading an initial set of items, and then providing a link to the next set (see Figure 3-5). This design emulates the way the iPhone Mail application works with incoming messages.

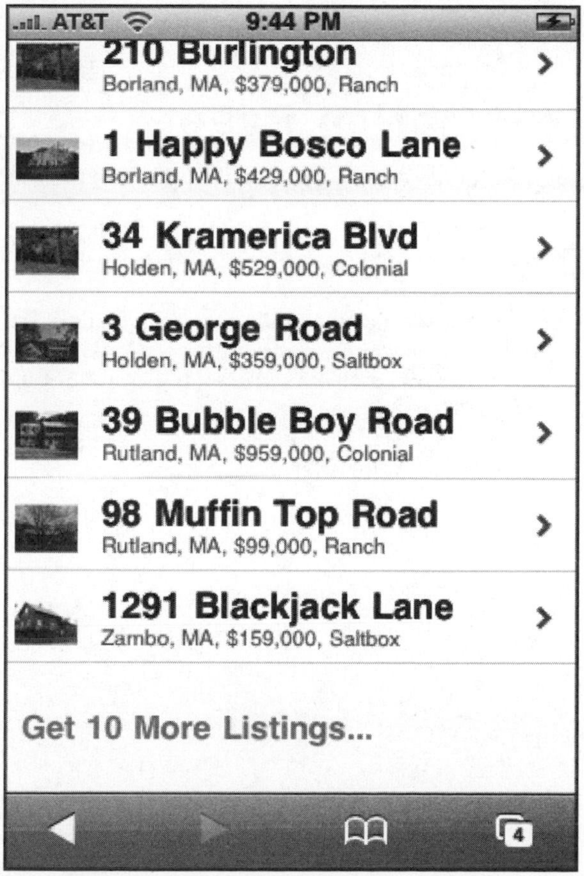

Figure 3-5: Loading additional listing

To provide this functionality in your application, create a link and add `target="_replace"` as an attribute. iUI will load the items from the URL replacing the current link. As with other AJAX links, the URL needs to point to a document fragment, not a complete HTML file. Here's the link added to the bottom of the listings `ul` list:

```
<li><a href="listings1.html" target="_replace">Get 10 More Listings...</a></li>
```

When using the `target="_replace"` attribute, you need to use a fragment of a `ul` element and not a different structure. For example, the following document fragment is valid to use with a `_replace` request:

```
<li>item 1</li>
<li>item 2</li>
<li>item 3</li>
```

However, the following document fragment would not be correct because it is not valid inside of a `ul` element:

```
<ul>
<li>item 1</li>
<li>item 2</li>
<li>item 3</li>
</ul>
```

Creating a Destination Page

Each of the MLS listings in iRealtor has its own individual destination page that is accessed by an AJAX-based link, such as:

```
<a class="listing" href="406509171.html">20 May Lane</a>
```

The design goal of the page is to provide a picture and summary details of the house listing. But, taking advantage of iPhone's services, you also want to add a button for looking up the address in the Map app and an external Web link to a site providing town information. Figures 3-6 and 3-7 show the end design for this destination page.

The document fragment for this page is as follows:

```
<div title="20 May Lane" class="panel">
  <div>
    <img src="images/406509171.png"/>
  </div>
  <h2>Details</h2>
  <fieldset>
      <div class="row">
        <label>mls #</label>
        <p>406509171</p>
      </div>
```

```
      <div class="row">
        <label>address</label>
        <p>20 May Lane</p>
      </div>
      <div class="row">
        <label>city</label>
        <p>Acton</p>
      </div>
      <div class="row">
        <label>price</label>
        <p>$318,000</p>
      </div>
      <div class="row">
        <label>type</label>
        <p>Single Family</p>
      </div>
      <div class="row">
        <label>acres</label>
        <p>0.27</p>
      </div>
      <div class="row">
        <label>rooms</label>
        <p>6</p>
      </div>
      <div class="row">
        <label>bath (f)</label>
        <p>1</p>
      </div>
      <div class="row">
        <label>bath (h)</label>
        <p>0</p>
      </div>
    </fieldset>
    <fieldset>
      <div class="row">
        <a  class="serviceButton" target="_self"
href="http://maps.google.com/maps?q=20+May+Lane,+Acton,+MA">Map To House</a>
      </div>
      <div class="row">
        <a  class="serviceButton" target="_self"
href="http://www.mass.gov/?pageID=mg2localgovccpage&L=3&L0=Home&L1=State%20Government
&L2=Local%20Government&sid=massgov2&selectCity=Acton">View Town Info</a>
      </div>
    </fieldset>
  </div>
```

There are several items of note. First, the div element is assigned the panel class, just as you did for the Meet Our Team page earlier in the chapter. Second, the individual items of the MLS listing data are contained in div elements with the row class. The set of div row elements is contained in a fieldset. Third, the button links to the map and external Web page are assigned a serviceButton class. Chapter 8, which is devoted to iPhone service integration, discusses these types of button links.

Figure 3-6: Top of listing page

Figure 3-7: Bottom of listing page

The styles for this page come from both iui.css and irealtor.css. First, here are the `row class` and `label` styles in iui.css (if you recall, the `fieldset` is defined earlier in the chapter):

```
.row  {
    position: relative;
    min-height: 42px;
    border-bottom: 1px solid #999999;
    -webkit-border-radius: 0;
    text-align: right;
}
fieldset > .row:last-child {
    border-bottom: none !important;
}
.row > label {
    position: absolute;
    margin: 0 0 0 14px;
    line-height: 42px;
    font-weight: bold;
}
```

The row class emulates the general look of an iPhone/iPod touch list row found in such locations as the built-in Settings and Contacts apps. The .row:last-child style removes the bottom border of the final row in a fieldset. The .row > label style defined in iui.css emulates the look of iPhone Settings, but as you will see in the following example, the code overrides this formatting to more closely emulate the Contacts look (right-aligned, black font).

The following styles are defined in irealtor.css to augment the base iUI styles:

```
.panel img {
    display: block;
    margin-left: auto;
    margin-right: auto;
    margin-bottom: 10px;
    border: 2px solid #666666;
    -webkit-border-radius: 6px;
}
.row > p {
    display: block;
    margin: 0;
    border: none;
    padding: 12px 10px 0 110px;
    text-align: left;
    font-weight: bold;
    text-decoration: inherit;
    height: 42px;
    color: inherit;
    box-sizing: border-box;
}
.row > label {
    text-align: right;
    width: 80px;
    position: absolute;
    margin: 0 0 0 14px;
    line-height: 42px;
    font-weight: bold;
    color: #7388a5;
}
.serviceButton {
    display: block;
    margin: 0;
    border: none;
    padding: 12px 10px 0 0px;
    text-align: center;
    font-weight: bold;
    text-decoration: inherit;
    height: 42px;
    color: #7388a5;
    box-sizing: border-box;
    -webkit-box-sizing: border-box;
}
```

The .panel > img centers the image with margin-left:auto and margin-right:auto and rounds the edges of the rectangle with -webkit-border-radius. (See Chapter 4 for more on this CSS style.)

The .row > p style is used to format the values of each MLS listing information. It is left-aligned and starts at 110px to the right of the left border of the element. The .row > label style adds specific formatting to emulate the Contacts UI look. The .serviceButton class style defines a link with a button look.

Adding a Dialog

The application pages that have been displayed have either been edge-to-edge navigation lists or destination panels for displaying content. iUI also enables you to define a modal dialog. When a user is in a dialog, they need to either perform the intended action (such as a search or submittal) or cancel out. Just like in any desktop environment, a dialog is ideal for form entry.

iRealtor needs dialog boxes for two parts of the application — Search and the Mortgage Calculator. The Search dialog is accessed by tapping the Search button on the top toolbar. Here's the calling link:

```
<a class="button" href="#searchForm">Search</a>
```

The link displays the internal link #searchForm. This references the form element with an id of searchForm:

```
<form id="searchForm" class="dialog" action="search.php">
    <fieldset>
        <h1>Search Listings</h1>
        <a class="button leftButton" type="cancel">Cancel</a>
        <a class="button blueButton" type="submit">Search</a>
        <select name="proptype" size="1">
          <option value="">Property Type</option>
          <option value="SF">Single-Family</option>
          <option value="CC">Condo</option>
          <option value="MF">Multi-Family</option>
          <option value="LD">Land</option>
          <option value="CI">Commercial</option>
          <option value="MM">Mobile Home</option>
          <option value="RN">Rental</option>
          <option value="BU">Business Opportunity</option>
        </select>
        <label class="altLabel">Min $:</label>
        <input class="altInput" type="text" name="minPrice"/>
        <label class="altLabel">Max $:</label>
        <input class="altInput" type="text" name="maxPrice"/>
        <label class="altLabel">MLS #:</label>
        <input class="altInput" type="text" name="mlsNumber"/>
    </fieldset>
</form>
```

The `dialog` class indicates that the form is a dialog. The form elements are wrapped inside of a `fieldset`. The action buttons for the dialog are actually defined as links. To be specific, the Cancel and Search links are defined as `button leftButton` and `button blueButton` classes respectively. iUI will display these two action buttons in the top toolbar of the dialog. It will also display the `h1` content as the dialog title.

A `select` list defines the type of properties that the user wants to choose from. Three `input` fields are defined for additional search criteria. Because the margin and padding styles are unique for this Search dialog, unique styles are specified for the `label` and `input` elements. You'll define those in a moment.

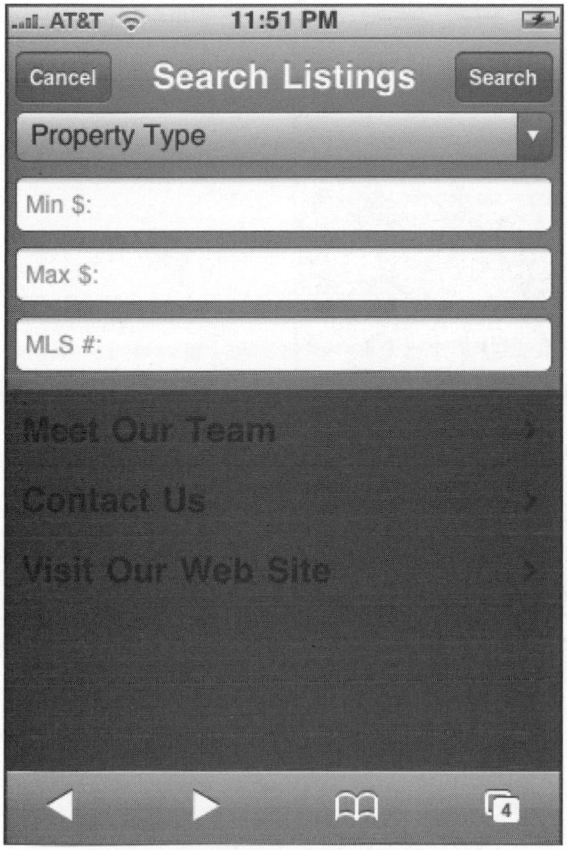

Figure 3-8: Search dialog box

Figure 3-9: Select list items

Figure 3-8 shows the form when displayed in the viewport. Per iPhone/iPod touch guidelines, the bottom part of the form is shaded to obscure the background page. Figure 3-9 displays the iPhone-specific selection list that is automatically displayed for you when the user taps into the `select` element. Finally, Figure 3-10 shows the pop-up keyboard that is displayed when the user taps into the `input` fields.

Figure 3-10: Text input of a form

Consider the CSS styles that are used to display this dialog. From iui.css, there are several rules to pay attention to:

```
body > .dialog {
    top: 0;
    width: 100%;
    min-height: 417px;
    z-index: 2;
    background: rgba(0, 0, 0, 0.8);
    padding: 0;
    text-align: right;
}
```

```
.dialog > fieldset {
    box-sizing: border-box;
    -webkit-box-sizing: border-box;
    width: 100%;
    margin: 0;
    border: none;
    border-top: 1px solid #6d84a2;
    padding: 10px 6px;
    background: url(toolbar.png) #7388a5 repeat-x;
}
.dialog > fieldset > h1 {
    margin: 0 10px 0 10px;
    padding: 0;
    font-size: 20px;
    font-weight: bold;
    color: #FFFFFF;
    text-shadow: rgba(0, 0, 0, 0.4) 0px -1px 0;
    text-align: center;
}
.dialog > fieldset > label {
    position: absolute;
    margin: 16px 0 0 6px;
    font-size: 14px;
    color: #999999;
}
input {
    box-sizing: border-box;
    -webkit-box-sizing: border-box;
    width: 100%;
    margin: 8px 0 0 0;
    padding: 6px 6px 6px 44px;
    font-size: 16px;
    font-weight: normal;
}
.blueButton {
    -webkit-border-image: url(blueButton.png) 0 5 0 5;
    border-width: 0 5px;
}
.leftButton {
    left: 6px;
    right: auto;
}
```

The body > .dialog rule places the form over the entire application, including the top toolbar. It also defines a black background with .8 opacity. Notice the way in which the .dialog > fieldset > label style is defined so that the label element appears to be part of the input element. The .blueButton and .leftButton styles define the action button styles.

Second, there are three styles that are defined in irealtor.css as an extension of iui.css:

```
.altLabel {
    position: absolute;
    margin: 16px 15px 0 6px;
    font-size: 14px;
```

(continued)

53

(continued)

```
      color: black;
  }
  .altInput {
    padding-left: 60px;
  }
  select {
    box-sizing: border-box;
    -webkit-box-sizing: border-box;
    width: 100%;
    margin: 15px 0 0 0;
    padding: 6px 6px 6px 144px;
    font-size: 16px;
    font-weight: normal;
  }
```

The `altLabel` and `altInput` rules are used to appropriately size and position the `label` and `input` elements. The `select` rule styles the `select` element.

When you submit this form, it is submitted via AJAX to allow the results slide from the side to provide a smooth transition.

You may, however, have other uses for dialogs beyond form submissions. For example, iRealtor will include a JavaScript-based mortgage calculator that is accessible from the top-level navigation menu. Here's the link:

```
<li><a href="calc.html">Mortgage Calculator</a></li>
```

The link accesses the document fragment contained in an external URL that contains the following form:

```
<form id="calculator" class="dialog">
  <fieldset>
      <h1>Mortgage Calculator</h1>
      <a class="button leftButton" type="cancel">Back</a>
      <label class="altLabel">Loan amount</label>
      <input class="calc" type="text" name="amt_zip" id="amt"/>
      <label class="altLabel">Interest rate</label>
      <input class="calc" type="text" name="ir_zip" id="ir"/>
      <label class="altLabel">Years</label>
      <input class="calc" type="text" name="amt_zip" id="term" onblur="calc()"/>
      <label class="altLabel">Monthly payment</label>
      <input class="calc" type="text" readonly="true" id="payment"/>
      <label class="altLabel">Total payment</label>
      <input class="calc" type="text" readonly="true" id="total"/>
  </fieldset>
</form>
```

All of the styles have been discussed already except for an additional one in irealtor.css:

```
input.calc {
    padding: 6px 6px 6px 120px;
}
```

This class style overrides the default padding to account for the longer labels used in the calculator.

The three input *elements have a dummy* name *attribute that includes* zip *in it. The zip string prompts the numeric keyboard to display rather than the alphabet keyboard.*

The purpose of the form is for the user to enter information in the first three input elements and then call the JavaScript function calc(), which then displays the results in the bottom two input fields. Because the calculation is performed inside of a client-side JavaScript, no submittal is needed with the server.

The JavaScript function calc() needs to reside in the document head of the main irealtor.html file, not the document fragment. Here's the scripting code:

```
<script type="application/x-javascript">
function calc() {
   var amt = document.getElementById('amt').value;
   var ir =  document.getElementById('ir').value / 1200;
   var term =  document.getElementById('term').value * 12;
   var total=1;
   for (i=0;i<term;i++) {
      total = total * (1 + ir);
   }
   var mp = amt * ir / ( 1 - (1/total));
   document.getElementById('payment').value = Math.round(mp*100)/100;
   document.getElementById('total').value = Math.round(mp * term *100)/100 ;
}
</script>
```

This routine performs a standard mortgage calculation and returns the results to the payment and total input fields. Figure 3-11 shows the result.

Designing a Contact Us Page with Integrated iPhone Services

The final destination page of iRealtor is a Contact Us page that provides basic contact information for the local realtor and integrates with the Mail, Phone, and Map services of iPhone. The code is shown here. iPhone service integration is fully explained in Chapter 7.

The document fragment that is loaded by an AJAX external link is as follows:

```
<div id="contact" title="Contact Us" class="panel">
    <div class="cuiHeader">
      <img class="cui" src="images/jordan_willmark.png"/>
      <h1 class="cui" style="text-overflow:ellipsis;">Jordan Willmark</h1>
      <h2 class="cui">J-Team Reality</h2>
    </div>
    <fieldset>
        <div class="row">
            <label class="cui">office</label>
            <a class="cuiServiceLink" target="_self" href="tel:(978) 555-1212"
onclick="return (navigator.userAgent.indexOf('iPhone') != -1)">(978) 555-1212</a>
        </div>
        <div class="row">
            <label class="cui">mobile</label>
           <a class="cuiServiceLink" target="_self" href="tel:(978) 545-1211"
onclick="return (navigator.userAgent.indexOf('iPhone') != -1)">(978) 545-1211</a>
        </div>
        <div class="row">
            <label class="cui">e-mail</label>
            <a class="cuiServiceLink" target="_self"
href="mailto:jordan@jteam3.com" onclick="return
(navigator.userAgent.indexOf('iPhone') != -1)">jordan@jteam3.com</a>
        </div>
    </fieldset>
    <fieldset>
        <div class="rowCuiAddressBox">
            <label class="cui">work</label>
            <p class="cui">15 Louis Street</p>
            <p class="cui">Princeton, MA 01541</p>
        </div>
    </fieldset>
    <fieldset>
        <div class="row">
            <a  class="serviceButton" target="_self"
href="http://maps.google.com/maps?q=15+Louis+St,+Princeton,+MA+(J-Team+Office)">Map
To Office</a>
        </div>
    </fieldset>
</div>
```

You'll notice that the code listing displays several styles prefixed with cui. These are defined in a separate style sheet called cui.css, which is fully explained in Chapter 7. However, in order to use these styles, the following style element needs to be added to the document head of irealtor.html:

```
<style type="text/css" media="screen">@import "../iui/cui.css";</style>
```

Figure 3-12 shows the panel when displayed on iPhone.

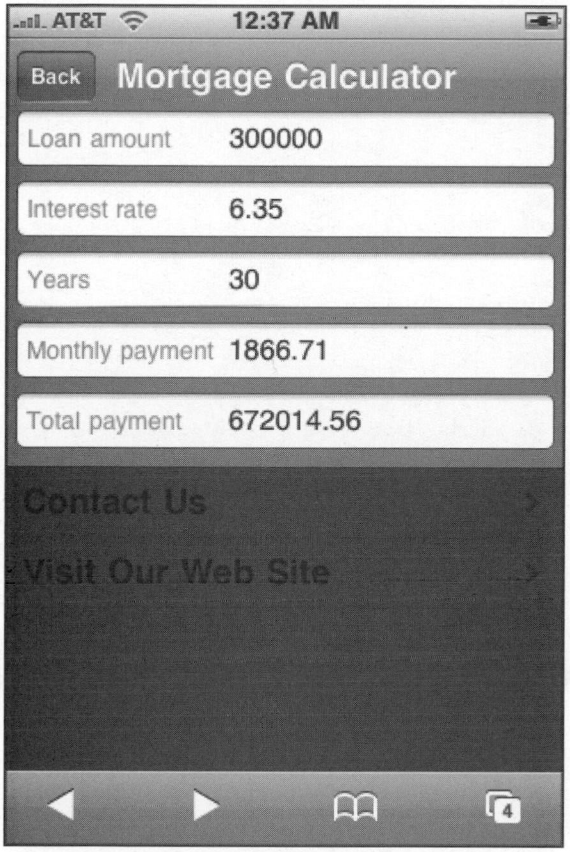

Figure 3-11: Text input of a form

Figure 3-12: IPhone-enabled Contact Us page

The following three listings provide a full code view of the major source files that have been discussed. Listing 3-1 displays irealtor.html, Listing 3-2 provides iui.css, and Listing 3-3 contains irealtor.css.

Listing 3-1: irealtor.html

```
<!DOCTYPE html PUBLIC "-//W3C//DTD XHTML 1.0 Strict//EN"
        "http://www.w3.org/TR/xhtml1/DTD/xhtml1-strict.dtd">
<html xmlns="http://www.w3.org/1999/xhtml">
<head>
<title>iRealtor</title>
```

(continued)

Listing 3-1 *(continued)*

```html
<meta name="viewport" content="width=device-width; initial-scale=1.0; maximum-
scale=1.0; user-scalable=0;"/>
<style type="text/css" media="screen">@import "../iui/iui.css";</style>
<style type="text/css" media="screen">@import "../iui/cui.css";</style>
<style type="text/css" media="screen">@import "irealtor.css";</style>
<script type="application/x-javascript" src="../iui/iui.js"></script>
<script type="application/x-javascript">
function calc() {
   var amt = document.getElementById('amt').value;
   var ir =  document.getElementById('ir').value / 1200;
   var term =  document.getElementById('term').value * 12;
   var total=1;
   for (i=0;i<term;i++) {
      total = total * (1 + ir);
   }
   var mp = amt * ir / ( 1 - (1/total));
  document.getElementById('payment').value = Math.round(mp*100)/100;
  document.getElementById('total').value = Math.round(mp * term *100)/100 ;
}
</script>
</head>
<body>
    <!-- Top toolbar -->
    <div class="toolbar">
        <h1 id="pageTitle"></h1>
        <a id="backButton" class="button" href="#"></a>
        <a class="button" href="#searchForm">Search</a>
    </div>
    <!-- Home menu -->
    <ul id="home" title="iRealtor" selected="true">
        <li><a href="featured.html">Featured Listings</a></li>
        <li><a href="listings.html">All Listings</a></li>
        <li><a href="#">Buying & Tips</a></li>
        <li><a href="calc.html">Mortgage Calculator</a></li>
        <li><a href="#meet_our_team">Meet Our Team</a></li>
        <li><a href="contact_us.html">Contact Us</a></li>
        <li><a href="index.html" target="_self">Visit Our Web Site</a></li>
    </ul>
    <div id="meet_our_team" class="panel" title="Meet Our Team">
        <h2>J-Team Reality</h2>
        <fieldset>
        <p class="normalText">Lorem ipsum dolor sit amet, consect etuer adipis cing
elit. Suspend isse nisl. Vivamus a ligula vel quam tinci dunt posuere. Integer
venen atis blandit est. Phasel lus ac neque. Quisque at augue. Phasellus purus. Sed
et risus. Suspe ndisse laoreet consequat metus. Nam nec justo vitae tortor
fermentum interdum. Aenean vitae quam eu urna pharetra ornare.</p>
        <p class="normalText">Pellent esque habitant morbi tristique senectus et
netus et malesuada fames ac turpis egestas. Aliquam congue. Pel lentesque pretium
fringilla quam. Integer libero libero, varius ut, faucibus et, facilisis vel, odio.
Donec quis eros eu erat ullamc orper euismod. Nam aliquam turpis. Nunc convallis
massa non sem. Donec non odio. Sed non lacus eget lacus hend rerit sodales.</p>
```

```
                </fieldset>
            </div>
            <form id="searchForm" class="dialog" action="search.php">
                <fieldset>
                    <h1>Search Listings</h1>
                    <a class="button leftButton" type="cancel">Cancel</a>
                    <a class="button blueButton" type="submit">Search</a>
                    <select name="proptype" size="1">
                      <option value="">Property Type</option>
                      <option value="SF">Single-Family</option>
                      <option value="CC">Condo</option>
                      <option value="MF">Multi-Family</option>
                      <option value="LD">Land</option>
                      <option value="CI">Commercial</option>
                      <option value="MM">Mobile Home</option>
                      <option value="RN">Rental</option>
                      <option value="BU">Business Opportunity</option>
                    </select>
                    <label class="altLabel">Min $:</label>
                    <input type="text" name="minPrice"/>
                    <label class="altLabel">Max $:</label>
                    <input type="text" name="maxPrice"/>
                    <label class="altLabel">MLS #:</label>
                    <input type="text" name="mlsNumber"/>
                </fieldset>
            </form>
    </body>
</html>
```

Listing 3-2: iui.css

```css
body {
    margin: 0;
    font-family: Helvetica;
    background: #FFFFFF;
    color: #000000;
    overflow-x: hidden;
    -webkit-user-select: none;
    -webkit-text-size-adjust: none;
}
body > *:not(.toolbar) {
    display: none;
    position: absolute;
    margin: 0;
    padding: 0;
    left: 0;
    top: 45px;
    width: 100%;
    min-height: 372px;
}
body[orient="landscape"] > *:not(.toolbar) {
    min-height: 268px;
}
```

(continued)

Listing 3-2 *(continued)*

```
body > *[selected="true"] {
    display: block;
}
a[selected], a:active {
    background-color: #194fdb !important;
    background-image: url(listArrowSel.png), url(selection.png) !important;
    background-repeat: no-repeat, repeat-x;
    background-position: right center, left top;
    color: #FFFFFF !important;
}
a[selected="progress"] {
    background-image: url(loading.gif), url(selection.png) !important;
}
/****************************************************************************************
**************/
body > .toolbar {
    box-sizing: border-box;
    -webkit-box-sizing: border-box;
    -moz-box-sizing: border-box;
    border-bottom: 1px solid #2d3642;
    border-top: 1px solid #6d84a2;
    padding: 10px;
    height: 45px;
    background: url(toolbar.png) #6d84a2 repeat-x;
}
.toolbar > h1 {
    position: absolute;
    overflow: hidden;
    left: 50%;
    margin: 1px 0 0 -75px;
    height: 45px;
    font-size: 20px;
    width: 150px;
    font-weight: bold;
    text-shadow: rgba(0, 0, 0, 0.4) 0px -1px 0;
    text-align: center;
    text-overflow: ellipsis;
    white-space: nowrap;
    color: #FFFFFF;
}
body[orient="landscape"] > .toolbar > h1 {
    margin-left: -125px;
    width: 250px;
}
.button {
    position: absolute;
    overflow: hidden;
    top: 8px;
    right: 6px;
    margin: 0;
    border-width: 0 5px;
    padding: 0 3px;
```

```
        width: auto;
        height: 30px;
        line-height: 30px;
        font-family: inherit;
        font-size: 12px;
        font-weight: bold;
        color: #FFFFFF;
        text-shadow: rgba(0, 0, 0, 0.6) 0px -1px 0;
        text-overflow: ellipsis;
        text-decoration: none;
        white-space: nowrap;
        background: none;
        -webkit-border-image: url(toolButton.png) 0 5 0 5;
}
.blueButton {
        -webkit-border-image: url(blueButton.png) 0 5 0 5;
        border-width: 0 5px;
}
.leftButton {
        left: 6px;
        right: auto;
}
#backButton {
        display: none;
        left: 6px;
        right: auto;
        padding: 0;
        max-width: 55px;
        border-width: 0 8px 0 14px;
        -webkit-border-image: url(backButton.png) 0 8 0 14;
}
.whiteButton,
.grayButton {
        display: block;
        border-width: 0 12px;
        padding: 10px;
        text-align: center;
        font-size: 20px;
        font-weight: bold;
        text-decoration: inherit;
        color: inherit;
}
.whiteButton {
        -webkit-border-image: url(whiteButton.png) 0 12 0 12;
        text-shadow: rgba(255, 255, 255, 0.7) 0 1px 0;
}
.grayButton {
        -webkit-border-image: url(grayButton.png) 0 12 0 12;
        color: #FFFFFF;
}
/*******************************************************************************
**************/
```

(continued)

Listing 3-2 *(continued)*

```css
body > ul > li {
    position: relative;
    margin: 0;
    border-bottom: 1px solid #E0E0E0;
    padding: 8px 0 8px 10px;
    font-size: 20px;
    font-weight: bold;
    list-style: none;
}
body > ul > li.group {
    position: relative;
    top: -1px;
    margin-bottom: -2px;
    border-top: 1px solid #7d7d7d;
    border-bottom: 1px solid #999999;
    padding: 1px 10px;
    background: url(listGroup.png) repeat-x;
    font-size: 17px;
    font-weight: bold;
    text-shadow: rgba(0, 0, 0, 0.4) 0 1px 0;
    color: #FFFFFF;
}
body > ul > li.group:first-child {
    top: 0;
    border-top: none;
}
body > ul > li > a {
    display: block;
    margin: -8px 0 -8px -10px;
    padding: 8px 32px 8px 10px;
    text-decoration: none;
    color: inherit;
    background: url(listArrow.png) no-repeat right center;
}
a[target="_replace"] {
    box-sizing: border-box;
    -webkit-box-sizing: border-box;
    padding-top: 25px;
    padding-bottom: 25px;
    font-size: 18px;
    color: cornflowerblue;
    background-color: #FFFFFF;
    background-image: none;
}
/****************************************************************************************
**************/
body > .dialog {
    top: 0;
    width: 100%;
    min-height: 417px;
```

```
        z-index: 2;
        background: rgba(0, 0, 0, 0.8);
        padding: 0;
        text-align: right;
}
.dialog > fieldset {
        box-sizing: border-box;
        -webkit-box-sizing: border-box;
        width: 100%;
        margin: 0;
        border: none;
        border-top: 1px solid #6d84a2;
        padding: 10px 6px;
        background: url(toolbar.png) #7388a5 repeat-x;
}
.dialog > fieldset > h1 {
        margin: 0 10px 0 10px;
        padding: 0;
        font-size: 20px;
        font-weight: bold;
        color: #FFFFFF;
        text-shadow: rgba(0, 0, 0, 0.4) 0px -1px 0;
        text-align: center;
}
.dialog > fieldset > label {
        position: absolute;
        margin: 16px 0 0 6px;
        font-size: 14px;
        color: #999999;
}
input {
        box-sizing: border-box;
        -webkit-box-sizing: border-box;
        width: 100%;
        margin: 8px 0 0 0;
        padding: 6px 6px 6px 44px;
        font-size: 16px;
        font-weight: normal;
}
/*****************************************************************************
**************/
body > .panel {
        box-sizing: border-box;
        -webkit-box-sizing: border-box;
        padding: 10px;
        background: #c8c8c8 url(pinstripes.png);
}
.panel > fieldset {
        position: relative;
        margin: 0 0 20px 0;
        padding: 0;
```

(continued)

Listing 3-2 *(continued)*

```
        background: #FFFFFF;
        -webkit-border-radius: 10px;
        border: 1px solid #999999;
        text-align: right;
        font-size: 16px;
}
.row  {
        position: relative;
        min-height: 42px;
        border-bottom: 1px solid #999999;
        -webkit-border-radius: 0;
        text-align: right;
}
fieldset > .row:last-child {
        border-bottom: none !important;
}
.row > input {
        box-sizing: border-box;
        -webkit-box-sizing: border-box;
        margin: 0;
        border: none;
        padding: 12px 10px 0 110px;
        height: 42px;
        background: none;
}
.row > label {
        position: absolute;
        margin: 0 0 0 14px;
        line-height: 42px;
        font-weight: bold;
}
.row > .toggle {
        position: absolute;
        top: 6px;
        right: 6px;
        width: 100px;
        height: 28px;
}
.toggle {
        border: 1px solid #888888;
        -webkit-border-radius: 6px;
        background: #FFFFFF url(toggle.png) repeat-x;
        font-size: 19px;
        font-weight: bold;
        line-height: 30px;
}
.toggle[toggled="true"] {
        border: 1px solid #143fae;
        background: #194fdb url(toggleOn.png) repeat-x;
}
```

```css
.toggleOn {
    display: none;
    position: absolute;
    width: 60px;
    text-align: center;
    left: 0;
    top: 0;
    color: #FFFFFF;
    text-shadow: rgba(0, 0, 0, 0.4) 0px -1px 0;
}
.toggleOff {
    position: absolute;
    width: 60px;
    text-align: center;
    right: 0;
    top: 0;
    color: #666666;
}
.toggle[toggled="true"] > .toggleOn {
    display: block;
}
.toggle[toggled="true"] > .toggleOff {
    display: none;
}
.thumb {
    position: absolute;
    top: -1px;
    left: -1px;
    width: 40px;
    height: 28px;
    border: 1px solid #888888;
    -webkit-border-radius: 6px;
    background: #ffffff url(thumb.png) repeat-x;
}
.toggle[toggled="true"] > .thumb {
    left: auto;
    right: -1px;
}
.panel > h2 {
    margin: 0 0 8px 14px;
    font-size: inherit;
    font-weight: bold;
    color: #4d4d70;
    text-shadow: rgba(255, 255, 255, 0.75) 2px 2px 0;
}
/*****************************************************************************
**************/
#preloader {
    display: none;
    background-image: url(loading.gif), url(selection.png),
        url(blueButton.png), url(listArrowSel.png), url(listGroup.png);
}
```

iui.css is open source code under the "new" Berkeley Software Distribution (BSD) license.

Listing 3-3: irealtor.css

```css
a.listing {
    padding-left: 54px;
    padding-right: 40px;
    min-height: 34px;
}
img.listingImg {
    display: block;
    position: absolute;
    margin: 0;
    left: 6px;
    top: 7px;
    width: 35px;
    height: 27px;
    padding: 7px 0 10px 0;
}
p.listingDetails {
    display: block;
    position: absolute;
    margin: 0;
    left: 54px;
    top: 27px;
    text-align: left;
    font-size: 12px;
    font-weight: normal;
    color: #666666;
    text-decoration: none;
    width: 100%;
    height: 13px;
    padding: 3px 0 0 0;
}
.panel img {
    display: block;
    margin-left: auto;
    margin-right: auto;
    margin-bottom: 10px;
     border: 2px solid #666666;
    -webkit-border-radius: 6px;
}
.row > p {
    display: block;
    margin: 0;
    border: none;
    padding: 12px 10px 0 110px;
     text-align: left;
    font-weight: bold;
    text-decoration: inherit;
    height: 42px;
    color: inherit;
    box-sizing: border-box;
    -webkit-box-sizing: border-box;
}
```

```css
.row > label {
    text-align: right;
    width: 80px;
    position: absolute;
    margin: 0 0 0 14px;
    line-height: 42px;
    font-weight: bold;
    color: #7388a5;
}
.serviceButton {
    display: block;
    margin: 0;
    border: none;
    padding: 12px 10px 0 0px;
     text-align: center;
    font-weight: bold;
    text-decoration: inherit;
    height: 42px;
    color: #7388a5;
    box-sizing: border-box;
    -webkit-box-sizing: border-box;
}
/********************************/
.panel p.normalText {
    text-align: left;
    padding: 0 10px 0 10px;
}
.panel > h2 {
    margin: 3px 0 10px 10px;
}
input.calc {
    padding: 6px 6px 6px 120px;
}
/********************************/
.altLabel {
  position: absolute;
  margin: 16px 15px 0 6px;
  font-size: 14px;
  color: black;
}
.altInput {
  padding-left: 60px;
}
select {
  box-sizing: border-box;
  -webkit-box-sizing: border-box;
  width: 100%;
  margin: 15px 0 0 0;
  padding: 6px 6px 6px 144px;
  font-size: 16px;
  font-weight: normal;
}
```

Scripting UI Behavior with iui.js

When you use the iUI framework, iui.js powers all of the UI behavior for you once you include it in your document head. However, because the iUI framework does take control over many aspects of the environment, it is important that you have a solid understanding of the library's internals.

The iui.js consists of a JSON object `window.iui`, three listeners for `load` and `click` events, and several supporting routines. All of the JavaScript code is enclosed in an anonymous function with several constants and variables defined:

```
(function() {
var slideSpeed = 20;
var slideInterval = 0;
var currentPage = null;
var currentDialog = null;
var currentWidth = 0;
var currentHash = location.hash;
var hashPrefix = "#_";
var pageHistory = [];
var newPageCount = 0;
var checkTimer;
// **** REST OF IUI CODE HERE ****
})();
```

The anonymous function creates a local scope to allow private semi-global variables and avoid name conflicts with applications that use iui.js.

On Document Load

When the HTML document loads, the following listener function is triggered:

```
addEventListener("load", function(event)
{
    var page = iui.getSelectedPage();
    if (page)
        iui.showPage(page);
    setTimeout(preloadImages, 0);
    setTimeout(checkOrientAndLocation, 0);
    checkTimer = setInterval(checkOrientAndLocation, 300);
}, false);
```

The `getSelectedPage()` method of the JSON object `iui` is called to get the selected page — the block element node that contains a `selected="true"` attribute. This node is then passed to `iui.showPage()`, which is the core routine to display content.

As Chapter 5 explains, `setTimeout()` is often used when calling certain JavaScript routines to prevent timing inconsistencies. Using `setTimeout()`, iUI calls an image preloader function to load application images and then a routine called checkOrientAndLocation(), which is an event handler used for detecting and handling viewport orientation changes. (Orientation change events are fully covered in Chapter 5.) The setInterval function then calls checkOrientAndLocation() every 300ms when the application runs. Note that the checkOrientAndLocation() also contains the code to hide the URL bar.

The iPhone update 1.1.1 added an orientationchange *event. However, for maximum compatibility with iPhone 1.0, I recommend continuing to use the* checkOrientAndLocation() *event.*

Getting back to iui.showPage(), its code is as follows:

```
showPage: function(page, backwards)
{
    if (page)
    {
        if (currentDialog)
        {
            currentDialog.removeAttribute("selected");
            currentDialog = null;
        }
        if (hasClass(page, "dialog"))
            showDialog(page);
        else
        {
            var fromPage = currentPage;
            currentPage = page;
            if (fromPage)
                setTimeout(slidePages, 0, fromPage, page, backwards);
            else
                updatePage(page, fromPage);
        }
    }
}
```

The currentDialog semi-global variable is evaluated to determine whether a dialog is already displayed. (currentDialog is set in the showDialog() function.) This variable would be null when the document initially loads because of the line var currentDialog = null; earlier in iui.js, which runs every time the document loads.

The node is then evaluated to determine whether it is a dialog (containing class="dialog" as an attribute) or a normal page. While the opening page of an iPhone/iPod touch is often a normal page, you may wish to have a login or initial search dialog.

Loading a Standard iUI Page

For normal pages, iUI will assign the value of currentPage to the variable fromPage and then reassign currentPage to the page parameter. If fromPage is not null (i.e., every page after the initial page), then iUI performs a slide-in animation with a function called slidePages(). The fromPage, page, and backwards variables are passed to slidePages().

However, because this is the first time running this routine (and `fromPage` will equal `null`), the `updatePage()` function is called:

```
function updatePage(page, fromPage)
{
    if (!page.id)
        page.id = "__" + (++newPageCount) + "__";
    location.href = currentHash = hashPrefix + page.id;
    pageHistory.push(page.id);
    var pageTitle = $("pageTitle");
    if (page.title)
        pageTitle.innerHTML = page.title;
    if (page.localName.toLowerCase() == "form" && !page.target)
        showForm(page);
    var backButton = $("backButton");
    if (backButton)
    {
        var prevPage = $(pageHistory[pageHistory.length-2]);
        if (prevPage && !page.getAttribute("hideBackButton"))
        {
            backButton.style.display = "inline";
            backButton.innerHTML = prevPage.title ? prevPage.title : "Back";
        }
        else
            backButton.style.display = "none";
    }
}
```

The `updatePage()` function is responsible for updating the `pageHistory` array, which is required for enabling the Mobile Safari Back button to work even in single-page applications. The value of the node's `title` attribute is then assigned to be the `innerHTML` of the top toolbar's h1 `pageTitle`.

If the page name contains the string `form` in it, then the `showForm()` function is called. Otherwise, the routine continues on, looking to see if a `backButton` element is defined in the toolbar. If so, then the page history is updated and button title is updated.

Subsequent pages will always bypass the direct call to `updatePage()` and use the `slidePages()` function instead. Here is the code:

```
function slidePages(fromPage, toPage, backwards)
{
    var axis = (backwards ? fromPage : toPage).getAttribute("axis");
    if (axis == "y")
        (backwards ? fromPage : toPage).style.top = "100%";
    else
        toPage.style.left = "100%";
    toPage.setAttribute("selected", "true");
    scrollTo(0, 1);
    clearInterval(checkTimer);
    var percent = 100;
```

```
        slide();
        var timer = setInterval(slide, slideInterval);
        function slide()
        {
            percent -= slideSpeed;
            if (percent <= 0)
            {
                percent = 0;
                if (!hasClass(toPage, "dialog"))
                    fromPage.removeAttribute("selected");
                clearInterval(timer);
                checkTimer = setInterval(checkOrientAndLocation, 300);
                setTimeout(updatePage, 0, toPage, fromPage);
            }
            if (axis == "y")
            {
                backwards
                    ? fromPage.style.top = (100-percent) + "%"
                    : toPage.style.top = percent + "%";
            }
            else
            {
                fromPage.style.left = (backwards ? (100-percent) : (percent-100)) + "%";
                toPage.style.left = (backwards ? -percent : percent) + "%";
            }
        }
    }
```

The primary purpose of slidePages() is to emulate the standard iPhone/iPod touch slide animation effect when you move between pages. It achieves this by using JavaScript timer routines to incrementally update the style.left property of the fromPage and the toPage. The updatePage() function (discussed previously) is called inside of a setTimeout routine.

Handling Link Clicks

Because most of the user interaction with an iPhone/iPod touch application is tapping the interface to navigate the application, iUI's event listener for link clicks is, in many ways, the "mission control center" for iui.jss. Check out the code:

```
addEventListener("click", function(event)
{
    var link = findParent(event.target, "a");
    if (link)
    {
        function unselect() { link.removeAttribute("selected"); }
        if (link.href && link.hash && link.hash != "#")
        {
            link.setAttribute("selected", "true");
            iui.showPage($(link.hash.substr(1)));
            setTimeout(unselect, 500);
        }
```

(continued)

71

(continued)

```
            else if (link == $("backButton"))
                history.back();
            else if (link.getAttribute("type") == "submit")
                submitForm(findParent(link, "form"));
            else if (link.getAttribute("type") == "cancel")
                cancelDialog(findParent(link, "form"));
            else if (link.target == "_replace")
            {
                link.setAttribute("selected", "progress");
                iui.showPageByHref(link.href, null, null, link, unselect);
            }
            else if (!link.target)
            {
                link.setAttribute("selected", "progress");
                iui.showPageByHref(link.href, null, null, null, unselect);
            }
            else
                return;
            event.preventDefault();
        }
    }, true);
```

This routine evaluates the type of link that it is:

❑ If it is an internal URL, then the page is passed to `iui.showPage()`.

❑ If the `backButton` is tapped, then `history.back()` is triggered.

❑ Dialog forms typically contain a Submit and Cancel button. If a Submit button is tapped, then `submitForm()` is called. If a Cancel button is tapped, then `cancelDialog()` is called. (The `submitForm()` and `cancelDialog()` functions are discussed later in the chapter.)

❑ External URLs that have `target="_replace"` or that do not have target defined are AJAX links. Both of these call the `iui.showPageByHref()` method.

❑ If it is none of these, then it is an external link with a `target="_self"` attribute defined and the default iUI behavior is suspended and the link is treated as normal.

Handling AJAX Links

When an AJAX link is tapped by the user, the click event listener (shown previously) calls the `iui.showPageByHref()` method:

```
        showPageByHref: function(href, args, method, replace, cb)
        {
            var req = new XMLHttpRequest();
            req.onerror = function()
            {
                if (cb)
                    cb(false);
            };
            req.onreadystatechange = function()
            {
                if (req.readyState == 4)
```

```
                    {
                        if (replace)
                            replaceElementWithSource(replace, req.responseText);
                        else
                        {
                            var frag = document.createElement("div");
                            frag.innerHTML = req.responseText;
                            iui.insertPages(frag.childNodes);
                        }
                        if (cb)
                            setTimeout(cb, 1000, true);
                    }
                };
                if (args)
                {
                    req.open(method || "GET", href, true);
                    req.setRequestHeader("Content-Type", "application/x-www-form-
            urlencoded");
                    req.setRequestHeader("Content-Length", args.length);
                    req.send(args.join("&"));
                }
                else
                {
                    req.open(method || "GET", href, true);
                    req.send(null);
                }
            }
```

The routine calls XMLHttpRequest() to assign the req object. If the args parameter is not null (that is, when an AJAX form is submitted), then the form data is sent to the server. If args is null, then the supplied URL is sent to the server. The processing of incoming text takes place inside of the onreadystatechange handler.

If replace is true (meaning that target="_replace" is specified in the calling link), then the replaceElementWithSource() function is called. As the following code shows, the calling link node (the replace parameter) is replaced with the source (the AJAX document fragment):

```
function replaceElementWithSource(replace, source)
{
    var page = replace.parentNode;
    var parent = replace;
    while (page.parentNode != document.body)
    {
        page = page.parentNode;
        parent = parent.parentNode;
    }
    var frag = document.createElement(parent.localName);
    frag.innerHTML = source;
    page.removeChild(parent);
    while (frag.firstChild)
        page.appendChild(frag.firstChild);
}
```

If a click is generated from a normal AJAX link, then the contents of the external URL will be displayed in a new page. Therefore, a div is created and the document fragment is added as the innerHTML of the element. The iui.insertPages() method adds the new nodes to create a new page, and then this page is passed to iui.showPage():

```
insertPages: function(nodes)
    {
        var targetPage;
        for (var i = 0; i < nodes.length; ++i)
        {
            var child = nodes[i];
            if (child.nodeType == 1)
            {
                if (!child.id)
                    child.id = "__" + (++newPageCount) + "__";
                var clone = $(child.id);
                if (clone)
                    clone.parentNode.replaceChild(child, clone);
                else
                    document.body.appendChild(child);
                if (child.getAttribute("selected") == "true" || !targetPage)
                    targetPage = child;
                --i;
            }
        }
        if (targetPage)
            iui.showPage(targetPage);
    }
```

Loading an iUI Dialog

If the node that is passed into the main showPage() function is a dialog (class="dialog"), then the showDialog() function is called, which in turn calls showForm(). These two functions are shown in the following code:

```
function showDialog(page)
{
    currentDialog = page;
    page.setAttribute("selected", "true");
    if (hasClass(page, "dialog") && !page.target)
        showForm(page);
}
function showForm(form)
{
    form.onsubmit = function(event)
    {
        event.preventDefault();
        submitForm(form);
    };
```

```
        form.onclick = function(event)
        {
            if (event.target == form && hasClass(form, "dialog"))
                cancelDialog(form);
        };
    }
```

The showForm() function assigns event handlers to the onsubmit and onclick events of the form. When a form is submitted, the submitForm() function submits the form data via AJAX. When an element on the form is clicked, then the dialog is closed. The following code shows the routines that are called:

```
function submitForm(form)
{
    iui.showPageByHref(form.action || "POST", encodeForm(form), form.method);
}
function cancelDialog(form)
{
    form.removeAttribute("selected");
}
function encodeForm(form)
{
    function encode(inputs)
    {
        for (var i = 0; i < inputs.length; ++i)
        {
            if (inputs[i].name)
                args.push(inputs[i].name + "=" + escape(inputs[i].value));
        }
    }
    var args = [];
    encode(form.getElementsByTagName("input"));
    encode(form.getElementsByTagName("select"));
    return args;
}
```

The entire code for iui.js is provided in Listing 3-4.

Listing 3-4: iui.js

```
  (function() {
var slideSpeed = 20;
var slideInterval = 0;
var currentPage = null;
var currentDialog = null;
var currentWidth = 0;
var currentHash = location.hash;
var hashPrefix = "#_";
var pageHistory = [];
var newPageCount = 0;
var checkTimer;
//
********************************************************************************
**************
```

(continued)

Listing 3-4 *(continued)*

```javascript
window.iui =
{
    showPage: function(page, backwards)
    {
        if (page)
        {
            if (currentDialog)
            {
                currentDialog.removeAttribute("selected");
                currentDialog = null;
            }
            if (hasClass(page, "dialog"))
                showDialog(page);
            else
            {
                var fromPage = currentPage;
                currentPage = page;
                if (fromPage)
                    setTimeout(slidePages, 0, fromPage, page, backwards);
                else
                    updatePage(page, fromPage);
            }
        }
    },
    showPageById: function(pageId)
    {
        var page = $(pageId);
        if (page)
        {
            var index = pageHistory.indexOf(pageId);
            var backwards = index != -1;
            if (backwards)
                pageHistory.splice(index, pageHistory.length);
            iui.showPage(page, backwards);
        }
    },
    showPageByHref: function(href, args, method, replace, cb)
    {
        var req = new XMLHttpRequest();
        req.onerror = function()
        {
            if (cb)
                cb(false);
        };
        req.onreadystatechange = function()
        {
            if (req.readyState == 4)
            {
                if (replace)
                    replaceElementWithSource(replace, req.responseText);
```

```
                else
                {
                    var frag = document.createElement("div");
                    frag.innerHTML = req.responseText;
                    iui.insertPages(frag.childNodes);
                }
                if (cb)
                    setTimeout(cb, 1000, true);
            }
        };
        if (args)
        {
            req.open(method || "GET", href, true);
            req.setRequestHeader("Content-Type", "application/x-www-form-
urlencoded");
            req.setRequestHeader("Content-Length", args.length);
            req.send(args.join("&"));
        }
        else
        {
            req.open(method || "GET", href, true);
            req.send(null);
        }
    },
    insertPages: function(nodes)
    {
        var targetPage;
        for (var i = 0; i < nodes.length; ++i)
        {
            var child = nodes[i];
            if (child.nodeType == 1)
            {
                if (!child.id)
                    child.id = "__" + (++newPageCount) + "__";
                var clone = $(child.id);
                if (clone)
                    clone.parentNode.replaceChild(child, clone);
                else
                    document.body.appendChild(child);
                if (child.getAttribute("selected") == "true" || !targetPage)
                    targetPage = child;
                --i;
            }
        }
        if (targetPage)
            iui.showPage(targetPage);
    },
    getSelectedPage: function()
    {
        for (var child = document.body.firstChild; child; child = child.
nextSibling)
```

(continued)

Listing 3-4 *(continued)*

```
        {
            if (child.nodeType == 1 && child.getAttribute("selected") == "true")
                return child;
        }
    }
};
//
********************************************************************************
**************
addEventListener("load", function(event)
{
    var page = iui.getSelectedPage();
    if (page)
        iui.showPage(page);
    setTimeout(preloadImages, 0);
    setTimeout(checkOrientAndLocation, 0);
    checkTimer = setInterval(checkOrientAndLocation, 300);
}, false);
addEventListener("click", function(event)
{
    var link = findParent(event.target, "a");
    if (link)
    {
        function unselect() { link.removeAttribute("selected"); }
        if (link.href && link.hash && link.hash != "#")
        {
            link.setAttribute("selected", "true");
            iui.showPage($(link.hash.substr(1)));
            setTimeout(unselect, 500);
        }
        else if (link == $("backButton"))
            history.back();
        else if (link.getAttribute("type") == "submit")
            submitForm(findParent(link, "form"));
        else if (link.getAttribute("type") == "cancel")
            cancelDialog(findParent(link, "form"));
        else if (link.target == "_replace")
        {
            link.setAttribute("selected", "progress");
            iui.showPageByHref(link.href, null, null, link, unselect);
        }
        else if (!link.target)
        {
            link.setAttribute("selected", "progress");
            iui.showPageByHref(link.href, null, null, null, unselect);
        }
        else
            return;
        event.preventDefault();
```

```
        }
    }, true);
    addEventListener("click", function(event)
    {
        var div = findParent(event.target, "div");
        if (div && hasClass(div, "toggle"))
        {
            div.setAttribute("toggled", div.getAttribute("toggled") != "true");
            event.preventDefault();
        }
    }, true);
    function checkOrientAndLocation()
    {
        if (window.innerWidth != currentWidth)
        {
            currentWidth = window.innerWidth;
            var orient = currentWidth == 320 ? "profile" : "landscape";
            document.body.setAttribute("orient", orient);
            setTimeout(scrollTo, 100, 0, 1);
        }
        if (location.hash != currentHash)
        {
            var pageId = location.hash.substr(hashPrefix.length)
            iui.showPageById(pageId);
        }
    }
    function showDialog(page)
    {
        currentDialog = page;
        page.setAttribute("selected", "true");
        if (hasClass(page, "dialog") && !page.target)
            showForm(page);
    }
    function showForm(form)
    {
        form.onsubmit = function(event)
        {
            event.preventDefault();
            submitForm(form);
        };
        form.onclick = function(event)
        {
            if (event.target == form && hasClass(form, "dialog"))
                cancelDialog(form);
        };
    }
    function cancelDialog(form)
    {
        form.removeAttribute("selected");
    }
```

(continued)

Listing 3-4 *(continued)*

```javascript
function updatePage(page, fromPage)
{
    if (!page.id)
        page.id = "__" + (++newPageCount) + "__";
    location.href = currentHash = hashPrefix + page.id;
    pageHistory.push(page.id);
    var pageTitle = $("pageTitle");
    if (page.title)
        pageTitle.innerHTML = page.title;
    if (page.localName.toLowerCase() == "form" && !page.target)
        showForm(page);
    var backButton = $("backButton");
    if (backButton)
    {
        var prevPage = $(pageHistory[pageHistory.length-2]);
        if (prevPage && !page.getAttribute("hideBackButton"))
        {
            backButton.style.display = "inline";
            backButton.innerHTML = prevPage.title ? prevPage.title : "Back";
        }
        else
            backButton.style.display = "none";
    }
}
function slidePages(fromPage, toPage, backwards)
{
    var axis = (backwards ? fromPage : toPage).getAttribute("axis");
    if (axis == "y")
        (backwards ? fromPage : toPage).style.top = "100%";
    else
        toPage.style.left = "100%";
    toPage.setAttribute("selected", "true");
    scrollTo(0, 1);
    clearInterval(checkTimer);
    var percent = 100;
    slide();
    var timer = setInterval(slide, slideInterval);
    function slide()
    {
        percent -= slideSpeed;
        if (percent <= 0)
        {
            percent = 0;
            if (!hasClass(toPage, "dialog"))
                fromPage.removeAttribute("selected");
            clearInterval(timer);
            checkTimer = setInterval(checkOrientAndLocation, 300);
            setTimeout(updatePage, 0, toPage, fromPage);
        }
```

```
            if (axis == "y")
            {
                backwards
                    ? fromPage.style.top = (100-percent) + "%"
                    : toPage.style.top = percent + "%";
            }
            else
            {
                fromPage.style.left = (backwards ? (100-percent) : (percent-100)) + "%";
                toPage.style.left = (backwards ? -percent : percent) + "%";
            }
        }
    }
}
function preloadImages()
{
    var preloader = document.createElement("div");
    preloader.id = "preloader";
    document.body.appendChild(preloader);
}
function submitForm(form)
{
    iui.showPageByHref(form.action || "POST", encodeForm(form), form.method);
}
function encodeForm(form)
{
    function encode(inputs)
    {
        for (var i = 0; i < inputs.length; ++i)
        {
            if (inputs[i].name)
                args.push(inputs[i].name + "=" + escape(inputs[i].value));
        }
    }
    var args = [];
    encode(form.getElementsByTagName("input"));
    encode(form.getElementsByTagName("select"));
    return args;
}
function findParent(node, localName)
{
    while (node && (node.nodeType != 1 || node.localName.toLowerCase() !=
localName))
        node = node.parentNode;
    return node;
}
function hasClass(self, name)
{
    var re = new RegExp("(^|\\s)"+name+"($|\\s)");
    return re.exec(self.getAttribute("class")) != null;
}
```

(continued)

Listing 3-4 *(continued)*

```javascript
function replaceElementWithSource(replace, source)
{
    var page = replace.parentNode;
    var parent = replace;
    while (page.parentNode != document.body)
    {
        page = page.parentNode;
        parent = parent.parentNode;
    }
    var frag = document.createElement(parent.localName);
    frag.innerHTML = source;
    page.removeChild(parent);
    while (frag.firstChild)
        page.appendChild(frag.firstChild);
}
function $(id) { return document.getElementById(id); }
function ddd() { console.log.apply(console, arguments); }
})();
```

iui.js is open source code under the BSD license.

4

Styling with CSS

Like its Mac and Windows cousins, Mobile Safari provides some of the best CSS support of all Web browsers. As you develop iPhone and iPod touch applications, you can utilize CSS to make powerful user interfaces.

Mobile Safari provides support for several of the more advanced -webkit- styles that are not part of the W3C CSS standard. (A -webkit- prefix is added to the names of these properties.) For a normal Web application, developers will typically stay away from these experimental properties or at least not rely upon them for their application's design. However, because you know that an iPhone and iPod touch user will be using Mobile Safari, you can safely use these more advanced styles as you create your UI.

CSS Selectors Supported in Mobile Safari

Many would contend that the real power of CSS is not so much in the properties that you can apply, but in CSS's ability select the exact elements within a DOM that you want to work with. If you have worked with CSS before, you are probably well familiar with the standard type, class, and id selectors. However, Mobile Safari provides selector support that includes many new selectors that are part of the CSS3 specification. Table 4-1 lists a set of CSS selectors that Mobile Safari provides support for, while Table 4-2 lists the set of pseudo-classes and pseudo-elements that Mobile Safari works with.

Note that the following CSS3 selectors are not supported with Mobile Safari:

- ❏ :last-child
- ❏ :only-child
- ❏ nth-child()
- ❏ nth-last-child()
- ❏ last-of-type

- ❏ only-of-type
- ❏ :nth-of-type()
- ❏ :nth-last-of-type()
- ❏ empty

Table 4-1: Mobile Safari CSS Selectors

Selector	Definition
E	Type selector
.class	Class selector
#id	ID selector
*	Universal selector (all elements)
E F	Descendant selector
E > F	Child selector
E + F	Adjacent sibling selector
E ~ F	Indirect adjacent selector[a]
E[attr]	attr is defined
E[attr=val]	attr value matches val
E[attr~=val]	One of many attribute value selectors[b]
E[attr|=val]	attr value is a hyphen-separated list and begins with val[b]
E[attr^=val]	attr value begins with val[a,b]
E[attr$=val]	attr value ends with val[a,b]
E[attr*=val]	attr value contains at least one instance of val[a,b]

[a]New to CSS3
[b]Case sensitive, even when unnecessary

Table 4-2: Mobile Safari Pseudo-Classes and Pseudo-Elements

Pseudo-Class/ Pseudo-Element	Definition
E:link	Unvisited link
E:visited	Visited link
E:lang([Code])	Selector content uses the language code specified
E:before	Content before an element
E::before	Content before an element (new double-colon notation in CSS3)[a]
E:after	Content after an element
E::after	Content after an element (new double-colon notation in CSS3)[a]
E:first-letter	First letter of element

Pseudo-Class/ Pseudo-Element	Definition
E::first-letter	First letter of element (new double-colon notation in CSS3)[a]
E:first-line	First line of element
E::first-line	First line of element (new double-colon notation in CSS3)[a]
E:first-child	First child[b]
E:first-of-type	First child of type[a,b]
E:root	Root[a]
E:not()	Negation[a]
E:target	Target[a]
E:enabled	Enabled state[a]
E:disabled	Disabled state[a]
E:checked	Checked state[a]

[a]New to CSS3
[b]When new first child/child of type is created programmatically using JavaScript, the previous maintains the :first-child or :first-of-type attributes.

Text Styles

When you are styling text inside your iPhone and iPod touch applications, keep in mind three text-related styles that are important to effective UI design: -webkit-text-size-adjust, text-overflow, and text-shadow. These properties are explained in this section.

Controlling Text Sizing with -webkit-text-size-adjust

When a page is rendered, Mobile Safari will automatically size the page's text based on the width of the text block. However, by using the -webkit-text-size-adjust property, you can override this setting. The none option turns off auto-sizing of text:

```
body { -webkit-text-size-adjust: none; }
```

Or, you can specify a specific multiplier:

```
body { -webkit-text-size-adjust: 140%; }
```

Finally, you can set it to the default value of auto:

```
body { -webkit-text-size-adjust: auto; }
```

Figures 4-1, 4-2, and 4-3 show the results of these three options on the same page.

Figure 4-1: No text adjustment

Figure 4-2: Text is increased to 125%.

Figure 4-3: Text is adjusted based on width of the
content block.

For a normal Web site, -webkit-text-size-adjust: auto is recommended for improving
the readability of text. However, if you are developing an application, you will almost always want to
use -webkit-text-size-adjust: none to maintain precise control over the text sizing, particularly
when you go between portrait and landscape modes.

Handling Overflowed Text with text-overflow

Because the width of the viewport in Mobile Safari is either 320 (portrait) or 480 (landscape) pixels, effectively managing the physical length of dynamic text on UI elements can be tricky. This is particularly important for headings or button text in which a fixed amount of real estate is available. The best example of the need to handle text overflow is in the top toolbar that is a standard part of iPhone application interface. By default, any content that does not fit inside of the container box of the element is clipped, which can potentially lead to confusion, such as the example shown in Figure 4-4.

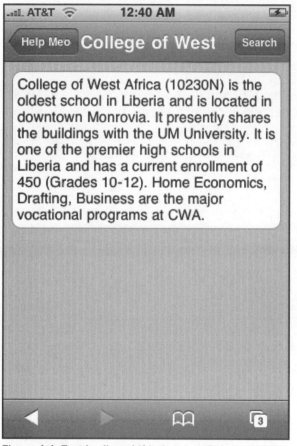

Figure 4-4: Text is clipped if it does not fit into available space.

Therefore, to prevent this situation from happening, you will want to provide a visual hint that the text has been clipped. Fortunately, the `text-overflow` property enables developers to specify what they wish to have done when the text runs on. The two values are `ellipsis` and `clip`. The `ellipsis` value trims the content and adds an ellipsis character (. . .) to the end. Suppose you assign the following property to the toolbar's button and heading element:

```
text-overflow: ellipsis;
```

Now, when text overflows, an ellipsis is added, as shown in Figure 4-5.

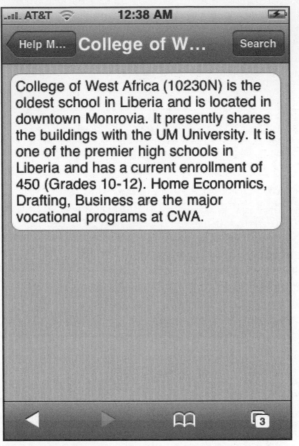

Figure 4-5: Ellipsis provides a visual indicator that the text has been clipped.

The `text-overflow` property is particularly useful for iPhone and iPod touch because a heading that displays fully in landscape mode may need to be clipped in the much thinner portrait mode.

The use of `text-overflow` may require specifying additional CSS properties to display as intended. The following code, for example, needs to have `overflow` or `white-space` properties set to ensure that the `text-overflow` property works:

```
<html>
<meta name="viewport" content="width=320; initial-scale=1.0; maximum-scale=1.0;">
<style>
.ellipsis {
text-overflow: ellipsis;
width: 200px;
```

```
    white-space: nowrap;
    overflow: hidden;
}
.ellipsisBroken1 {
text-overflow: ellipsis;
width: 200px;
/* white-space: nowrap; */
overflow: hidden;
}
.ellipsisBroken2 {
text-overflow: ellipsis;
width: 200px;
white-space: nowrap;
/* overflow: hidden; */
}
</style>
<body>
<div class="ellipsis"> this is a test this is a test this is a test
this is a test this is a test this is a testthis is a test </div>
<br><br>
<div class="ellipsisBroken1"> this is a test this is a test this is a test
this is a test this is a test this is a testthis is a test </div>
<br><br>
<div class="ellipsisBroken2"> this is a test this is a test this is a test
this is a test this is a test this is a testthis is a test </div>
</body>
</html>
```

Subtle Shadows with text-shadow

In the iPhone UI, Apple makes subtle use of text shadows, particularly on buttons and larger heading text. In addition to aesthetics, text shadows are also useful in making text more readable by increasing its contrast with the background.

You can add drop shadows to your text through the text-shadow property. The basic declaration is as follows:

```
text-shadow: #666666 0px -1px 0;
```

The first value is the color of the shadow. The next two give the shadow's offset position — the second value being the *x*-coordinate and the third is the *y*-coordinate. (Negative values move the shadow left and up.) The fourth parameter indicates the shadow's Gaussian blur radius. So, in the preceding example, a gray shadow is added 1px above the element's text with no blur.

However, text shadows can be a distraction and look tacky if they are too noticeable. Therefore, an rgba (red, green, blue, alpha) color value can be used in place of a solid color value in order to define the transparency value of the shadow. (See the "Setting Transparencies" section later in this chapter.) Therefore, the following declaration defines a white shadow with a .7 alpha value (0.0 is fully transparent, while 1.0 is fully opaque) that is positioned 1 pixel under the element's text:

```
text-shadow: rgba(255, 255, 255, 0.7) 0 1px 0;
```

Figures 4-6 and 4-7 show the subtle difference of adding a text shadow.

Figure 4-6: No text shadow defined   Figure 4-7: Text shadow defined

Styling Block Elements

There are several styles that you can apply to block elements to transform their appearance that go beyond the typical CSS2 styles. These include three so-called experimental properties (-webkit-border-image, -webkit-border-radius, and -webkit-appearance) and a CSS3 enhancement of the background property. These are described in this section.

Image-Based Borders with -webkit-border-image

The -webkit-border-image property enables you to use an image to specify the border rather than the border-style properties. The image appears behind the content of the element, but on top of the background. For example:

```
-webkit-border-image: url(image.png) 7 7 7 7;
```

The four numbers that follow the image URL represent the number of pixels in the image that should be used as the border. The first number indicates the height of the top (both the corners and edge) of the image used. Per CSS conventions, the remaining three numbers indicate the right, bottom, and left sides. Pixel is the default unit, though you can specify percentages.

If the image URL you provide cannot be located or the style is set to none, then border-style properties are used instead.

One or two keywords can be optionally specified at the end of the declaration. These determine how the images for the sides and the middle are scaled and tiled. The valid keywords are stretch or round. If stretch is used as the first keyword, the top, middle, and bottom parts of the image are scaled to the same width as the element's padding box. Far less common for iPhone use, round can also be used as the first keyword. When used, the top, middle, and bottom images are reduced in width so that a whole number of the images fit in the width of the padding box. The second keyword acts on the height of the left, middle, and right images. If both keywords are omitted, then stretch stretch is implied.

When rendered, the Mobile Safari browser looks at the -webkit-border-image property and divides up the image based on the four numbers specified.

The -webkit-border-image property plays an important role in creating CSS-based iPhone buttons, which is explained later in this chapter.

Rounded Corners with -webkit-border-radius

The `-webkit-border-radius` is used to specify the radius of the corners of an element. Using this property, you can easily create rounded corners on your elements rather than resorting to image-based corners. For example:

```
-webkit-border-radius: 10px;
```

This declaration specifies a 10px radius for the element, which is the standard radius value for the Rounded Rectangle design for destination pages (see Chapter 3). You can also specify the radius of each individual corner using the following properties:

```
-webkit-border-top-left-radius
-webkit-border-top-right-radius
-webkit-border-bottom-left-radius
-webkit-border-bottom-right-radius
```

If, for example, you wanted to create a `div` with rounded top corners, but square bottom corners, the style code would look like the following:

```
div.roundedTopBox {
   -webkit-border-top-left-radius: 10px;
   -webkit-border-top-right-radius: 10px;
   -webkit-border-bottom-left-radius: 0px;
   -webkit-border-bottom-right-radius: 0px;
}
```

Results are shown in Figure 4-8.

Gradient Push Buttons with -webkit-appearance

The `-webkit-appearance` property is designed to transform the appearance of an element into a variety of different controls. Mobile Safari supports just two of the possible values: `push-button` and `button`. But it is the `push-button` that holds the most promise for iPhone application developers. Suppose, for example, you would like to turn a link element into a gradient push button. You could do it with an image, but `-webkit-appearance: push-button` allows you to do it entirely within CSS. To demonstrate, begin with a link assigned to a class named `special`:

```
<a href="tel:202-555-1212" class="special">Call Headquarters</a>
```

Then, define the `a.special` style:

```
a.special {
    display: block;
    width: 246px;
    font-family: Helvetica;
    font-size: 20px;
    font-weight: bold;
    color: #000000;
    text-decoration: none;
    text-shadow: rgba(255, 255, 255, 0.7) 0 1px 0;
```

(continued)

91

(continued)

```
        text-align: center;
        line-height: 36px;
        margin: 15px auto;
        -webkit-border-radius:10px;
        -webkit-appearance: push-button;
    }
```

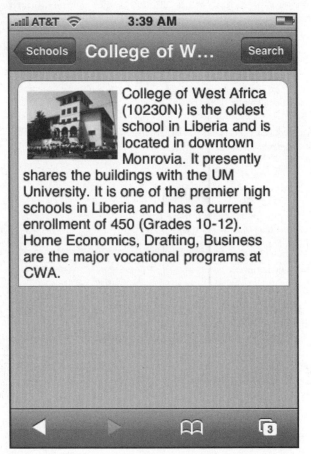

Figure 4-8: Rounded top, square bottom

The `display:block` and `width:246px` properties give the link a wide rectangular block shape.
The `-webkit-appearance: push-button` property transforms the appearance to have a gradient gray
push button look. The `-webkit-border-radius` rounds the edges using the standard 10px value.
While the shape of the push button is now set, the text needs to be tweaked using not just standard text

formatting properties, but also a `line-height` property of 36px, which vertically centers the 20px text in the middle of the push button. If you add a simple `background-color: #000000` style to the body tag, then you get the result shown in Figure 4-9.

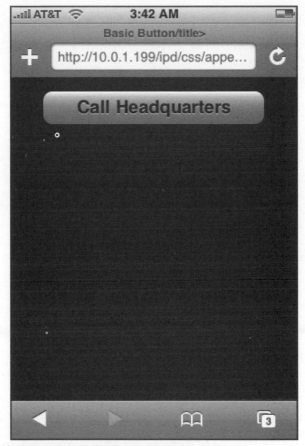

Figure 4-9: Gradient push button

Multiple Background Images

In earlier versions of CSS, there was always a 1:1 correspondence between an element and a background image. While that capability worked for most purposes, some page designs could not work effectively with a single background image defined. So, in order to get around the 1:1 limitation, designers would resort to adding extra `div` tags here or there just to achieve the intended visual design.

CSS3 addresses this issue by giving you the ability to define multiple background images for a given element. Most browsers don't support this feature yet, but fortunately for iPhone application developers, Mobile Safari does.

You define a set of background images by listing them in order after the background property name declaration. Images are rendered with the first one declared on top, the second image behind the first, and so on. You can also specify the background-repeat and background-position values for each of the images. If background-color is defined, then this color is painted below all of the images. For example:

```
div.banner {
background: url(header_top.png) top left no-repeat,
    url(banner_main.png) top 6px no-repeat,
    url(header_bottom.png) bottom left no-repeat,
    url(middle.png) left repeat-y;
}
```

In this code, the header_top.png serves as the background image aligned to the top left portion of the div element. The banner_main.png is positioned 6px from the top, while the header_bottom.png image is positioned at the bottom of the div. Finally, the middle.png is treated as a repeating background.

Setting Transparencies

Developers have long used rgb to specify an RGB color value for text and backgrounds. CSS3 adds the ability to set an alpha value when specifying an RGB color with the new rgba declaration. Using the rgba declaration, you can add translucent color overlays without transparent PNGs or GIFs. The syntax is:

```
rgba(r, g, b, alpha)
```

The r, g, and b values are integers between 0-255 that represent the red, green, and blue values, while alpha is a value between 0 and 1 (0.0 is fully transparent, while 1.0 is fully opaque). For example, to set a red background with a 50 percent transparency, you would use:

```
background: rgba(255, 0, 0, 0.5);
```

The alpha value in the rgba declaration is not the same as the opacity property. rgba sets the opacity value only for the current element, while opacity sets the value for the element and its descendants.

The following example shows five div elements, each with a different alpha value for the black background:

```
<!DOCTYPE html PUBLIC "-//W3C//DTD XHTML 1.0 Strict//EN"
        "http://www.w3.org/TR/xhtml1/DTD/xhtml1-strict.dtd">
<html xmlns="http://www.w3.org/1999/xhtml">
<head>
<title>RGBA Declaration</title>
```

```
<meta name="viewport" content="width=320; initial-scale=1.0; maximum-scale=1.0;
user-scalable=0;">
<style type="text/css" media="screen">
div.colorBlock {
    width: 50px;
    height: 50px;
    float: left;
    margin-bottom: 10px;
    font-family: Helvetica;
    font-size: 20px;
    text-align:center;
    color:white;
    text-shadow: rgba(0,0, 0, 0.7) 0 1px 0;
    line-height: 46px;
}
</style>
</head>
<body>
<div style="margin: 10px 0 0 30px;">
<div class="colorBlock" style="background: rgba(0, 0, 0, 0.2);"><span
>20%</span></div>
<div class="colorBlock" style="background: rgba(0, 0, 0,
0.4);"><span>40%</span></div>
<div class="colorBlock" style="background: rgba(0, 0, 0,
0.6);"><span>60%</span></div>
<div class="colorBlock" style="background: rgba(0, 0, 0,
0.8);"><span>80%</span></div>
<div class="colorBlock" style="background: rgba(0, 0, 0,  1.0)
;"><span>100%</span></div>
</div>
</body>
</html>
```

Figure 4-10 shows the page in Mobile Safari.

Creating CSS-Based iPhone Buttons

Using -webkit-border-image, you can create push buttons that closely emulate Apple's standard push button design. This technique, inspired by developer Matthew Krivanek, involves using a pill-shaped button image (available for download at www.wrox.com), stretching the middle of the button image, but ensuring that the left and side sides of the button are not distorted in the process.

Begin by defining a normal link with a fullSizedButton class:

```
<a href="mailto:rich@digitalwalk.net" class="fullSizedButton">Send to Client</a>
```

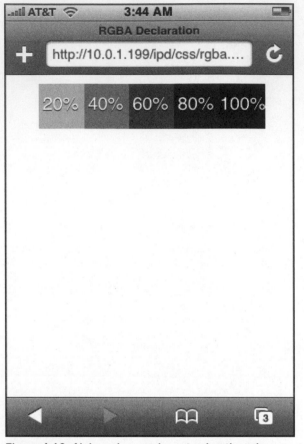

Figure 4-10: Alpha value can be set using the rgba declaration.

Next, define the a.fullSizedButton style:

```
a .fullSizedButton {
    font-family: Helvetica;
    font-size: 20px;
    display: block;
    width: 246px;
    line-height: 46px;
    margin: 15px auto;
    text-align:center;
    text-decoration: none;
    font-weight: bold;
    color: #000000;
    text-shadow: rgba(255, 255, 255, 0.7) 0 1px 0;
    border-width: 0 14px 0 14px;
    -webkit-border-image: url(images/whiteButton.png) 0 14 0 14;
}
```

In the preceding code, the `display` property is set to `block` and the width is set to 246px, the width of the buttons used by Apple. The `line-height` is set to 46px, which gives the block element the standard height and vertically centers the button text. A `border-width` property sets the left and right borders to 14px and eliminates the borders for the top and bottom by defining their values as 0.

Now that everything else is set up, look at the `-webkit-border-image` property definition. In this example, 0 pixels are used from whiteButton.png on the top and bottom. However, the first 14 pixels of the image are used for the left border of the element, while the 14 rightmost pixels are used for the right border. Because the whiteButton.png image is 29 pixels in width, a 1-pixel section is used as the middle section. This middle section is then repeated over and over to fill the width of the element. Figure 4-11 shows how `-webkit-border-image` divides up the image.

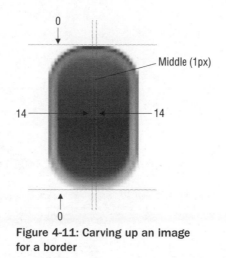

Figure 4-11: Carving up an image for a border

Figure 4-12 shows the button when rendered by Mobile Safari.

Here is the full source code for this example:

```
<!DOCTYPE html PUBLIC "-//W3C//DTD XHTML 1.0 Strict//EN"
        "http://www.w3.org/TR/xhtml1/DTD/xhtml1-strict.dtd">
<html xmlns="http://www.w3.org/1999/xhtml">
<head>
<title>Basic Button/title>
<meta name="viewport" content="width=320; initial-scale=1.0; maximum-scale=1.0;
user-scalable=0;">
<style type="text/css" media="screen">
a.fullSizedButton {
    font-family: Helvetica;
    font-size: 20px;
    display: block;
    width: 246px;
    margin: 15px auto;
    text-align:center;
```

(continued)

(continued)

```
        text-decoration: none;
        line-height: 46px;
        font-weight: bold;
        color: #000000;
        text-shadow: rgba(255, 255, 255, 0.7) 0 1px 0;
        border-width: 0 14px 0 14px;
        -webkit-border-image: url(images/whiteButton.png) 0 14 0 14;
}
body {
 background-color: black;
}
</style>
</head>
<body>
<a href="mailto:me@company.net" class="fullSizedButton">Send to Client</a>
</body>
</html>
```

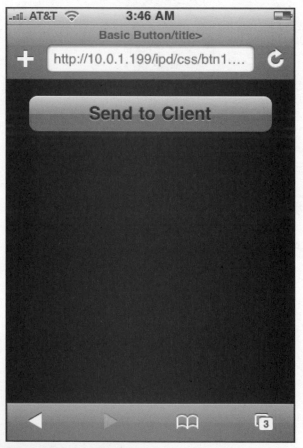

Figure 4-12: A border image

Identifying Incompatibilities

While Mobile Safari is closely related to its Mac and Windows counterparts, it is not identical in terms of CSS support. The latest versions of Safari for Mac and Windows support most of the newer CSS3 and experimental properties (prefixed with -webkit-). Mobile Safari provides limited support of several properties.

The following CSS properties are not supported (or have limited support) in Mobile Safari:

- ❑   box-shadow
- ❑   -webkit-box-shadow
- ❑   text-stroke
- ❑   -webkit-text-stroke
- ❑   text-fill-color
- ❑   -webkit-text-fill-color
- ❑   -website-appearance (push-button supported, but no other values are)

Handling Touch Interactions and Events

An essential part of any Web 2.0 application is the ability to respond to events triggered by the user or by a condition that occurs on the client. The clicking of a button. The pressing of a key. The scrolling of a window. While the user interacts with an HTML element, the entire document, or the browser window, JavaScript serves as the watchful eye behind the scenes that monitors all of this activity taking place and fires off events as they occur.

With its touch screen interface, iPhone is all about direct interactivity with the user. As a result, you would expect any iPhone/iPod touch application you create to be able to handle the variety of finger taps, flicks, swipes, and pinches that a user naturally performs as they interact with their mobile device. However, because of the current capabilities of Mobile Safari browser, you have to work with these interactions differently than what you might expect.

How iPhone Handles Events

When working with touch interactions and events for iPhone, keep in mind that the finger is not a mouse. As a result, the traditional event model that Web developers are so used to working with does not always apply in this new context. This is both good news and bad news for the application developer. The good news is that much of the touch interaction that iPhone and iPod touch are famous for is built right into Mobile Safari. As a result, you do not need to write any code to handle the basic touch interactions of the user. Flick-scrolling, pinching and unpinching, and one-finger scrolling are those sorts of user inputs that come for free. The bad news is that the developer is greatly constrained in his or her ability to work with the full suite of JavaScript events and override built-in behavior. As a result, certain user interactions that have become a staple to Web developers now are impossible to utilize or require tricky, dumbed-down workarounds.

The general rule of thumb for iPhone event handling is that no events trigger *until* the user's finger leaves the touch screen. The implications are significant:

❑ The onmousedown event handler fires only after a mouse up event occurs (but before onmouseup is triggered). As a result, the onmousedown event is rendered useless.

❑ The onmousemove event handler is unsupported. However, on rare occasions, our tests show that Mobile Safari may trigger an onmousemove event, so developers should not assume that these handlers will never be called.

❑ :hover does not work.

In addition, you cannot trap for zoom events associated with the window. First, Mobile Safari provides no built-in event handler support for zooming out or zooming in. Second, you cannot perform a work-around by polling the window for width changes, since the width remains the same regardless of the current zoom factor.

You cannot trap for events associated with a user switching between pages in Mobile Safari. The onfocus and onblur events of the window object are not triggered when the focus moves off or on a page. Additionally, when another page becomes the active page, JavaScript events (including polling events created with setInterval()) are not fired. However, the onunload event of the window object is triggered when the user loads a new page in the current window.

Table 5-1 lists the events that are fully supported and unsupported. Table 5-2 identifies the events that are partially supported.

Table 5-1: JavaScript Event Compatibility

Supported events	Unsupported events
formfield.onblur	document.onkeydown
formfield.onchange	document.onkeypress
formfield.onclick	document.onkeyup
formfield.onfocusformfield.onkeydown	form.onsubmit
formfield.onkeyup	formfield.ondblclick
formfield.onkeypress	formfield.onmouseenter
formfield.onmouseout	formfield.onmouseleave
formfield.onmouseover	formfield.onmousemove
formfield.onmouseup	formfield.onselect
form.onreset	window.oncontextmenu
window.onload	window.onerror
window.onmousewheel	window.onresize
window.onorientationchange	window.onscroll

Table 5-2: Partially Supported JavaScript Events

Event	Level of support
document.onmousedown	Occurs after a mouseup event occurs but before onmouseup is fired

Besides the anomaly of the timing of the onmousedown event, the rest of the supported mouse and key events fire in Mobile Safari in the same sequence as a standard Web browser. Table 5-3 shows the event sequences that occur when both a block level element and a form element are clicked. The form element column also displays the order of key events if the user types in the on-screen keyboard.

Table 5-3: Event Sequencing

Block-level elements (e.g., div)	Form element (e.g., textarea, input)
onmouseover	onmouseover
onmousedown	onmousedown
onmouseup	onfocus
onclick	onmouseup
onmouseout	onclick
	onkeydown
	onkeypress
	onkeyup
	onchange
	onblur
	onmouseout

Detecting an Orientation Change

One of the unique events that an iPhone application developer will need to be able to trap for is the change between vertical and horizontal orientation. Newer versions of Mobile Safari (iPhone 1.1.1 and later) provide support for the onorientationchange event handler of the window object. This event is triggered each time the device is rotated by the user. The following code shows how to configure the onorientationchange event:

```
<!DOCTYPE html PUBLIC "-//W3C//DTD XHTML 1.0 Strict//EN"
        "http://www.w3.org/TR/xhtml1/DTD/xhtml1-strict.dtd">
<html xmlns="http://www.w3.org/1999/xhtml">
<head>
<title>Orientation Change Example</title>
```

(continued)

(continued)

```
<meta name="viewport" content="width=320; initial-scale=1.0; maximum-scale=1.0;
user-scalable=0;">
<script type="application/x-javascript">
    function orientationChange() {
      var str = "Orientation: ";
      switch(window.orientation) {
          case 0:
              str += "Portrait";
          break;

          case -90:
              str += "Landscape (right, screen turned clockwise)";
          break;

          case 90:
              str += "Landscape (left, screen turned counterclockwise)";
          break;

          case 180:
            str += "Portrait (upside-down portrait)";
          break;
      }
      document.getElementById("mode").innerHTML = str;
    }
</script>
</head>
<body onload="orientationChange();" onorientationchange="orientationChange();">
<h4 id="mode">Ras sed nibh.</h4>
<p>
Donec semper lorem ac dolor ornare interdum. Praesent condimentum. Suspendisse
lacinia interdum augue. Nunc venenatis ipsum sed ligula. Aenean vitae lacus. Sed
sit amet neque. Vestibulum ante ipsum primis in faucibus orci luctus et ultrices
posuere cubilia Curae; Duis laoreet lorem quis nulla. Curabitur enim erat, gravida
ac, posuere sed, nonummy in, tortor. Donec id orci id lectus convallis egestas.
Duis ut dui. Aliquam dignissim dictum metus.
</p>
</body>
</html>
```

An onorientationchange attribute is added to the body element and assigned the JavaScript function orientationChange(). The orientationChange() function evaluates the window.orientation property to determine the current state: 0 (Portrait), -90 (Landscape, clockwise), 90 (Landscape counterclockwise), or 180 (Portrait, upside down). The current state string is then output to the document.

However, note that the onorientationchange event is not triggered when the document loads. Therefore, in order to evaluate the document orientation at this time, assign the orientationChange() function to the onload event.

While the onorientationchange event works great for iPhone 1.1.1 and later, earlier versions of Mobile Safari did not support this event. Therefore, if you are designing an application that works on all versions of Mobile Safari, you need to perform a workaround to emulate this functionality.

The `window.onresize` event handler would seem like a logical candidate to trap for an orientation change. For example, consider the following code:

```
<!DOCTYPE html PUBLIC "-//W3C//DTD XHTML 1.0 Strict//EN"
        "http://www.w3.org/TR/xhtml1/DTD/xhtml1-strict.dtd">
<html xmlns="http://www.w3.org/1999/xhtml">
<head>
<head>
<title>On Resize</title>
<meta name="viewport" content="width=320; initial-scale=1.0; maximum-scale=1.0;
user-scalable=0;">
<script type="application/x-javascript">
    window.onresize = function( ) {
        alert( "window.onresize detected: "+ document.body.offsetWidth +"x"+
document.body.offsetHeight );
    };
</script>
</head>
<body>
<h1>Cras sed nibh.</h1>
<p>
Donec semper lorem ac dolor ornare interdum. Praesent condimentum. Suspendisse
lacinia interdum augue. Nunc venenatis ipsum sed ligula. Aenean vitae lacus. Sed
sit amet neque. Vestibulum ante ipsum primis in faucibus orci luctus et ultrices
posuere cubilia Curae; Duis laoreet lorem quis nulla. Curabitur enim erat, gravida
ac, posuere sed, nonummy in, tortor. Donec id orci id lectus convallis egestas.
Duis ut dui. Aliquam dignissim dictum metus.
</p>
</body>
</html>
```

In this example, a function is added as the handler for `window.onresize`, which calls an `alert()` dialog box each time a window resize is detected. While this is a logical option, the problem with using `window.onresize` to detect an orientation change is that this event is triggered inconsistently. It does not fire off every time. In fact, it usually does not fire until after the *third* time the orientation changes. As a result, until Mobile Safari corrects this issue, avoid using `onresize`.

A much better solution is to poll the browser for orientation changes using the `setInterval()` function. Here's a basic example:

```
<!DOCTYPE html PUBLIC "-//W3C//DTD XHTML 1.0 Strict//EN"
        "http://www.w3.org/TR/xhtml1/DTD/xhtml1-strict.dtd">
<html xmlns="http://www.w3.org/1999/xhtml">
<head>
<title>Orientation Change Example #1</title>
<meta name="viewport" content="width=320; initial-scale=1.0; maximum-scale=1.0;
user-scalable=0;">
<script type="application/x-javascript">
    // add timer event
    addEventListener("load", function() {
        setTimeout(orientationChange, 0);
    }, false);
    var currentWidth = 0;
```

(continued)

105

(continued)

```
        // handler for orientation changes
        function orientationChange() {
            if (window.innerWidth != currentWidth) {
          currentWidth = window.innerWidth;
          var orient = (currentWidth == 320) ? "portrait" : "landscape";
          // do something useful here
            document.getElementById('mode').innerHTML = 'Current mode: ' + orient;
        }
      setInterval(orientationChange, 400);
    </script>
    </head>
    <body>
    <h4 id="mode">Ras sed nibh.</h4>
    <p>
    Donec semper lorem ac dolor ornare interdum. Praesent condimentum. Suspendisse
    lacinia interdum augue. Nunc venenatis ipsum sed ligula. Aenean vitae lacus. Sed
    sit amet neque. Vestibulum ante ipsum primis in faucibus orci luctus et ultrices
    posuere cubilia Curae; Duis laoreet lorem quis nulla. Curabitur enim erat, gravida
    ac, posuere sed, nonummy in, tortor. Donec id orci id lectus convallis egestas.
    Duis ut dui. Aliquam dignissim dictum metus.
    </p>
    </body>
    </html>
```

`addEventListener()` is used to fire the `orientationChange()` function when the window is loaded. The `orientationChange()` function is then called continuously using `setInterval()` at the end of the script to poll the browser.

The `orientationChange()` function itself works by detecting changes in the `innerWidth` property of the `window`. The function compares the `innerWidth` against its previously known value, which is stored in the `currentWidth` variable. If the `innerWidth` has changed, then the `currentWidth` variable is updated to the new `innerWidth` value and the `orient` variable is set with the current orientation. If the `currentWidth` equals 320 (the width of iPhone when held in portrait mode), then the `orient` variable is assigned the string value of `portrait`. Otherwise, it receives a string value of `landscape`. For this example, the `orient` string value is added to the `innerHTML` property of the h4 element in the text.

When the vast majority of iPhone users have upgraded to 1.1.1 and later, use of `onorientationchange` is recommended. However, until then, the `setInterval()` workaround is a safer solution.

Changing a Style Sheet When Orientation Changes

The most common procedure that iPhone developers will want to use an `orientationChange()` handler for is to specify a style sheet based on the current viewport orientation. To do so, you can expand upon the previous `orientationChange()` handler by updating the `orient` attribute of the body element based on the current orientation, and then updating the active CSS styles off of that attribute value.

To add this functionality, you first begin with a basic XHTML document. The following code, based on Joe Hewitt's liquid layout template, uses a series of `div` elements to imitate a basic iPhone interface, consisting of a top toolbar, content area, and bottom toolbar. The content inside of the `center div` is going to be used for testing purposes only. Here's the code:

```
<!DOCTYPE html PUBLIC "-//W3C//DTD XHTML 1.0 Strict//EN"
        "http://www.w3.org/TR/xhtml1/DTD/xhtml1-strict.dtd">
<html xmlns="http://www.w3.org/1999/xhtml">
<head>
<title>Change Stylesheet based on Orientation</title>
<meta name="viewport" content="width=320; initial-scale=1.0; maximum-scale=1.0;
user-scalable=0;">
</head>
<body>
    <div id="canvasMain" class="container">
        <div class="toolbar anchorTop">
            <div class="main">
                <div class="header">AppTop</div>
            </div>
        </div>
        <div class="center">
      <p>Orientation mode:<span id="iMode"></span></p>
        <p>Width:<span id="iWidth"></span></p>
        <p>Height:<span id="iHeight"></span></p>
        <p>Bottom toolbar height:<span id="iToolbarHeight"></span></p>
        <p>Bottom toolbar top:<span id="iToolbarTop"></span></p>
        </div>
        <div id="bottomToolbar" class="toolbar anchorBottom">
            <div class="main">
                <div class="header">
                    AppBottom
                </div>
            </div>
        </div>
    </div></body>
</html>
```

Next, add CSS rules to the document head. However, notice the selector for the final four rules are dependent upon the state of the `orient` attribute of `body`:

```
<style type="text/css" media="screen">
    body {
        margin: 0;
        padding: 0;
        width: 320px;
        height: 416px;
        font-family: Helvetica;
        -webkit-user-select: none;
        cursor: default;
        -webkit-text-size-adjust: none;
    background: #000000;
```

(continued)

(continued)

```css
      color: #FFFFFF;
    }
    .container {
            position: absolute;
            width: 100%;
    }
    .toolbar {
            position: absolute;
            width: 100%;
            height: 60px;
            font-size: 28pt;
    }
    .anchorTop {
            top: 0;
    }
    .anchorBottom {
            bottom: 0;
    }
    .center {
            position: absolute;
            top: 60px;
            bottom: 60px;
    }
    .main {
        overflow: hidden;
        position: relative;
    }
    .header {
        position: relative;
        height: 44px;
        -webkit-box-sizing: border-box;
        box-sizing: border-box;
        background-color: rgb(111, 135, 168);
        border-top: 1px solid rgb(179, 186, 201);
        border-bottom: 1px solid rgb(73, 95, 144);
        color: white;
        font-size: 20px;
        text-shadow: rgba(0, 0, 0, 0.6) 0 -1px 0;
        font-weight: bold;
        text-align: center;
        line-height: 42px;
    }
/* Styles adjusted based on orientation  */
    body[orient='portrait'] .container {
            height: 436px;
    }
    body[orient='landscape'] .container {
            height: 258px;
```

```
        }
        body[orient='landscape'] .toolbar {
                height: 30px;
                font-size: 16pt;
        }
        body[orient='landscape'] .center {
                top: 50px;
                bottom: 30px;
        }
    </style>
```

Based on the body element's orient value, the container CSS class changes its height, the top and bottom toolbars adjust their height and font-size, and the main content area (the center class) is repositioned to fit with the sizing changes around it.

With the XHTML and CSS styles in place, you are ready to add the JavaScript code inside of the document head:

```
<script type="application/x-javascript">
    addEventListener('load', function() {
        setTimeout(orientationChange, 0);
    }, false);
    var currentWidth = 0;
    function orientationChange() {
        if (window.innerWidth != currentWidth) {
           currentWidth - window.innerWidth;
              var orient = currentWidth == 320 ? 'portrait' : 'landscape';
            document.body.setAttribute('orient', orient);

         setTimeout(function() {
                        document.getElementById('iMode').innerHTML = orient;
                        document.getElementById('iWidth').innerHTML = currentWidth
 + 'px';
                        document.getElementById('iHeight').innerHTML =
document.getElementById('canvasMain').offsetHeight + 'px';
                        document.getElementById('iToolbarHeight').innerHTML =
document.getElementById('bottomToolbar').offsetHeight +'px';
                        document.getElementById('iToolbarTop').innerHTML =
document.getElementById('bottomToolbar').offsetTop +'px';
         }, 100);

        setTimeout(function() {
            window.scrollTo(0, 1);
        }, 100);
      }
    }
    setInterval(orientationChange, 400);
</script>
```

If you worked through the previous example, the shell of this code looks pretty familiar. The orientationChange() function is called by the addEventListener() function when the window is loaded, and then setInterval() is used to poll the browser every 400 milliseconds. The orientationChange() function evaluates window.innerWidth, checking to see if any change has occurred since the previous test. If a change is detected, then the body element's orient attribute is updated to either portrait or landscape.

This example also outputs some of the changing div size and position values into a series of span elements for information purposes. Notice that the getElementById() calls are enclosed inside of a setTimeout() function. Without setTimeout(), the values do not correctly display the first time orientationChange() is called when the document loads.

Finally, to hide the URL bar, window.scrollTo() is called. Once again, to prevent timing problems, this call is enclosed inside of a setTimeout() function.

Figures 5-1 and 5-2 show the document loaded in both portrait and landscape modes, respectively.

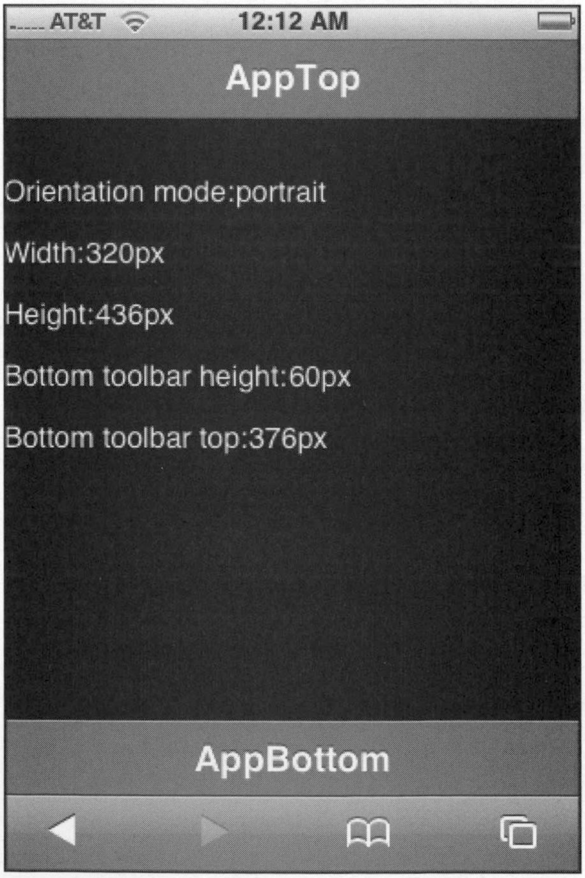

Figure 5-1: Portrait mode

Figure 5-2: Landscape mode

Changing Element Positioning Based on Orientation Change

Once you begin to understand the basic interaction between an `orientationChange()` polling function and orientation-dependent styles, you can begin to dynamically position elements of the UI based on whether the current viewport is in portrait or landscape mode. Suppose, for example, you would like to align an arrow image to the bottom left side of a page. Here's the `img` declaration:

```
<img id="pushBtn" src="bottombarknobgray.png"/>
```

To align the graphic in portrait mode, you could specify the CSS rule as:

```
#pushbtn {
    position: absolute;
    left: 10px;
    top: 360px;
}
```

However, if you leave the positioning as is, the button would go offscreen when the user tilted the viewport to landscape mode. Therefore, a second landscape-specific rule is needed for the button image with an adjusted `top` value:

```
body[orient="landscape"] #pushBtn {
    left: 10px;
    top: 212px;
}
```

To adjust the image positioning based on the orientation, add the core `orientationChange()` polling functionality:

```
addEventListener("load", function() {
    setTimeout(orientationChange, 0);
}, false);
```

(continued)

(continued)

```
        var currentWidth = 0;
        function orientationChange() {
            if (window.innerWidth != currentWidth) {
            currentWidth = window.innerWidth;
          var orient = (currentWidth == 320) ? "portrait" : "landscape";
          document.body.setAttribute('orient', orient);
            setTimeout(function() {
                        window.scrollTo(0, 1);
            }, 100);
        }
        }
        setInterval(orientationChange, 400);
```

As Figures 5-3 and 5-4 show, the button image aligns to the bottom left of the page document in both portrait and landscape modes respectively.

Figure 5-3: Push button aligned in portrait mode

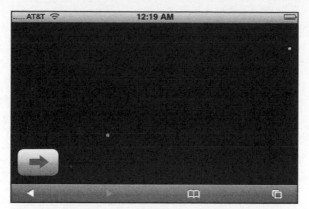

Figure 5-4: Push button aligned in landscape mode

Capturing Two-Finger Scrolling

Pinching and flicking are arguably the most popular touch inputs for iPhone and iPod touch, but as a developer, you have no way to capture these events for your own purposes. You have to go along with what Mobile Safari does by default. However, you do have a way to manipulate a less popular touch input — the two-finger scroll. While a one-finger scroll is used to move an entire page around, the two-finger scroll can be used to scroll inside any scrollable region of a page, such as a textarea. Because Mobile Safari supports the overriding of the window.onmousewheel event, you can use the two-finger scroll for your own purposes.

Suppose, for example, you would like to control the vertical position of a ball image based on the two-finger scroll input of the user inside of a scrollable region. When the user scrolls up, you want the ball to move up. When the user scrolls down, you want the ball to move down. Figure 5-5 shows the UI layout for this example.

Start with the page layout and styles:

```
<!DOCTYPE html PUBLIC "-//W3C//DTD XHTML 1.0 Strict//EN"
        "http://www.w3.org/TR/xhtml1/DTD/xhtml1-strict.dtd">
<html xmlns="http://www.w3.org/1999/xhtml">
<head>
<title>ScrollPad</title>
<meta name="viewport" content="width=320; initial-scale=1.0; maximum-scale=1.0;
user-scalable=0;">
<style type="text/css" media="screen">
    body {
        margin: 0;
        padding: 0;
        width: 320px;
      height: 416px;
        font-family: Helvetica;
        -webkit-user-select: none;
        cursor: default;
```

(continued)

(continued)

```
            -webkit-text-size-adjust: none;
    background: #000000;
    color: #FFFFFF;
     }
     #leftPane {
          position: absolute;
          width: 160px;
          height: 100%;
     }
     #rightPane {
          position: absolute;
          width: 140px;
          left: 161px;
          height:100%;
     }
  #scrollPad {
          width: 148px;
          top: 3px;
          height: 300px;
          border-style: none;
          background-image: url( 'fs.png' );
     }
     #blueDot {
               position: absolute;
               left: 50px;
               top: 10px;
     }
</style>
</head>
<body>
    <div id="leftPane">
        <p>Use a two-finger scroll in the scrollpad to move the blue dot.</p>
        <form>
        <textarea id="scrollPad" readonly="readonly" disabled="true"></textarea>
        </form>
    </div>
    <div id="rightPane">
        <img id="blueDot" src="compose_atom_selected.png"/>
    </div>
</body>
</html>
```

The `scrollPad` `textarea` element is used as the *hot* scrollable region. It is enclosed inside of a `div` on the left half of the page and sized large enough so that a two-finger scroll is easy for people to perform inside of its borders. To ensure that the `textarea` is easy to identify on the screen, an arrow PNG is added as the background image and a solid border is defined. The `disabled="true"` attribute value must be added to prevent keyboard input in the control. On the other side of the page, the `blueDot` `img` is enclosed inside of a `div` on the right.

The interactivity comes by capturing `window.onmousewheel`, which is the event Mobile Safari triggers when a user performs a two-finger scroll. You do that through an `addEventListener()` call:

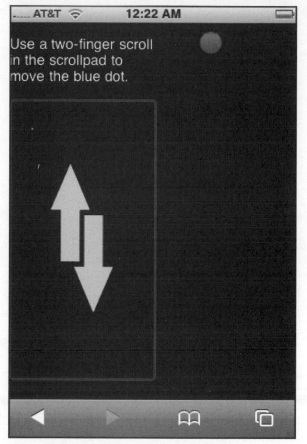

Figure 5-5: UI for the ScrollPad application

```
addEventListener('load', function() {
    window.onmousewheel = twoFingerScroll;
  setTimeout(function() {
      window.scrollTo(0, 1);
  }, 100);
}, false);
```

As shown in the preceding example, a function called `twoFingerScroll()` is assigned to be the event handler for `window.onmousewheel`. And, as is now typical for iPhone applications, a `window.scrollTo()` is called inside `setTimeout()` to hide the URL bar.

Next, here's the code for `twoFingerScroll()`:

```
function twoFingerScroll(wEvent) {
    var delta = wEvent.wheelDelta/120;
    scrollBall(delta);
    return true;
}
```

115

The wheelDelta property returns -120 when the scroll movement is upward and a positive 120 when the movement is downward. This value is divided by 120 and assigned to the delta variable, which is then passed onto the scrollBall() function.

The scrollBall() function is used to manipulate the vertical position of the ball:

```
var currentTop = 1;
var INC = 8
function scrollBall(delta) {
    currentTop = document.getElementById('blueDot').offsetTop;
    if (delta < 0)
              currentTop = currentTop-INC;
    else if (delta > 0)
          currentTop = currentTop+INC;
    if (currentTop > 390)
          currentTop = 390;
    else if (currentTop < 1 )
          currentTop = 1;
  document.getElementById('blueDot').style.top = currentTop + 'px';
  setTimeout(function() {
              window.scrollTo(0, 1);
      }, 100);
}
```

The currentTop variable is used to store the current top position of the blueDot img. The delta variable is then evaluated. If the number is less than 0, then currentTop decreases by the value of INC. If greater than 0, then it increases by the same amount. While INC can be any value, 8 seems the most natural for touch interaction in this example. To ensure the blueDot does not scroll off the top or bottom of the viewport, the currentTop value is evaluated and adjusted as needed. The blueDot style.top property is updated to the new value. Finally, to ensure that inadvertent touch inputs do not cause the URL bar to display, window.scrollTo() is called.

This technique enables you to effectively utilize the two-finger scroll in your own applications. However, there are two caveats to using this touch input:

❑ The biggest downfall to implementing the two-finger scroll in your application is that it is a tricky touch input for a user to pull off consistently. If one of the fingers lifts up off of the glass surface, Mobile Safari is unforgiving. It immediately thinks the user is performing a one-finger scroll and begins to scroll the entire page.

❑ There is no way to effectively program a flicking action in association with a two-finger scroll to accelerate the rate of movement of the element you are manipulating. Instead, there is always a 1:1 correspondence between the firing of an onmousescroll event and the position of the element.

Finally, I should mention that this demo works only in portrait mode and is not enabled for landscape.

Simulating a Drag-and-Drop Action

I mentioned already that Mobile Safari does not provide support for drag-and-drop actions. However, it is possible to use the two-finger scrolling technique to implement a poor man's version of drag-and-drop. Therefore, instead of manipulating another object as shown in the previous example, you can dynamically reposition the scrollable region when the user performs a two-finger scroll on it. However, in addition to the two-finger scroll limitations previously discussed, keep in mind the following constraints to simulating drag-and-drop:

- ❑   A two-finger scroll is not a standard drag- and-drop input for iPhone.

- ❑   The dragging element can only move around in a vertical position. There is no way to programmatically move in a horizontal position based on a user's two-finger scroll input.

- ❑   Because the two-finger scroll is happening on the element being moved, this interaction has a tendency to cause inadvertent page scrolling.

With those constraints in mind, consider the following example, which uses a two-finger scroll to move a globe image (see Figure 5-6) from the top to the bottom of a page. As the globe hits the bottom of the page, the image is changed to simulate the animation of a melting globe (see Figure 5-7).

Figure 5-6: The globe can move up or down based on a two-finger scroll.

Figure 5-7: When the globe hits the bottom of the viewport, it begins to melt.

The full source code for this example follows:

```
<!DOCTYPE html PUBLIC "-//W3C//DTD XHTML 1.0 Strict//EN"
        "http://www.w3.org/TR/xhtml1/DTD/xhtml1-strict.dtd">
<html xmlns="http://www.w3.org/1999/xhtml">
<head>
<title>Poor Man's Drag & Drop</title>
<meta name="viewport" content="width=320; initial-scale=1.0; maximum-scale=1.0;
user-scalable=0;">
<style type="text/css" media="screen">
    body {
        margin: 0;
        padding: 0;
        width: 320px;
        height: 416px;
        font-family: Helvetica;
```

```
                -webkit-user-select: none;
                cursor: default;
                -webkit-text-size-adjust: none;
                background: #000000;
                color: #FFFFFF;
        }
    #dropItem {
                position: absolute;
                left: 10px;
                top: 10px;
                width: 300px;
                height: 303px;
                border-color: #000000;
                background-image: url( 'globe.png' );
        }
</style>
<script type="application/x-javascript">
        addEventListener('load', function() {
                setTimeout(function() {
                        window.scrollTo(0, 1);
                }, 100);
        }, false);
</script>
</head>
<body>
<form>
<textarea id="dropItem" readonly="readonly" disabled="true"></textarea>
</form>
<script type="application/x-javascript">
    var dropItem = document.getElementById('dropItem');
    window.onmousewheel = moveItem;
    function moveItem(wEvent) {
            var delta = wEvent.wheelDelta/120;
            var currentTop = parseInt(dropItem.style.top) || 0;
            currentTop = currentTop + delta;
            dropItem.style.top = (currentTop) + "px";
            setTimeout(function() {
              if ( currentTop > 195 )
                  dropItem.style.backgroundImage = 'url( globemelt.png)';
              else if ( currentTop < 195 )
                  dropItem.style.backgroundImage = 'url( globe.png)';
                }, 100);
            setTimeout(function() {
              window.scrollTo(0, 1);
                }, 100);
    }
</script>
</body>
</html>
```

Since it provides support for a two-finger scroll, a textarea is used as the draggable element. It is sized big enough (300 × 303px) so that an average user can easily place two-fingers on it. (If you make the element too small — say 60 × 60 — then it becomes virtually impossible to get two-fingers on it.) The border of the element is hidden and a background image is assigned to it. A disabled="true" attribute value is added to textarea to prevent the keyboard from displaying when the user selects the element.

Next, this example shows an alternative way to trap for the window.onmousewheel event. Note that the JavaScript code is placed in a script element at the bottom of the page rather than in the document header so that it loads after everything else on the page. The moveItem() function is used to adjust the vertical positioning of the textarea based on the wheelDelta value received from the onmousewheel event. The current position is then evaluated to determine the correct background image to display. This code is wrapped inside of a setTimeout() to prevent timing issues from occurring.

Trapping for Key Events with the On-Screen Keyboard

As with an ordinary Web page, you can validate keyboard input by trapping the onkeydown event. To illustrate, suppose you have an input field in which you wish to prevent the user from entering in a numeric value. To trap for this, begin by adding an onkeydown handler to the input element:

```
<input onkeydown="return validate(event)" />
```

In the document header, add a script element with the following code inside of it:

```
function validate(e) {
    var keynum = e.which;
    var keychar = String.fromCharCode(keynum);
    var chk = /\d/;
    return !chk.test(keychar)
}
```

As a standard JavaScript validation routine, this function tests the current character code value to determine whether it is a number. If a non-number is found, then true is returned to the input field. Otherwise, a false is sent back and the character is disallowed.

Advanced Programming Topics: Canvas and Video

The unique platform capabilities of iPhone and iPod touch enable developers to create innovative applications inside of Mobile Safari that go beyond the normal "Web app" fare. Mobile Safari's support for the canvas element opens drawing and animation capabilities in an ordinary HTML page that was previously available only by using Flash or Java. What's more, deep inside the heart of these two Apple devices lies the best portable audio and video media player that money can buy. As an application developer, you can take advantage of these iPod capabilities by seamlessly integrating multimedia into your mobile applications.

However, once you begin to open up these capabilities of Mobile Safari or the device itself, you need to be sure that you are working with an iPhone and iPod touch rather than a desktop browser. So, I'll start by showing you how to identify the user agent for iPhone and iPod touch.

Identifying the User Agent for iPhone and iPod touch

When you are trying to identify the capabilities of the browser requesting your Web site or application, you generally want to avoid detecting the user agent and use object detection instead. However, if you are developing an application designed exclusively for iPhone/iPod touch or need Safari-specific features, such as canvas, then user agent detection is a valid option. Therefore, this chapter assumes you are creating a Mobile Safari–specific application. Chapter 8 discusses using media queries in general Web contexts.

The Mobile Safari user agent string for iPhone closely resembles the user agent for Safari on other platforms. However, it contains an iPhone platform name and the mobile version number. Depending on the version of Mobile Safari, it will look something like this:

```
Mozilla/5.0 (iPhone; U; CPU like Mac OS X; en) AppleWebKit/420+ (KHTML, like Gecko)
Version/3.0 Mobile/1A543a Safari/419.3
```

Here's a breakdown of the various components of the user agent:

❑   The platform string: `(iPhone; U; CPU like Mac OS X; en)`. Notice the "`like Mac OS X`" line, which reveals some the underpinnings of the iPhone.

❑   The WebKit engine build number: `AppleWebKit/420+`. This Safari version number is provided on all platforms (including Mac and Windows).

❑   The marketing version: `(Version/3.0)`. This Safari version number is provided on all platforms (including Mac and Windows).

❑   OS X build number: `Mobile/1A543a`.

❑   Safari build number: `Safari/419.3`.

The iPod touch user agent is similar, but distinct with `iPod` as the platform:

```
Mozila/5.0 (iPod; U; CPU like Mac OS X; en) AppleWebKit/420.1 (KHTML, like Geckto)
Version/3.0 Mobile/3A101a Safari/419.3
```

The version numbers will change, obviously, when Apple updates Mobile Safari, but the string structure stays the same.

To test to whether the device is an iPhone/iPod touch or not, you need to perform a string search on `iPhone` and `iPod`. The following function returns `true` if the user agent is either an iPhone or iPod touch:

```
function isAppleMobile() {
  result ((navigator.platform.indexOf("iPhone") != -1) ||
          (navigator.userAgent.indexOf('iPod') != -1))
}
```

Be sure not to test for the string `Mobile` within the user agent, because a non-Apple mobile device (such as Nokia) might be based on the WebKit-based browser.

If you need to do anything beyond basic user agent detection and test for specific devices or browser versions, however, consider using WebKit's own user agent detection script available for download at `trac.webkit .org/projects/webkit/wiki/DetectingWebKit`. By linking WebKitDetect.js to your page, you can test for specific devices (iPhone and iPod touch) as well as software versions. Here's a sample detection script:

```
<!DOCTYPE html PUBLIC "-//W3C//DTD XHTML 1.0 Strict//EN"
          "http://www.w3.org/TR/xhtml1/DTD/xhtml1-strict.dtd">
<html xmlns="http://www.w3.org/1999/xhtml">
<head>
<title>User Agent Detection via WebKit Script</title>
<meta name="viewport" content="width=320; initial-scale=1.0; maximum-scale=1.0;
user-scalable=0;">
<script type="application/x-javascript" src="WebKitDetect.js"></script>
</head>
```

```
<body>
<p id="log"></p>
</body>
<script type="application/x-javascript">
function addTextNode(str) {
  var t = document.createTextNode(str);
  var p = document.getElementById("log");
  p.appendChild(t);
}
if ( WebKitDetect.isMobile() ) {
  var device = WebKitDetect.mobileDevice();
  // String found in Settings/General/About/Version
  var minSupport = WebKitDetect.mobileVersionIsAtLeast("1C28");
  switch( device ) {
    case 'iPhone' :
      if ( minSupport ) {
        addTextNode('If this were a real app, I launch its URL right now.');
        break;
      }
      else {
        addTextNode('Please upgrade your iPhone to the latest update before
running this application.');
        break;
      }
    case 'iPod' :
      addTextNode('If this were a real app, I would launch its iPod touch
version.');
    default :
      addTextNode( 'This mobile device is not supported by this application.
Go to your nearest Apple store and get an iPhone.');
  }
}
else {
  addTextNode( 'Desktop computers are so 1990s. Go to your nearest Apple store and
get an iPhone.' );
}
</script>
</html>
```

With the WebKitDetect.js script included, the WebKitDetect object is accessible. Begin by calling its isMobile() method to determine whether the device is or is not a mobile device. Next, check to ensure that the mobile version is the latest release and save that result in the minSupport variable. The switch statement then evaluates the mobile devices. If it is an iPhone, then it checks to see if minSupport is true. If so, then a real application would begin here. If minSupport is false, then the user is notified to update his or her iPhone to the latest software version. The remaining two case statements evaluate for an iPhone or else an unknown mobile device. The final else statement is called if the device is not a mobile computer.

Programming the iPhone Canvas

C++ and other traditional software programmers have long worked with a *canvas* on which they could draw graphics. In contrast, Web developers typically program the presentation layer using HTML and CSS. But unless they used Flash or Java, they had no real way to actually draw graphical content on a

Web page. However, both desktop and mobile versions of Safari support the canvas element to provide a resolution-dependent bitmap region for drawing arbitrary content. The canvas element defines a drawing region on your Web page that you then draw on using a corresponding JavaScript canvas object. The canvas element is part of the Web Hypertext Application Technology Working Group (WHATWG) specification for HTML 5.0.

The canvas frees you up as an application developer to not only draw anything you want to, but also to use canvas as a way to render graphs, program games, or add special effects. On Mac OS X, the canvas is often used for creating Dashboard widgets. On iPhone, Apple makes use of the canvas for both the Clock and Stocks built-in applications.

Canvas programming can be a mindset difference for Web developers used to manipulating existing graphics rather than creating them from scratch. It is the loose equivalent of a Photoshop expert beginning to create content using an Adobe Illustrator–like program in which all of the graphics are created in a nonvisual manner.

Defining the Canvas Element

The canvas is defined using the canvas element:

```
<canvas id="theCanvas" width="300" height="300"/>
```

Except for the src and alt attributes, the canvas element supports all of the same attributes as the img tag. However, the id, width, and height attributes are not required, but should be defined as a sound programming practice. The width and height are usually defined in pixels, although it could also be a percentage of the viewport.

You can place multiple canvas elements on a page, just as long as each one has its own unique id.

Getting a Context

Once a canvas region is defined on your Web page, you can then draw inside of the flat two-dimensional surface using JavaScript. Just like a Web page, the canvas has an origin (0,0) in the top left corner. By default, all of the x,y coordinates you specify are relative to this position.

As the first step in working with the canvas, you first need to get a 2d context object. This object, which is responsible for managing the canvas' graphics state, is obtained by calling the getContext() method of the canvas object:

```
var canvas = document.GetElementById("theCanvas");
var context = canvas.getContext("2d");
```

Or, because you don't normally work directly with the canvas object, you can also combine the two lines:

```
var context = document.GetElementById("theCanvas").getContext("2d");
```

All of the drawing properties and methods you work with are called from the context object. The context object has many properties (see Table 6-1) that determine how the drawing looks on the page.

Table 6-1: Context Properties

Property	Description
fillStyle	Provides CSS color or style (gradient, pattern) of the fill of a path.
globalAlpha	Specifies the level of transparency of content drawn on the canvas. Floating point value is between 0.0 (fully transparent) and 1.0 (fully opaque).
globalCompositeOperation	Specifies the compositing mode to determine how the canvas is displayed relative to background content. Values include copy, darker, destination-atop, destination-in, destination-out, destination-over, lighten, source-atop, source-in, source-out, source-over, xor.
lineCap	Defines the end style of a line. String values include butt for flat edge, round for rounded edge, square for square ends. (Defaults to butt.)
lineJoin	Specifies the way lines are joined together. String values include round, bevel, miter. (Defaults to miter.)
lineWidth	Specifies the line width. Floating point value is greater than 0.
miterLimit	Specifies the miter limit for drawing a juncture between line segments.
shadowBlur	Defines the width that a shadow covers.
shadowColor	Provides CSS color for the shadow.
shadowOffsetX	Specifies the horizontal distance of the shadow from the source.
shadowOffsetY	Specifies the vertical distance of the shadow from the source.
strokeStyle	Defines the CSS color or style (gradient, pattern) when stroking paths.

Drawing a Simple Rectangle

There are several techniques for drawing on the canvas. Perhaps the most straightforward is by drawing a rectangle. To do so, you work with three context methods:

❑ context.fillRect(x,y,w,h) draws a filled rectangle.

❑ context.strokeRect(x,y,w,h) draws a rectangular outline.

❑ context.clearRect(x,y,w,h) clears the specified rectangle and makes it transparent.

For example, suppose you would like to draw a rectangular box with a set of squares inside of it and a rectangular outline on the outside. Here's a JavaScript function that draws that shape:

```
function draw(){
  var canvas = document.getElementById('myCanvas');
  var context = canvas.getContext('2d');
    context.strokeRect(10,10,150,140);
    context.fillRect(15,15,140,130);
    context.clearRect(30,30,30,30);
    context.clearRect(70,30,30,30);
    context.clearRect(110,30,30,30);
    context.clearRect(30,100,30,30);
    context.clearRect(70,100,30,30);
    context.clearRect(110,100,30,30);
}
```

Once the `context` is obtained, then `strokeRect()` creates a rectangular outline starting at the coordinate (10,10) and is 150 × 140 pixels in size. The `fillRect()` method paints a 140 × 130 rectangle starting at coordinate (15,15). The six `clearRect()` calls clear areas previously painted by `fillRect()`. Figure 6-1 shows the result.

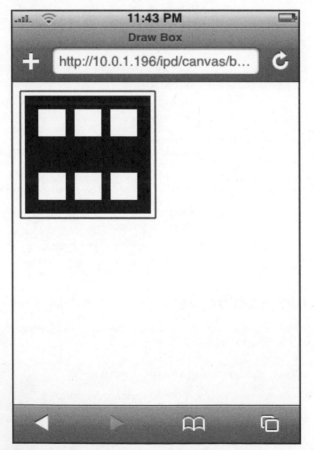

Figure 6-1: Rectangular blocks drawn on a canvas

The full page source is shown in the following code:

```
<!DOCTYPE html PUBLIC "-//W3C//DTD XHTML 1.0 Strict//EN"
        "http://www.w3.org/TR/xhtml1/DTD/xhtml1-strict.dtd">
<html xmlns="http://www.w3.org/1999/xhtml">
<head>
<title>Draw Box</title>
<meta name="viewport" content="width=320; initial-scale=1.0; maximum-scale=1.0;
user-scalable=0;">
<script type="application/x-javascript">
function draw(){
    var canvas = document.getElementById('myCanvas');
    var context = canvas.getContext('2d');
    context.strokeRect(10,10,150,140);
    context.fillRect(15,15,140,130);
    context.clearRect(30,30,30,30);
    context.clearRect(70,30,30,30);
    context.clearRect(110,30,30,30);
    context.clearRect(30,100,30,30);
    context.clearRect(70,100,30,30);
    context.clearRect(110,100,30,30);
}
</script>
</head>
<body onload="draw()">
<canvas id="myCanvas" width="300" height="300" style="position:absolute; left:0px;
top:0px; z-index:1"/>
</body>
</html>
```

Drawing Other Shapes

Non-rectangular shapes are drawn by creating a path for that shape, and then either *stroking* (drawing) a line along the specified path or else *filling* (painting) in the area inside of the path. Much like an Etch A Sketch drawing, paths are composed of a series of *subpaths*, such as a straight line or an arc that together form a shape.

When you work with paths, the following methods are used for drawing basic shapes:

❏   beginPath() creates a new path in the canvas and sets the starting point to the coordinate (0,0).

❏   closePath() closes an open path and attempts to draw a straight line from the current point to the starting point of the path. The use of closePath() is optional.

❏   stroke() draws a line along the current path.

❏   fill() closes the current path and paints the area within it. (Because fill() closes the path automatically, you don't need to call closePath() when you use it.)

❑ lineTo(x,y) adds a line segment from the current point to the specified coordinate.

❑ moveTo(x,y) moves the starting point to a new coordinate specified by the *x,y* values.

Using these methods, you can create a list of subpaths to form a shape. For example, the following code creates two triangles next to each other; one is empty and one is filled. An outer rectangle surrounds both triangles. Here's the code:

```
function drawTriangles(){
  var canvas = document.getElementById('myCanvas');
  var context = canvas.getContext('2d');
  // Empty triangle
  context.beginPath();
  context.moveTo(10,10);
  context.lineTo(10,75);
  context.lineTo(100,40);
  context.lineTo(10,10);
  context.stroke();
  context.closePath();
  // Filled triangle
  context.beginPath();
  context.moveTo(110,10);
  context.lineTo(110,75);
  context.lineTo(200,40);
  context.lineTo(110,10);
  context.fill();
  // Outer rectangle
  context.strokeRect(3,3,205,80);
}
```

Figure 6-2 shows the results.

If you are new to canvas programming, drawing complex shapes on the canvas can take some getting used to. You may find it helpful initially to go low tech and use a piece of graph paper to sketch out the shapes you are trying to draw and calculate the x,y coordinates using the paper grid.

The JavaScript canvas enables you to go well beyond drawing with straight lines, however. You can use the following methods to create more advanced curves and shapes:

❑ arc(x, y, radius, startAngle, endAngle, clockwise) adds an arc to the current sub-path using a radius and specified angles (measured in radians).

❑ arcTo(x1, y1, x2, y2, radius) adds an arc of a circle to the current subpath by using a radius and tangent points.

❑ quadratricCurveTo(cpx, cpy, x, y) adds a quadratic Bezier curve to the current subpath. It has a single control point (the point outside of the circle that the line curves toward) represented by cpx, cpy. The *x,y* values represent the new ending point.

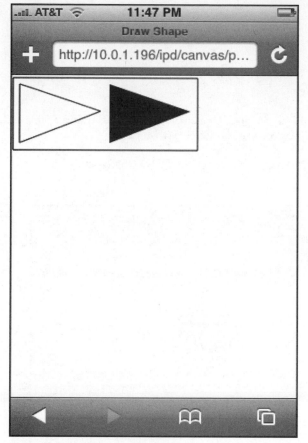

Figure 6-2: Drawing two triangles

❑ `bezierCurveTo(cp1x, cp1y, cp2x, cp2y, x, y)` adds a cubic Bezier curve to the current subpath using two control points.

Using `arc()`, I can create a filled circle inside of an empty circle using the following code:

```
function drawCircles(){
  var canvas = document.getElementById('myCanvas');
  var context = canvas.getContext('2d');
  // Create filled circle
  context.beginPath();
  context.arc(125,65,30,0, 2*pi, 0);
  context.fill();
```

(continued)

129

(continued)

```
    // Create empty circle
    context.beginPath();
    context.arc(125,65,35,0, 2*pi, 0);
    context.stroke();
    context.endPath();
}
```

The `arc()` method starts the arc shape at coordinate (125,65) and draws a 30px radius starting at 0 degrees and ending at 360 degrees at a counterclockwise path.

Figure 6-3 displays the circle shapes that are created when this script is run.

Figure 6-3: Using arc() to draw a circle

Drawing an Image

In addition to lines and other shapes, you can also draw an image onto your canvas by using the drawImage() method. The image can reference either an external image or another canvas element on the page. There are actually three ways in which you can call this method. The first variant simply draws an image at the specified coordinates using the size of the image:

```
context.drawImage(image, x, y)
```

The second method enables you to specify the dimensions of the image with the w and h arguments:

```
context.drawImage(image, x, y, width, height)
```

To do a basic image draw, define the Image object and assign an src. Next, you want to draw the image, but only after you are certain the image is fully loaded. Therefore, the drawImage() method is placed inside of the image's onload handler:

```
<!DOCTYPE html PUBLIC "-//W3C//DTD XHTML 1.0 Strict//EN"
          "http://www.w3.org/TR/xhtml1/DTD/xhtml1-strict.dtd">
<html xmlns="http://www.w3.org/1999/xhtml">
<head>
<title>Draw Image</title>
<meta name="viewport" content="width=320; initial-scale=1.0; maximum-scale=1.0;
user-scalable=0;">
<script type="application/x-javascript">
function drawImg(){
  var canvas = document.getElementById('myCanvas');
  var context = canvas.getContext('2d');
  var img = new Image();
  img.src = 'images/beach.jpg';
  img.onload = function() {
    context.drawImage( img, 0, 0 );
  }
}
</script>
</head>
<body onload="drawImg()">
<canvas id="myCanvas" width="300" height="300" style="position:absolute; left:0px;
top:0px; z-index:1"/>
</body>
</html>
```

Figure 6-4 shows the image displayed inside of the canvas. Keep in mind that this is not an HTML img element, but the external image file drawn onto the context of the canvas.

Figure 6-4: Drawing an image onto the canvas

Additionally, there is a final `drawImage()` option that is slightly more complex:

```
context.drawImage(image, sourcex, sourcey, sourceWidth, sourceHeight, destx, desty,
destWidth, destHeight)
```

In this variant, the method draws a subsection of the image specified by the source rectangle (`sourcex`, `sourcey`, `sourceWidth`, `sourceHeight`) onto a destination rectangle specified by the final arguments (`destx`, `desty`, `destWidth`, `destHeight`). For example, suppose you just wanted to display the rock thrower in Figure 6-4 rather than the entire picture. Using this expanded syntax of `drawImage()`, you want to extract a 79 × 131px rectangle from the original picture starting at the coordinate (151, 63). You then paint the same sized rectangle at coordinate (10, 10) on the canvas. Here is the updated code:

```
function drawImg(){
  var canvas = document.getElementById('myCanvas');
  var context = canvas.getContext('2d');
  var img = new Image();
```

```
img.src = 'images/beach.jpg';
img.onload = function() {
    context.drawImage( img, 151, 63, 79, 131, 10, 10, 79, 131 );
}
}
```

Figure 6-5 shows the result.

Figure 6-5: Painting a portion of an image

You can also use a data: URI encoded image (see Chapter 10 for more details on data: URI encoding) to eliminate the need for an external image file altogether for canvas painting. For example, start with an online image encoder, such as the one available at www.scalora.org/projects/uriencoder. Using this tool, you encode the image, as shown in Figure 6-6.

Figure 6-6: Encoding an image

The outputted encoded string can then be integrated into the script code as the image object's source (much of the encoded text for this example has been removed for space reasons):

```
function drawImg(){
var img_src = 'data:image/jpeg;base64,' +
'/9j/4AAQSkZJRgABAgAAZABkAAD/7AARRHVja3kAAQAEAAAAMAAA/+4ADkFkb2JlAGTAAAAAf/bAIQA' +
'CQYGBgcGCQcHCQ0IBwgNDwsJCQsPEQ4ODw4ERENDg4ODg0RERQUFhQUERoaHBwaGiYmJiYmKysrKysr' +
'KysrKwEJCAgJCgkMCgoMDww0DhMVDg4PDg4VGhMRERERExoGhYWFahoXHR0aGh0dJCQjJCQr' +
'KysrKysrKysr/8AAEQgA4AEsAwEiAAIRAQMRAf/EAJ8AAAEFAQEBAAAAAAAAAAAAIBAwQFBgAHCAEA' +
'AwEBAQAAAAAAAAAAAAAAECAwQFEAABAwIEAwUFBQcEAQUAAAABAAAIDEQQhMRIFQVETYXGBIgaRoTIj' +
'FLFCUnIzwdFiQyQ0B+GCkhWy0lODNRcRAAICAQMCBAUDBAMAAAAAAAABEQIhMRIDQVFhcYEikaGxEwTB' +
'MkLw4VIj0WKC/9oADAMBAAIRAxEAPwDyO2t5TdRAvJbqHFaWRkETzCMzia8VSMEocxw+HVg5WgIke0vq' +
'ZKLmtk6Ke0tYmgRNAypglK6MUiaOQXEKCgSkSlImIRWcA+U3uVaFaQj5be5AMKi6iVcgQKSiJIgBKLkq' +
'5ACLkq5ACLkq5ACJEq5ACJKJVyABXFKkQAiQhKUiAEKSiIpKIpKIAhCQjSEIAoSEZQlAgaLqJaJQEDGbg' +
'VhcOYT00A9N/IHBPXf6Du5DtbKQuPBxr7kpyOMD9x+i/8pWQ/m+P7VsLr+3k/KVj/wCZ4p9GLsT/APp9' +
'OmIIzR8p0jsHErPNYljQxowbgpW5TOudxkfm2LyN7zi5R8u5IlvIJAPYhPvRHNDkfsTEXnpO1tXXcu4X' +
'rOpY7TC671jOT3g6YYj+Z5CsLL1B6lvPUcTTdyPmmma18IPyg2vnb08tLW1Xendsu7v08+K2idI7cdwg' +
'hl0jAQwMMz9R4CrhmrqT07centnvNyaz6neJ201Ob8NvHJ+oWfiIriV2cfHfZV11Je+zX0+BwcvLx77q' +
'0Ws/9dE/r4Z1M5u8zX7zaQwnRbwuj6IpgOrKZtQH+9Qt7AG87g0ClLmYAf8AyOVptdp1vU9iJcI7SOG4' +
'm1cGQRNld/4qpguDcbg64lo8zPkmdq/FR0gPtWPIpTnG6+PRf3N+PDUZ28cv/wBP+wF8a3cnGhDa9rQG' +
'n7FHfknnwwyCBk7h5JXDXDXE4ktpqqw8V13Z3VqYy23MToTK3qMDsKtOFfaFg02248fidCaSSnw+AwE5FHJK' +
'8MYKuOPIADMk8AOKft7a7EzIxZOnlkAfHG5j6uacjpbQlpVlJuh28fTRWVtb3rD/AFB6OsUFCI/nl3eV' +
'VeNRNnCXgTbkcxVbm/H5kaBn09jNcwQNuomPZFLdPJDWudiGRsqCa0zPsUKW7nlFCQxnFjAGtFewLZv9' +
'Y3EOxWt4yxtRNPM+Jw0DSTG0fM0tpj5lRyerdzeySLo2jYpfijFtHT3hbcleNKqXI9JhV7mPFFls7N8S' +
'w4127YfQoySSTmTxS0XONXF1AKmtAKDwCTCq5TqDM0jm6SQRliATQDTnRABRKEqG2wwhF3euK5AAkJT7' +
'lyRACJOK41CD5jjkgQYxNEkhp5R4pNWkVGaCpOJzKcBIuCRKkOaBirqmlOGdF1SuwSGenAp+U/IPco4K' +
'duHhls9xya0krZHP0Kbc7k9Nlow4yCslPw8vFdZQgDLioUTnTSumdm817hwVrbUHgsnlnVVbak6BoACl' +
```

```
  'tywUWM44J809ipCZz60VLvc/Tt3mvBWssoaM1nN3c65kZA3OV7WD/caIYkZ6/wBpvdvbFJcN8103qxyD' +
  'I6vNpPaFDIBHby5r1q9261vLF1jcN1RaQ0c2loo1ze0LzDddtn2y8fazCtMWP4PacnBJCsoK84Yc8ihJ' +
  '4HNE7t45psk6gDmEyGeibFul7snoq07tdIDhcyOLhUdR0sUMOHZ51VbDvO4Xd/fyXtw+4611OJNZqMhS' +
  'jchSvBO31yGf4422AHGa5fXuY6R32kLP7XeiyuxM8F0T2vilAz0SN0mnaM12X5HW3Cpaqq1b7ZOKnErU' +
  '57bU709kn1wzf7fBt9pDPudwDNdbna6YoWsLi2GFjWSup/E61exQrR8M/pq93G7gbd3AdNBFduYGOdEG' +
  'lzHUAwAJIw71QWPq7dba4MshbdQuPmhkGAYRpc2NwoWVbhhgrrbmnfrXc4LS5kc6b6ZvSdGyJsMQkNWM' +
  'axxaaCuQFfFaU5aXxTWLe3u9ZMr8N+NbrvE19yelU4jwKpkcMVtbXWirLG0bcVPGaSWRsbSPzmvc1X+3' +
  'emYtw2fZru9A0NdNeX9w8+YxF3Uax1eD8yqrcd22yz3C92qe1N3tzGQWvy39N4NsDVzTjm5xVZuXqndL' +
  'xs9tFK6322UgMtGkUaxrQxrNVK0o3FZ7+Ljb3e6Ft2r/ACX6YNdnNyJbfZL3bn/jZaefuZ6BZ+p9svLG' +
  '43Nhi+rtnTR2keHUERLWMcWA6tJzPYsp61sWTGHeLZ8cwlAivei7W1k1ARjn5gciskCpdhul/t7nus5j' +
  'D1BpkAALXDhVrgRUcCov+WuSuy9YT6rv3gvj/D+1ffx2yuj0jtJO3d4isLHbqaZbQPM7eIllDZHA9orp' +
  '8FUpQ/W8ulJLnnU5+bqnEnE41SEAU0mtQCcKUPJc17bnPTReSwdVK7axq8tvxeWcVyTilUFnLly5AHJC' +
  'lJQlAjkhPtSoCUwEJQB2LkvFNu8rimhMPVq8EtUDCKdiJApCqhOaXguSKOCVCi4I6h0P/9k=';
  var canvas = document.getElementById('myCanvas');
  var context = canvas.getContext('2d');
  var img = new Image();
  img.src = img_src;
  img.onload = function() {
    context.drawImage( img, 10, 10 );
  }
}
```

Figure 6-7 shows the rendered image.

Figure 6-7: Encoded image

Adding Color and Transparency

The `fillStyle` and `strokeStyle` properties of the `context` object provides a way for you to set the color, alpha value, or style of the shape or line you are drawing. (See Table 6-1 for a list of all context properties.) If you would like to set a color value, you can use any CSS color, such as:

```
context.fillStyle="#666666";
context.strokeStyle=rgb(125,125,125);
```

Once you set `fillStyle` or `strokeStyle`, it becomes the default value for all new shapes in the canvas until you reassign it.

You can also use `rgba(r,g,b,a)` to assign an alpha value to the shape you are filling in. The `r`, `g`, and `b` parameters take an integer value between 0-255, while `a` is a float value between 0.0 and 1.0 (0.0 being fully transparent, and 1.0 being fully opaque). For example, the following code draws two circles in the canvas. The large circle has a 90 percent transparency value, while the smaller circle has a 30 percent transparency value:

```
function drawTransCircles() {
    var canvas = document.getElementById('myCanvas');
    var context = canvas.getContext('2d');
    // Large circle - 90% transparency
    context.fillStyle = "rgba(13,44,50, 0.9)";
    context.beginPath();
    context.arc(95,90,60,0, 2*pi, 0);
    context.fill();
    // Smaller circle - 30% transparency
    context.fillStyle = "rgba(0,0,255, 0.3)";
    context.beginPath();
    context.arc(135,120,40,0, 2*pi, 0);
    context.fill();
}
```

Figure 6-8 shows the two colored, semitransparent circles. Alternatively, you can set the `context .globalAlpha` property to set a default transparency value for all stroke or fill styles. Once again, value should be a float number between 0.0 and 1.0.

Adding Gradients

You can create both linear and radial gradients by using the following methods of the `context` object:

❑ `createLinerGradient(x1,y1,x2,y2)` creates a gradient from the starting point (x1,y1) to the end point (x2,y2).

❑ `createRadialGradient(x1,y1,r1,x2,y2,r2)` creates a gradient circle. The first circle is based on the x1, y1, and r1 values and the second circle based on the x2, y2, and r2 values.

Both of these methods return a `canvasGradient` object that can have colors assigned to it with the `addColorStop(position, color)` method. The `position` argument is a float number between 0.0 and 1.0 that indicates the position of the color in the gradient. The `color` argument is any CSS color.

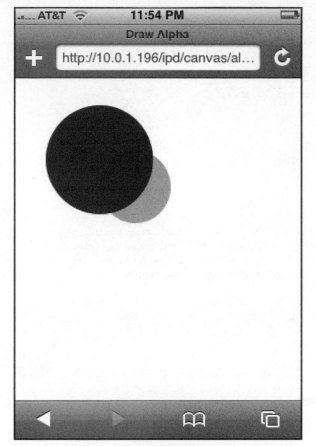

Figure 6-8: Working with alpha values

In the following example, a linear gradient is added to a square box on the canvas. The gradient starts on the left side, transitions to blue, and ends on the right in red. Here is the code for the entire HTML page:

```
<!DOCTYPE html PUBLIC "-//W3C//DTD XHTML 1.0 Strict//EN"
        "http://www.w3.org/TR/xhtml1/DTD/xhtml1-strict.dtd">
<html xmlns="http://www.w3.org/1999/xhtml">
<head>
<title>Draw Gradient</title>
<meta name="viewport" content="width=320; initial-scale=1.0; maximum-scale=1.0;
user-scalable=0;">
<script type="application/x-javascript">
function drawGradient(){
  var canvas = document.getElementById('myCanvas');
  var context = canvas.getContext('2d');
  var lg = context.createLinearGradient(0,125,250,125);
  context.globalAlpha="0.8";
  lg.addColorStop(0,'white');
  lg.addColorStop(0.75,'blue');
```

(continued)

(continued)

```
        lg.addColorStop(1,'red');
        context.fillStyle = lg;
        context.strokeStyle="#666666";
        context.lineWidth=".5";
        context.fillRect(10,10,250,250);
        context.strokeRect(10,10,250,250);
    }
</script>
</head>
<body onload="drawGradient()">
<canvas id="myCanvas" width="300" height="300" style="position:absolute; left:0px;
top:0px; z-index:1"/>
</body>
</html>
```

The first color stop is set to white, while the second is set to blue, and the third red. Once you assign these using the addColorStop() method, the lg linearGradient object is assigned as the fillStyle for the context. The fillRect() method is then called to paint the block. A gray border is added using the strokeRect() method. Figure 6-9 shows the results.

Figure 6-9: Linear gradient can be set on the canvas.

A radial gradient is created by using the `createRadialGradient()` method, and then adding color stops at the appropriate position. For example:

```
function drawRadialGradient(){
 var canvas = document.getElementById('myCanvas');
 var context = canvas.getContext('2d');
 var rg = context.createRadialGradient(45,45,10,52,50,35);
 rg.addColorStop(0, '#95b800');
 rg.addColorStop(0.9, '#428800');
 rg.addColorStop(1, 'rgba(220,246,196,0)');
 context.fillStyle = rg;
 context.fillRect(0,0,250,250);
}
```

The `createRadialGradient()` defines two circles, one with a 10px radius and the second with a 35px radius. Three color stops are added using `addColorStop()`, and then the `rg` `radialGradient` object is assigned to the `fillStyle` property. See Figure 6-10.

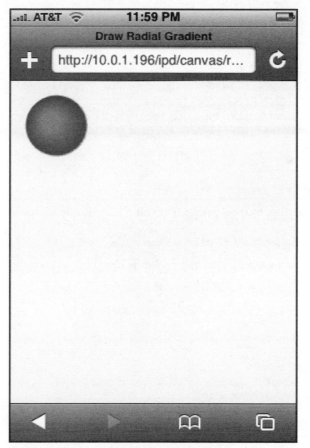

Figure 6-10: Creating a radial gradient

Creating an Image Pattern

You can use an external image to create an image pattern on the back of a canvas element using the createPattern() method. The syntax is:

```
patternObject = context.createPattern(image, type)
```

The image argument references an Image object or else a different canvas element. The type argument is one of the familiar CSS pattern types: repeat, repeat-x, repeat-y, and no-repeat. The method returns a Pattern object, as shown in the following example:

```
function drawPattern(){
  var canvas = document.getElementById('myCanvas');
  var context = canvas.getContext('2d');
  var pImg = new Image();
  pImg.src = 'images/tech.jpg';
  // call when image is fully loaded
  pImg.onload = function() {
    var pat = context.createPattern(pImg,'repeat');
    context.fillStyle = pat;
    context.fillRect(0,0,300,300)
  }
}
```

In this code, an Image object is created and assigned a source. However, before this image can be used in the pattern, you need to ensure it is loaded. Therefore, you place the rest of the drawing code inside of the Image object's onload event handler. Much like the gradient examples shown earlier, the Pattern object that is created with createPattern() is then assigned to fillStyle. Figure 6-11 shows the results.

Adding Shadows

The context object provides four properties that you can use for defining shadows on the canvas:

❑   shadowColor defines the CSS color of the shadow.

❑   shadowBlur specifies the width of the shadow blur.

❑   shadowOffsetX defines the horizontal offset of the shadow.

❑   shadowOffsetY specifies the vertical offset of the shadow.

The following code uses these properties to define a blurred shadow for an image:

```
function drawImg(){
  var canvas = document.getElementById('myCanvas');
  var context = canvas.getContext('2d');
```

```
context.shadowColor = "black";
context.shadowBlur = "10";
context.shadowOffsetX = "5";
context.shadowOffsetY = "5";
 var img3 = new Image();
 img3.src = 'images/nola.jpg';
 img3.onload = function() {
   context.drawImage( img3, 20, 30 );
 }
}
```

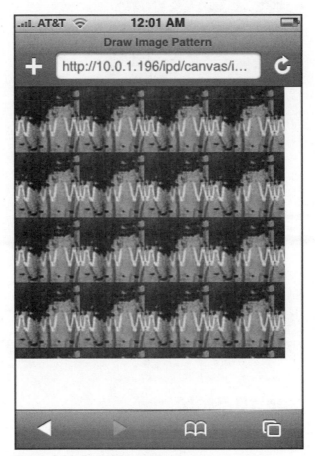

Figure 6-11: An image pattern drawn on a canvas

Figure 6-12 shows the result.

Figure 6-12: Shadow effects

Transforming a Canvas State

The `context` object has three methods you can use for transforming the state of a canvas:

❑   `translate(x, y)` changes the origin coordinate (0,0) of the canvas.

❑   `rotate(angle)` rotates the canvas around the current origin of a specified number of radians.

❑   `scale(x, y)` adjusts the scale of the canvas. The x parameter is a positive number that scales horizontally, while the y parameter scales vertically.

The following example uses `translate()` and `scale()` as it draws a circle successive times onto the canvas. Each time these methods are called, their parameters are adjusted:

```
function transform(){
  var canvas = document.getElementById('myCanvas');
  var context = canvas.getContext('2d');
  var s=1;
  for (i=1;i<6;i++){
    var t=i*8;
    context.translate(t,t);
    context.scale(s,s);
    context.fillStyle = "rgba(" + t*4 + ","+ t*6 + "," + t*8 + ", 0.3)";
    context.beginPath();
    context.arc(50,50,40,0,2*pi , false);
    context.fill();
    s=s-0.05;
  }
}
```

The t variable is 8 times the current iteration of the for loop, and then is used as the parameters for translate(). The scale() method uses the s variable, which is decremented by 0.05 after each pass. The fillStyle() method also uses the t variable to adjust the rgb color values for each circle drawn. Figure 6-13 shows the result of the transformation.

Figure 6-13: A series of transformed circles

The rotate() method rotates the canvas based on the specified angle. For example, in the following code, an image is drawn on the canvas three times, and each time the translate() and rotate() parameter values and the globalAlpha property are changed:

```
function rotateImg(){
  var canvas = document.getElementById('myCanvas');
  var context = canvas.getContext('2d');
  context.globalAlpha="0.5";
    var r=1;
  var img = new Image();
  img.src = 'images/jared.jpg';
  img.onload = function() {
    for (i=1;i<4;i++) {
      context.translate(50,-15);
      context.rotate(.15*r);
      context.globalAlpha=i*.33;
      context.drawImage(img, 20, 20);
      r+=1;
    }
  }
}
```

Figure 6-14 shows the layered result. Note the difference in transparency of the bottommost image to the topmost.

Saving and Restoring State

When you begin to work with more advanced drawings on the canvas, you will need to manage the drawing state. A drawing state includes the current path, the values of the major context properties (such as fillStyle and globalAlpha), and any transformations (such as rotating) that have been applied. To this end, you can use the save() and restore() methods. The save() method saves a snapshot of the canvas, which can then be retrieved later using the restore() method. The save() and restore() methods enable you to return to a default drawing state with minimal additional code and without needing to painstakingly recreate every setting.

Creating an Animation

You can use the context drawing capabilities discussed earlier in combination with JavaScript timer routines to create animations on the canvas. On first take, the potential for creating canvas-based animation sounds like a perfect lightweight substitute for Flash for iPhone and iPod touch. For some purposes, it can be ideal. However, any such excitement needs to be kept in reasonable check. Perhaps the chief shortcoming of the canvas drawing in JavaScript is that you need to repaint the entire canvas for each frame of your animation. As a result, complex animations risk becoming jerky on the mobile device. That being said, canvas animation can be a powerful tool to add to your development toolbox.

Like a motion picture or video clip, an animation is a series of frames that, when viewed one after the other, gives the appearance of movement. Therefore, when you code, your job is to show a drawing, clear it, draw the next frame in the series, clear it, and so on until your animation is completed or it loops back to the start. If you are changing any context settings and need to reset them for each new frame, you need to use the save() and restore() methods.

Figure 6-14: Image rotated using rotate()

The following HTML page shows a simple animation program in which a circle moves diagonally from the top left to the bottom right part of the canvas:

```
<!DOCTYPE html PUBLIC "-//W3C//DTD XHTML 1.0 Strict//EN"
        "http://www.w3.org/TR/xhtml1/DTD/xhtml1-strict.dtd">
<html xmlns="http://www.w3.org/1999/xhtml">
<head>
<title>Animate</title>
<meta name="viewport" content="width=320; initial-scale=1.0; maximum-scale=1.0;
user-scalable=0;">
<script type="application/x-javascript">
function init() {
  setInterval( animate, 100 );
}
var p = 0;
function animate(){
  var canvas - document.getElementById('myCanvas');
```

(continued)

(continued)

```
      var context = canvas.getContext('2d');
      context.clearRect(0, 0, 300, 300);
         context.fillStyle = "rgba(0,0,255, 0.3)";
         context.beginPath();
         context.arc(50+p,50+p,40,0, 2*pi, false);
         context.fill();
         p+=1;
}
</script>
</head>
<body onload="init()">
<canvas id="myCanvas" width="300" height="300" style="position:absolute; left:0px;
top:0px"/>
</body>
</html>
```

The `init()` function is called when the document is loaded, which sets off a timer to call `animate()` every 100 milliseconds. The `animate()` function clears the canvas, moves the orientation point, and draws a filled circle. The `p` variable is then incremented by one before repeating.

Canvas in Action

Several open source libraries that use canvas programming to create sophisticated charts and image effects, such as reflections, are available on the Web. Two particularly noteworthy libraries are the PlotKit and Reflection.js. PlotKit (see Figure 6-15) is a JavaScript Chart Plotting library (available at `www.liquidx.net/plotkit`), and Reflection.js enables you to add reflections to your images (available at `cow.neondragon.net/stuff/reflection`). The Reflection.js library uses canvas to render the reflection, but allows you to use it simply by adding a `reflect` class to an image.

Working with Video

If you are creating an application that incorporates multimedia, certainly one of the great benefits of developing for iPhone and iPod touch is their strong video and audio support. However, in order to take full advantage of streaming movies over Wi-Fi and EDGE networks, there are several issues that you need to keep in mind as you prepare your video for Internet usage.

Preparing iPhone/iPod touch–Friendly Video

iPhone and iPod touch support a variety of video formats, including H.264 (Baseline Profile Level 3.0), QuickTime, and MPEG-4 Part 2 (simple profile), and video files with the following extensions (.mov, .mp4, .m4v, and .3gp). However, in order to optimize the movie for Wi-Fi and EDGE networks, you should use videos encoded with the H.264 codec. H.264 is an open standard that is strong in providing high-quality video and audio in as small a file size as possible. However, because H.264 is not the native format for most video editing software, you will need to export or convert the media file for this codec.

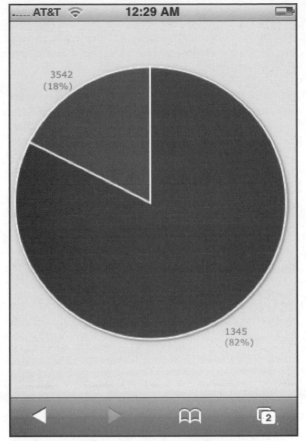

Figure 6-15: Plot dynamic graphs using PlotKit.

Deciding on Video Size and Bit Rate

Two critical factors that you need to decide upon when exporting videos for playback on iPhone or iPod touch are resolution (video size) and bit rate. When you play video, the native *resolution* of the iPhone and iPod touch screen is 480 × 320 pixels in landscape mode. However, as Table 6-2 shows, the device is actually able to handle video resolutions up to 640 × 480, converting the higher resolution to a suitable output resolution for playback on the device.

Table 6-2: iPhone and iPod touch Video Support

Type	Maximum Size and Bit Rate
Output on iPhone and iPod touch display	480 × 320
H.264 videos	640 × 480, 1.5 Mbps
MPEG-4 videos	640 × 480, 2.5 Mbps

The *bit rate* refers to the amount of data that is encoded into one second of video. In general, it is the bit rate that largely determines the file size — the higher the bit rate, the higher the file size. Standard iPod-content is at 1.5 Mbps, although, as will be discussed shortly, any content you wish to stream over the Internet should be done so at a lower bit rate. That's because the bit rate often is the key determinant in the quality of playback when streaming over the Internet.

As you would expect, the higher the resolution and bit rates, the better quality the video will be. However, if your users will *only* be streaming the videos for playback on iPhone and iPod touch displays, then it makes no sense to set the resolution and bit rates beyond their capabilities. As mentioned, the iPhone and iPod touch will scale down videos that are larger than their native 480 × 320 resolutions anyway, so encoding them at a higher resolution is a waste of bandwidth.

Considering Aspect Ratio

An additional issue to consider when working with video is the aspect ratio of the video. The *aspect ratio* is the width:height ratio of the video image. Table 6-3 lists the three standard aspect ratios.

Table 6-3: Popular Video Aspect Ratios

Aspect ratio	Description
16:9 (1.78:1)	*Widescreen TV.* Widescreen aspect ratio usually used by HDTV and widescreen televisions.
4:3 (or 1.33:1)	*Standard TV.* Traditional "box" aspect ratio standard for TV.
2:35:1	*Cinemascope widescreen.* A "super widescreen" aspect ratio used in Cinemascope and Panavision motion pictures.

The aspect ratio of the video may not directly correspond with the aspect ratio of the display. In particular, the iPhone and iPod touch displays have an aspect ratio of 1.5:1 (480/320=1.5). To display for 1.78:1 and 2.35:1 aspect ratios, iPhone or iPod touch will *letterbox*, or add black bars to the top and bottom. To display standard 1.33:1 videos, the device will *pillarbox*, or add black bars to the left and right sides of the video.

However, iPhone and iPod touch also allow users to crop the video to fit the 1.5:1 aspect ratio of the display by clicking the zoom button in video playback mode (see Figure 6-16). Zooming crops the video image to fill the entire screen in any aspect ratio. Widescreen content is expanded in height to fill the display and has its width chopped off that cannot fit into the display. For 4:3 videos, the top and bottom are cut off so that the sides go edge to edge on the display.

When you are deciding the resolution size of your video, you will want to preserve the original aspect ratio of your video, and then choose a resolution based on your needs (see Table 6-4). If your goal is usability over the Internet, then choose a recommended size from the Wi-Fi or EDGE columns. Or, if your objective is highest possible quality (perhaps for output display on a television), then choose the maximum resolution supported for your aspect ratio.

Figure 6-16: Zoom button toggles between original aspect ratio and cropped.

Table 6-4: Aspect Ratios for iPhone and iPod touch

Aspect ratio	Maximum resolution supported	Recommended resolution for Wi-Fi videos	Recommended resolution for EDGE videos
16:9 (1.78:1)	640 × 360	480 × 260	176 × 99
4:3 (or 1.33:1)	640 × 480	480 × 360	176 × 144
2.35:1	640 × 272	480 × 204	176 × 75

Some newer video tools and devices support *anamorphic encoding*. When a video is anamorphic encoded, it does not have a single hardcoded aspect ratio. Instead, the output device processes the anamorphic pixel aspect ratio (PAR) information stored in the video and displays it based on its native aspect ratio. However, currently iPhone and iPod touch cannot handle PAR and will display any anamorphic videos in a distorted manner. Therefore, avoid anamorphic encoded videos.

Exporting for Wi-Fi and EDGE

If users of your application will access the videos over both Wi-Fi and EDGE networks, you will want to export two different versions of the video — one that is optimized for Wi-Fi and one optimized for EDGE. The easiest solution is to use QuickTime Pro 7.2, which supports a Movie to iPhone export command to optimize the movie for Wi-Fi and a Movie to iPhone (Cellular) to prepare a movie for EDGE network. (Note that QuickTime Pro is paid program.) If you are using another exporting tool, refer to Table 6-5 to see the recommended settings for the two media files.

iPhone and iPod touch do not support RTP/RTSP streaming. Therefore, if you are using an earlier version of QuickTime or a third-party tool, be sure to turn off any streaming option that uses RTP/RTSP.

Table 6-5: Optimizing Video for iPhone and iPod touch

Connection	Video	Audio	File type
Wi-Fi	H.264 Baseline 900 kbit bit rate 480 × 360 resolution 30 fps Preserve aspect ratio: Fit within size	128kbit, AAC-LC	.m4v
EDGE	H.264 64 kbit bit rate 176 × 144 resolution 10 or 15fps Preserve aspect ratio: Letterbox or crop	16kbit, AAC-LC	.3gp

Creating a Reference Movie

Because you are creating Wi-Fi and EDGE versions of the same video, you could provide links to each of these files in your application and leave it up to the user to determine which one to play back. However, quite obviously, that's a weak solution. A much better option is to embed a reference movie that manages the versioning for you. A *reference movie* is a movie file that points to other movie files, each of which is at a different data rate (the EDGE .3gp file, the Wi-Fi .m4v file). When Mobile Safari requests the reference movie, QuickTime tests each of the movie URLs and determines which version is most appropriate based on the current network speed. Once a movie URL is found that best passes the tests, then that movie is sent to iPhone or iPod touch, which is then opened in the movie playback mode.

MakeRefMovie is a free downloadable OS X tool developed by Apple that you can use to create reference movies. You can add file or URL references from the Movies ⇨ Add URL menu item, rank their priority by dragging and dropping them to the appropriate position on the list, and even specify whether or not the movie is only available on iPhone (and iPod touch) in its Mobility option (see Figure 6-17). Once you save this file, you then reference it in your application. You can download MakeRefMovie at `developer .apple.com/quicktime/quicktimeintro/tools`. At the time of this writing, MakeRefMovie is not available for Microsoft Windows platforms.

A second alternative for making reference movies is with the PhpMovieRef (`www.zkm.de/static/ phprefmovie.html`). At the cost of more complexity, it's free, cross-platform, and can generate reference movies dynamically.

> *Make sure the Web server that hosts the video files supports byte-range requests (which are sometimes referred to as content-range or partial-range requests). And, as indicated before, RTP/RTSP is not supported.*

> *In addition, configure your server to send the correct MIME type for the following file types: .mov (video/QuickTime), .mp4 (video/mp4), .m4v (video/x-m4v), and .3gp (video/3gpp). For example on Apache, you can set these by configuring your mime.types file or using the AddType directive in a .htaccess file.*

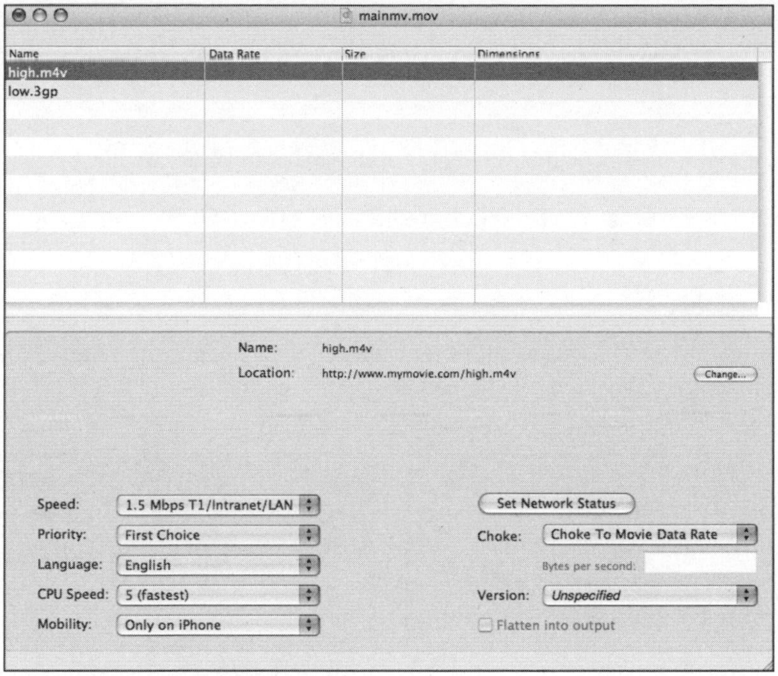

Figure 6-17: MakeRefMovie

Embedding Video or Audio Files

Once you have the video files converted, reference movie created, and your Web server configured to handle video files (see the "Hosting Media Files" section), you are ready to reference them in your Web page or application.

You link a video or audio file to your Web page using an embed element. The embed element is defined as:

```
<embed href="http://www.mysite.com/vid2.m4v" type="video/x-m4v" src="video.png"
target="myself" height="84" width="84" scale="1"/>
```

At the time of this writing, using embed with a poster image and specifying a relative URL for the href attribute produced inconsistent results. I recommend using an absolute path.

The href and type define the source and MIME type of the video file. The src attribute allows you to optionally define a poster image to display in the embed block. If no src attribute is displayed, then a QuickTime box is displayed. The height and width are used to determine the dimensions of the poster image.

Because iPhone and iPod touch do not support inline playback, media playback does not begin until the user enters movie playback mode. As a result, to play the video, a user clicks the play button displayed on the embed element to enter playback mode. The `target="myself"` attribute-value pair is used for this linkage.

Here's a code snippet from a page that references both video and audio media:

```
<embed href="vid-ref.mov" src="vid.png" type="video/quicktime" target="myself"
height="84" width="84" scale="1"/>
<embed href="aud.mp3" src="aud.png" type="audio/x-mp3" target="myself" height="84"
width="84" scale="1"/>
```

Figure 6-18 shows how Mobile Safari renders these embedded elements inside of a page. Figure 6-19 then shows the iPhone displayed in playback mode.

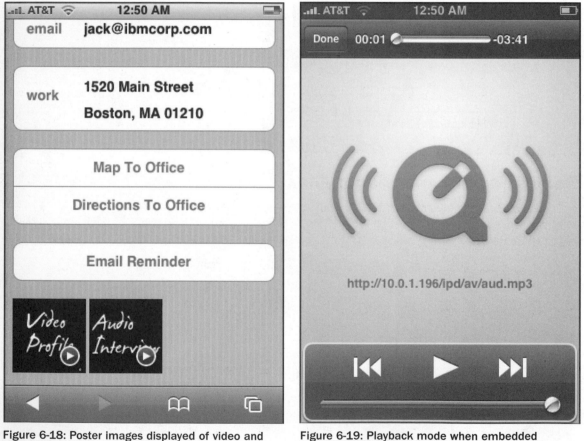

Figure 6-18: Poster images displayed of video and audio media

Figure 6-19: Playback mode when embedded element is pressed

7

Integrating with iPhone Services

One of the most intriguing ideas when creating a Web 2.0 application for iPhone is integrating the application with core mobile services, such as dialing phone numbers or sending e-mails. After all, once you break those inside the browser barriers, the application becomes more than just a Web app and extends its functionality across the mobile device.

However, iPhone service integration is a mixed bag; it's a "good news, bad news" situation. On the upside, perhaps the three most important mobile functions (Phone, Mail, and Google Maps) are accessible to the developer. On the downside, there are no means of tapping into other core services, such as SMS messaging, Calendar, Address Book, Camera, Clock, iPod, and Settings.

In order to demonstrate the integration with iPhone services, you'll be working with a sample application called iProspector, which is a mocked up contact management system that emulates the iPhone Contact UI (see Figure 7-1). To create the UI, you will be starting with Joe Hewitt's iUI framework, which is discussed fully in Chapter 3. However, because it does not provide support for the specific controls needed for the Contact UI, this chapter will show you how to extend iUI as service integration is discussed.

Because iPod touch does not provide support for Phone and Mail services, any iPhone-specific integration should degrade gracefully when running on iPod touch.

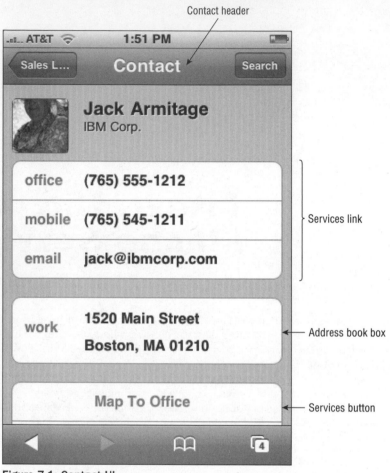

Figure 7-1: Contact UI

Preparing the iProspector Application Shell

Before integrating services and adding custom UI controls for them, you first need to prepare the iProspector application shell. The following XHTML document contains a standard iUI setup for a hierarchical list-based, side-scrolling interface:

```
<!DOCTYPE html PUBLIC "-//W3C//DTD XHTML 1.0 Strict//EN"
        "http://www.w3.org/TR/xhtml1/DTD/xhtml1-strict.dtd">
<html xmlns="http://www.w3.org/1999/xhtml">
<head>
<title>iProspector</title>
<meta name="viewport" content="width=device-width; initial-scale=1.0;
maximum-scale=1.0; user-scalable=0;"/>
<style type="text/css" media="screen">@import "../iui/iui.css";</style>
```

```
<style type="text/css" media="screen">@import "../iui/cui.css";</style>
<script type="application/x-javascript" src="../iui/iui.js"></script>
</head>
<body>
    <!-- Top iUI toolbar -->
    <div class="toolbar">
        <h1 id="pageTitle"></h1>
        <a id="backButton" class="button" href="#"></a>
        <a class="button" href="#searchForm">Search</a>
    </div>
    <!-- Top-level menu -->
    <!-- Customers, Orders, Settings, and About menus not enabled for this sample -->
    <ul id="home" title="iProspector" selected="true">
        <li><a href="#leads">Sales Leads</a></li>
        <li><a href="#customers">Customers</a></li>
        <li><a href="#orders">Order Fulfillment</a></li>
        <li><a href="#settings">Settings</a></li>
        <li><a href="#about">About</a></li>
    </ul>
    <!-- Sales Leads menu -->
    <ul id="leads" title="Sales Leads">
        <li class="group">A</li>
        <li><a href="#Jack_Armitage">Jack Armitage</a></li>
        <li><a href="#Jason_Armstrong">Jason Armstrong</a></li>
        <li class="group">B</li>
        <li><a href="#Bob_Balancia">Bob Balancia</a></li>
        <li><a href="#Sara_Billingsly">Sara Billingsly</a></li>
        <li><a href="#Uri_Bottle">Uri Bottle</a></li>
        <li><a href="#Larry_Brainlittle">Larry Brainlittle</a></li>
        <li class="group">C</li>
        <li><a href="#Carl_Carlsson">Carl Carlsson</a></li>
        <li><a href="#John_Charleston">John Charleston</a></li>
        <li class="group">D</li>
        <li><a href="#Bill_Drake">Bill Drake</a></li>
        <li><a href="#Randy_Dulois">Randy Dulois</a></li>
    </ul>
     <!-- Contact panel -->
     <div id="Jack_Armitage" title="Contact" class="panel">
        <h2>This page is intentionally blank.</h2>
     </div>
    <!-- iUI Search form -->
    <form id="searchForm" class="dialog" action="search.php">
        <fieldset>
            <h1>Contact Search</h1>
            <a class="button leftButton" type="cancel">Cancel</a>
            <a class="button blueButton" type="submit">Search</a>
            <label>Name:</label>
            <input type="text" name="name"/>
            <label>Company:</label>
            <input type="text" name="company"/>
        </fieldset>
    </form>
</body>
</html>
```

In the document head, begin by adding a link to a style sheet named cui.css, stored in the same directory as iui.css. You'll begin defining cui.css shortly.

The iUI framework uses a series of `ul` lists to compose a list-based navigation UI. The `home ul` list provides the top-level menu for the iProspector application (see Figure 7-2). Because you're concerned here with the functionality of working with a specific contact rather than the nuts and bolts of an entire contact management system, the Sales Leads link is the only one defined.

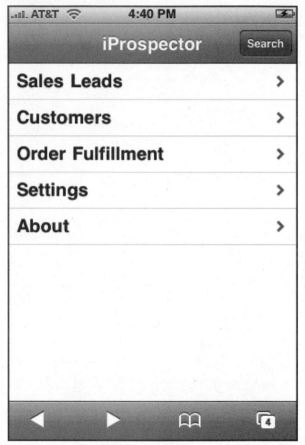

Figure 7-2: iProspector top-level menu

The `leads ul` list provides a canned list of sales leads (see Figure 7-3). Each of the list items contains a link that, in the real world, would be mapped to a unique Contact panel. The `Jack_Armitage` link is connected to the one Contact panel provided in the example document. From a code standpoint, the Contact panel is a `div` element with the `panel` class assigned to it, which displays a generic iPhone-style page (see Figure 7-4).

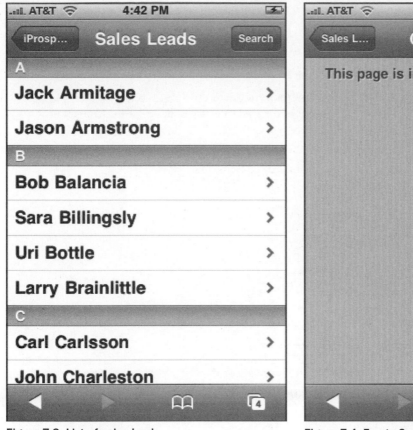

Figure 7-3: List of sales leads

Figure 7-4: Empty Contact panel

Creating the Contact Header

With the application shell functionality in place, the Contact panel is now ready to be filled in. At the top of a typical iPhone Contacts page is a thumbnail image of the contact along with the contact name and company. The HTML document is set up by replacing the dummy h2 text with a div element with a cuiHeader class that you'll define shortly. Inside of the div, three elements are defined, each of which is assigned a cui class. Here's the code:

```
<div id="Jack_Armitage" title="Contact" class="panel">
    <div class="cuiHeader">
        <img class="cui" src="jackarmitage.png"/>
        <h1 class="cui">Jack Armitage</h1>
        <h2 class="cui">IBM Corp.</h2>
    </div>
</div>
```

The img element will hold the thumbnail image. The h1 element will contain the name, while the h2 element will show the company.

Creating the cui.css Style Sheet

Next, it is time to create the cui.css file (or download it from www.wiley.com). When you use the style conventions originally defined in iui.css, four additional rules are defined for the Contact header:

```
.panel h1.cui {
    margin: 5px 0 0px 80px;
    font-size: 20px;
    font-weight: bold;
    color: black;
    text-shadow: rgba(255, 255, 255, 0.75) 2px 2px 0;
    top: 5px;
    clear: none;
}
.panel h2.cui {
    margin: 0 0 30px 80px;
    font-size: 14px;
    font-weight: normal;
    color: black;
    text-shadow: rgba(255, 255, 255, 0.75) 2px 2px 0;
    top: 43px;
    clear: none;
}
.panel img.cui {
    margin: 0px 15px 5px 0px;
    border: 1px solid #666666;
    float: left;
    -webkit-border-radius: 5px;
}
.panel > div.cuiHeader {
    position: relative;
    margin-bottom: 0px 0px 10px 14px;
}
```

The first three rules position the h1, h2, and img elements in the appropriate location. The final rule adds spacing between the header panel and the rest of the page. Figure 7-5 shows the current state of the Contact panel.

With all of the preparatory UI in place, you can begin to add the service integration.

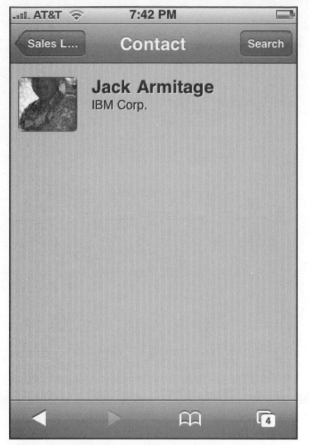

Figure 7-5: Adding the Contact header

Making Phone Calls
from Your Application

You can make a phone call from your application simply through a special telephone link. A telephone link is specified through the tel: protocol. The basic syntax is:

```
<a href="tel:1-507.555-5555">1-507.555-5555</a>
```

When a user clicks the link, the phone does not automatically dial. Instead, iPhone displays a confirmation box (see Figure 7-6) that allows the user to click Call or Cancel.

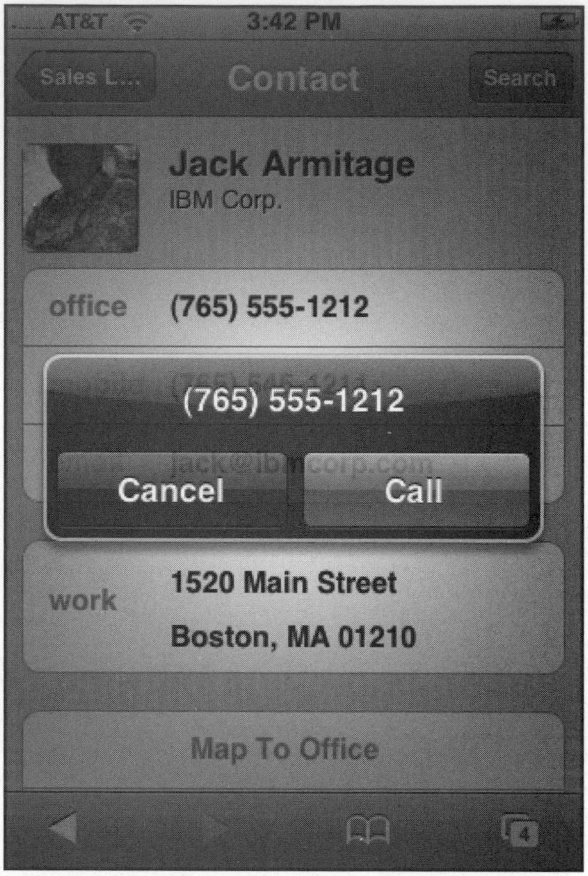

Figure 7-6: User needs to confirm a telephone link before a call is initiated.

Telephone links can go beyond ordinary numbers. iPhone provides partial support for the RFC 2086 protocol (www.ietf.org/rfc/rfc2806.txt), which enables you to develop some sophisticated telephone-based URLs. For example, the following link calls the U.S. Postal Service, pauses for 2 seconds, and then presses 2 to get a Spanish version:

```
<a href="tel:+1-800-ASK-USPS;pp2">USPS (Espanol)</a>
```

Note that p creates a 1-second pause, so pp will cause a 2-second pause before continuing. Mobile Safari will also automatically create telephone links for you in your pages. Any number that takes the form of a phone is displayed as a link. Therefore, if you ever have a situation in which you do not want to link a telephone number (or a number that could be interpreted as a phone number), then add the format-detection meta tag (for iPhone 1.1.1 and above) to the document head:

```
<meta name = "format-detection" content = "telephone=no">
```

For legacy support, you can also break up the number sequence using a span element. For example,

```
<p>Your ID is 5083212202.</p>
```

would become

```
<p>Your ID is <span>5083</span>212202.</p>
```

Creating Service Links

In adding this telephone link functionality into iProspector, you want to emulate the telephone links inside of the iPhone Contact UI. To do so, begin by adding a fieldset in prospector.html and enclosing two row div elements inside of it. Inside of the div elements, add a label and a link. Here's the code:

```
<fieldset>
    <div class="row">
        <label class="cui">office</label>
        <a class="cuiServiceLink" target="_self" href="tel:(765) 555-1212"
onclick="return (navigator.userAgent.indexOf('iPhone') != -1)">(765) 555-1212</a>
    </div>
    <div class="row">
        <label class="cui">mobile</label>
        <a class="cuiServiceLink" target="_self" href="tel:(765) 545-1211"
onclick="return (navigator.userAgent.indexOf('iPhone') != -1)">(765) 545-1211</a>
    </div>
</fieldset>
```

The a links, which are referred to as service links in this book, are assigned a cuiServiceLink class and use the tel: protocol in the href value. The target="_self" attribute is needed to override default iUI behavior, which would prevent the link from calling the Phone application. Also, to degrade gracefully when running on iPod touch, the onclick handler ensures that the link works only if running on iPhone. Finally, the label is assigned a cui class.

The fieldset and row class styling are already defined in the iui.css. However, several additional styles need to be defined inside of the cui.css file. First, styles need to be defined for the labels and service links. Second, a set of styles needs to be added to emulate the push-down effect of the services link when a user presses it with a finger. The rules are shown in the following code:

```
.row > label.cui {
    position: absolute;
    margin: 0 0 0 14px;
    line-height: 42px;
    font-weight: bold;
    color: #7388a5;
}
```

(continued)

(continued)

```css
.cuiServiceLink {
    display: block;
    margin: 0;
    border: none;
    padding: 12px 10px 0 80px;
    text-align: left;
    font-weight: bold;
    text-decoration: inherit;
    height: 42px;
    color: inherit;
    box-sizing: border-box;
}
.row[cuiSelected]  {
    position: relative;
    min-height: 42px;
    border-bottom: 1px solid #999999;
    -webkit-border-radius: 0;
    text-align: right;
    background-color: #194fdb !important;
    color: #FFFFFF !important;
}
.row[cuiSelected] > label.cui  {
    position: absolute;
    margin: 0 0 0 14px;
    line-height: 42px;
    font-weight: bold;
    color: #FFFFFF;
}
fieldset > .row[cuiSelected]:last-child  {
    border-bottom: none !important;
}
```

The bottom three rules are used to change the `row` and `label` styling when the `row` `div` has a `cuiSelected` attribute set to true (the element's background becomes blue, and the label font is set to white).

Although the styles are now ready for these elements, the service links are not yet functional within the iUI framework. By default, iUI intercepts all link click events inside of iui.js in order to change a link's selection state and to disable the default action of a link. Therefore, you need to add a handler for service link buttons coming through this routine. Here's the modified version of the `addEventListener` `("click", function(event))` handler:

```javascript
addEventListener("click", function(event)
{
    var link = findParent(event.target, "a");
    if (link)
    {
        function unselect() { link.removeAttribute("selected"); }
```

```
        if (link.href && link.hash && link.hash != "#")
        {
            link.setAttribute("selected", "true");
            iui.showPage($(link.hash.substr(1)));
            setTimeout(unselect, 500);
        }
        // Begin cui insertion
        else if ( link.getAttribute("class") == "cuiServiceLink" )
        {
            var curRow = findParent( link, "div" );
            curRow.setAttribute("cuiSelected", "true");
                            setTimeout(function() {
                                curRow.removeAttribute("cuiSelected");
                }, 500);
            return;
        }
        // End cui insertion
        else if (link == $("backButton"))
            history.back();
        else if (link.getAttribute("type") == "submit")
            submitForm(findParent(link, "form"));
        else if (link.getAttribute("type") == "cancel")
            cancelDialog(findParent(link, "form"));
        else if (link.target == "_replace")
        {
            link.setAttribute("selected", "progress");
            iui.showPageByHref(link.href, null, null, link, unselect);
        }
        else if (!link.target)
        {
            link.setAttribute("selected", "progress");
            iui.showPageByHref(link.href, null, null, null, unselect);
        }
        else
            return;
        event.preventDefault();
    }
}, true);
```

The first `else if` conditional block is inserted to check for all links that have a class of
`cuiServiceLink`. If so, then the parent `div` is retrieved and its instance assigned to `curRow`. A
`cuiSelected` attribute is then added to the `curRow` and then removed. When paired with the styles
set up in cui.css, this code changes the colors of the service link's parent `div` for 500 milliseconds, and
then sets them back to normal. The visual effect simulates, as much as possible, the default behavior
of iPhone. Finally, a `return` statement is added at the end of the block to ensure that the
`preventDefault()` command is not called (which would prevent the services link from
working correctly).

The telephone links of the Contact panel, shown in Figure 7-7, are now styled and fully functional.

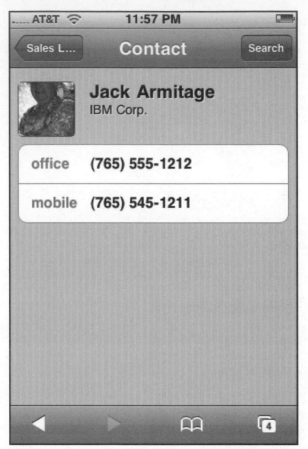

Figure 7-7: Telephone links added to the Contact panel

Sending Emails

Emails can also be sent from your application through links using the familiar `mailto:` protocol, as shown in the following example:

```
<a href="mailto:jack@ibmcorp.com">Jack Armitage</a>
```

When this link is clicked by the user, Mail opens and a new message window is displayed, as shown in Figure 7-8. The user can then fill out the subject and body of the message and send it. As you would expect, you cannot automatically send an email message using the `mailto:` protocol without user intervention. The `mailto:` protocol always takes the user to a new message window.

Figure 7-8: Sending a mail message from an application

Following the `mailto:` protocol, you can also include parameters to specify the subject, cc address, bcc address, and message body. Table 7-1 lists these options.

Table 7-1: Optional mailto: Attributes

Option	Syntax
Multiple recipients	, (comma separating email addresses)
Message subject	subject=Subject Text
Cc recipients	cc=name@address.com
Bcc recipients	bcc=name@address.com
Message text	body=Message text

Per HTTP conventions, precede the initial parameter with a ? (such as ?subject=) and precede any additional parameters with an &.

The `mailto:` protocol normally allows line breaks in the `body` attribute value using `%0A` for a line break and `%0A%0A` for a line break followed by a blank line. However, iPhone ignores the `%0A` codes and puts all of the text on one line.

As a work-around, iPhone enables you to embed HTML in your message body, therefore enabling you to add `br` tags for line breaks and even other tags (such as `strong`) for formatting.

When you combine several parameters, the following element provides everything a user needs to send a reminder message:

```
<a  class="cuiServiceButton" target="_self" onclick="return
(navigator.userAgent.indexOf('iPhone') != -1)"
href="mailto:jack@ibmcorp.com?subject=Meeting&body=Dear Jack,<br/>I look forward to
our upcoming meeting together <strong>this Friday at
8am.</strong><br/>Sincerely,<br/>Jason Malone&cc=jason@iphogcorp.com">Email
Reminder</a>
```

As Figure 7-9 shows, all the user needs to do is press the Send button.

Figure 7-9: Populating an email message data from an application

Adding an email link to the iProspector application is straightforward. Because the look and functionality of an email link are identical to those of telephone links in the native iPhone Contact UI, you can piggyback on top of the styles and functionality you already defined earlier in this chapter. With that in mind, add an email link just under the two telephone links inside of the same `fieldset`:

```
<fieldset>
    <div class="row">
        <label class="cui">office</label>
        <a class="cuiServiceLink" target="_self" href="tel:(765) 555-1212"
onclick="return (navigator.userAgent.indexOf('iPhone') != -1)">(765) 555-1212</a>
    </div>
    <div class="row">
        <label class="cui">mobile</label>
        <a class="cuiServiceLink" target="_self" href="tel:(765) 545-1211"
onclick="return (navigator.userAgent.indexOf('iPhone') != -1)">(765) 545-1211</a>
    </div>
    <div class="row">
        <label class="cui">email</label>
        <a class="cuiServiceLink" target="_self" onclick="return
(navigator.userAgent.indexOf('iPhone') != -1)" href="mailto:jack@ibmcorp.com">
jack@ibmcorp.com</a>
    </div>
</fieldset>
```

Pointing on Google Maps

While Google Maps does not have its own custom `href` protocol, Mobile Safari on iPhone is smart enough to reroute any request to `maps.google.com` to the built-in Maps application rather than going to the public Google Web site. (On iPod touch, Mobile Safari links directly to the public Google Web site.) As a result, you can create a link to specify either a specific location or driving directions between two geographical points.

You cannot specify whether to display the map in Map or Satellite view. The location you specify will be displayed in the last selected view of the user.

Keep in mind the basic syntax conventions when composing a Google Maps URL:

❑ For normal destinations, start with the q= parameter, and then type the location as you would a normal address, substituting + signs for blank spaces.

❑ For clarity, include commas between address fields.

Here's a basic URL to find a location based on city and state:

```
<a href="http://maps.google.com/maps?q=Boston,+MA">Boston</a>
```

Here's the syntax used for a full street address:

```
<a href="http://maps.google.com/maps?q=1000+Massachusetts+Ave,+Boston,+MA">Jack
Armitage's Office</a>
```

When the address shown previously is located in Google Maps, the marker is generically labeled `1000 Massachusetts Ave Boston MA`. However, you can specify a custom label by appending the URL with `+(Label+Text)`, as shown in the following example:

```
<a href="http://maps.google.com/maps?q=1000+Massachusetts+Ave,+Boston,+MA+(Jack
+Armitage's+Office)">Jack Armitage's Office</a>
```

Figure 7-10 shows the custom label in Google Maps.

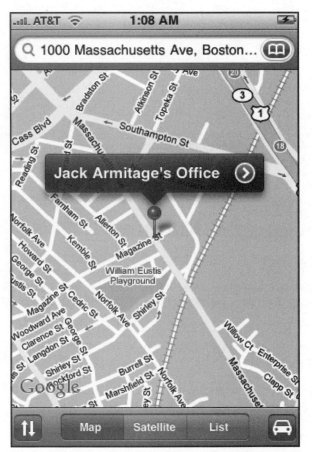

Figure 7-10: Customizing the Google Maps label

You can specify a location using latitude and longitude coordinates as well:

```
<a href="http://maps.google.com/maps?q=52.123N,2.456W">Jack's Summer Retreat</a>
```

To get directions, use the saddr= parameter to indicate the starting address and daddr= parameter to specify the destination address, as shown in the following example:

```
<a href="http://maps.google.com/maps?saddr=Holden+MA&daddr=1000+Massachusetts+Ave,
+Boston,+MA">Directions To Office</a>
```

Figure 7-11 displays the map view when this link is clicked.

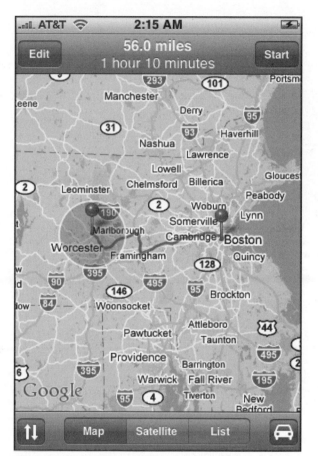

Figure 7-11: Programming driving directions

Google Maps on its public Web site has an extensive set of parameters. However, except where noted previously, none of these are supported at this time. You cannot, for example, use the t= parameter to specify the Satellite map, the z= parameter to indicate the map zoom level, or even layer=t to turn on the Traffic display. The user needs to perform those steps interactively.

In order to add Google Maps integration with iProspector, two new capabilities need to be added to its Contact panel. First, multiline, read-only address information needs to be displayed in its own box. Second, a new action button style needs to be created to emulate the button functionality of the native iPhone Contact UI.

Creating a Contacts Address Box

To define an address box, define a `div` with a new style named `rowCuiAddressBox`. Inside of it, add a `cui label` and then `cui p` elements for each line of the address:

```
<fieldset>
    <div class="rowCuiAddressBox">
            <label class="cui">work</label>
            <p class="cui">1520 Main Street</p>
            <p class="cui">Boston, MA 01210</p>
    </div>
</fieldset>
```

Next, going back to cui.css, four new styles need to be defined:

```
.rowCuiAddressBox    {
    position: relative;
    min-height: 24px;
    border-bottom: 1px solid #999999;
    -webkit-border-radius: 0;
    text-align: left;
}
.rowCuiAddressBox > p.cui {
    box-sizing: border-box;
    margin: 0;
    border: none;
    text-align: left;
    padding: 2px 10px 0 80px;
    height: 30px;
    background: none;
    font-weight: bold;
}
fieldset > .rowCuiAddressBox:first-child  {
     padding-top: 12px;
    border-bottom: none !important;
}
fieldset > .rowCuiAddressBox:last-child  {
    min-height: 25px;
    text-align: left;
    border-bottom: none !important;
}
```

The `:first-child` and `:last-child` styles are used to ensure proper padding and sizing of the contents of the box.

To style the address box label, one additional selector needs to be added onto the previously defined `.row > label.cui` rule:

```
.row > label.cui, .rowCuiAddressBox > label.cui  {
    position: absolute;
    margin: 0 0 0 14px;
    line-height: 42px;
    font-weight: bold;
    color: #7388a5;
}
```

The display-only address box is now ready.

Creating Service Buttons

Two new links are needed to add Google Maps integration. One link will display a map of the contact and a second will provide driving directions. Here is the `fieldset` definition:

```
<fieldset>
    <div class="row">
        <a   class="cuiServiceButton" target="_self"
href="http://maps.google.com/maps?q=1000+Massachusetts+Ave,+Boston,+MA">Map To
Office</a>
        </div>
        <div class="row">
            <a class="cuiServiceButton" target="_self"
href="http://maps.google.com/maps?saddr=Holden+MA&daddr=1000+Massachusetts+Ave,
+Boston,+MA">Directions To Office</a>
        </div>
    </fieldset>
```

These two links are assigned to the `cuiServiceButton` class. The first link displays a map of the specified address in Boston, while the second link provides driving directions between Holden, MA and the Boston address. Once again, to get around the way iUI handles events in iui.jss, you need to specify the `target="_self"` parameter.

Back over in cui.css, one new style needs to be added:

```
.cuiServiceButton {
    display: block;
    margin: 0;
    border: none;
    padding: 12px 10px 0 0px;
```

(continued)

(continued)

```
        text-align: center;
        font-weight: bold;
        text-decoration: inherit;
        height: 42px;
        color: #7388a5;
        box-sizing: border-box;
    }
```

This style emulates the look of the action buttons (centered blue text, and so on) in the native iPhone Contact UI.

There is one final tweak that needs to be made to iui.jss before the `cuiServiceButton` links work as expected. If you recall, an `else if` condition is added to trap for service links inside of the `addEventListener( "click", event(function) )` function. You need to add an additional test so that both `cuiServiceLink` and `cuiServiceButton` classes are evaluated. To do so, modify the line of code as specified here:

```
else if ( (link.getAttribute("class") == "cuiServiceLink" )  ||
( link.getAttribute("class") == "cuiServiceButton") )
```

Now that the `cuiServiceButton` link class is ready to go, you need to add one last button to the iProspector Contact panel to finish it off — a services button that automatically composes a reminder email to the Contact. The following HTML code combines `mailto:` link functionality and the `cuiServiceButton` style:

```
        <fieldset>
            <div class="row">
                <a  class="cuiServiceButton" target="_self" href="mailto:
jack@ibmcorp.com?subject=Meeting&body=Dear Jack, I look forward to our
upcoming meeting together this Friday at 8am. Sincerely, Jason
Malone&cc=jason@iphogcorp.com">Email Reminder</a>
            </div>
        </fieldset>
```

Figure 7-12 shows the display of these `cuiServiceButton` links inside of iProspector.

The iProspector Contact panel is now fully enabled to emulate both the look and functionality of the built-in iPhone Contact UI.

Listing 7-1 displays the prospector.html file, Listing 7-2 displays the cui.css file, and Listing 7-3 displays the modified function block inside of iui.jss.

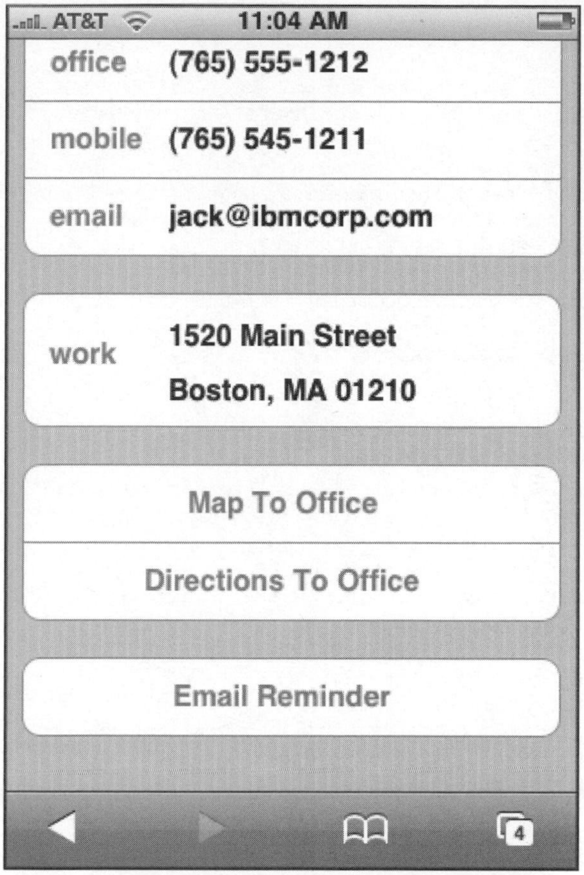

Figure 7-12: Enabled Contact buttons that integrate with Google Maps and Mail

Listing 7-1: prospector.html

```
<!DOCTYPE html PUBLIC "-//W3C//DTD XHTML 1.0 Strict//EN"
        "http://www.w3.org/TR/xhtml1/DTD/xhtml1-strict.dtd">
<html xmlns="http://www.w3.org/1999/xhtml">
<head>
<title>iProspector</title>
<meta name="viewport" content="width=320; initial-scale=1.0; maximum-scale=1.0;
user-scalable=0;"/>
<style type="text/css" media="screen">@import "../iui/iui.css";</style>
<style type="text/css" media="screen">@import "../iui/cui.css";</style>
<script type="application/x-javascript" src="../iui/iui.js"></script>
</head>
<body>
        <!-- Top iUI toolbar -->
    <div class="toolbar">
        <h1 id="pageTitle"></h1>
```

(continued)

Listing 7-1 *(continued)*

```
            <a id="backButton" class="button" href="#"></a>
            <a class="button" href="#searchForm">Search</a>
    </div>
    <!-- Top-level menu -->
    <!-- Customers, Orders, Settings, and About menus not enabled for this sample -->
    <ul id="home" title="iProspector" selected="true">
        <li><a href="#leads">Sales Leads</a></li>
        <li><a href="#customers">Customers</a></li>
        <li><a href="#orders">Order Fulfillment</a></li>
        <li><a href="#settings">Settings</a></li>
        <li><a href="#about">About</a></li>
    </ul>
    <!-- Sales Leads menu -->
    <ul id="leads" title="Sales Leads">
        <li class="group">A</li>
        <li><a href="#Jack_Armitage">Jack Armitage</a></li>
        <li><a href="#Jason_Armstrong">Jason Armstrong</a></li>
        <li class="group">B</li>
        <li><a href="#Bob_Balancia">Bob Balancia</a></li>
        <li><a href="#Sara_Billingsly">Sara Billingsly</a></li>
        <li><a href="#Uri_Bottle">Uri Bottle</a></li>
        <li><a href="#Larry_Brainlittle">Larry Brainlittle</a></li>
        <li class="group">C</li>
        <li><a href="#Carl Carlsson">Carl Carlsson</a></li>
        <li><a href="#John_Charleston">John Charleston</a></li>
        <li class="group">D</li>
        <li><a href="#Bill_Drake">Bill Drake</a></li>
        <li><a href="#Randy_Dulois">Randy Dulois</a></li>
    </ul>
        <!-- Contact panel -->
    <div id="Jack_Armitage" title="Contact" class="panel">
                <div class="cuiHeader">
                        <img class="cui" src="jackarmitage.png"/>
            <h1 class="cui">Jack Armitage</h1>
            <h2 class="cui">IBM Corp.</h2>
        </div>
        <fieldset>
            <div class="row">
                <label class="cui">office</label>
                <a class="cuiServiceLink" target="_self" href="tel:(765) 555-1212"
onclick="return (navigator.userAgent.indexOf('iPhone') != -1)">(765) 555-1212</a>
            </div>
            <div class="row">
                <label class="cui">mobile</label>
                <a class="cuiServiceLink" target="_self" href="tel:(765) 545-1211"
onclick="return (navigator.userAgent.indexOf('iPhone') != -1)">(765) 545-1211</a>
            </div>
            <div class="row">
                <label class="cui">email</label>
                <a class="cuiServiceLink" target="_self"
href="mailto:jack@ibmcorp.com" onclick="return
(navigator.userAgent.indexOf('iPhone') != -1)">jack@ibmcorp.com</a>
            </div>
```

```
            </fieldset>
            <fieldset>
                <div class="rowCuiAddressBox">
                            <label class="cui">work</label>
                            <p class="cui">1520 Main Street</p>
                            <p class="cui">Boston, MA 01210</p>
                </div>
            </fieldset>
            <fieldset>
                <div class="row">
                        <a   class="cuiServiceButton" target="_self"
href="http://maps.google.com/maps?q=1000+Massachusetts+Ave,+Boston,+MA">Map To
Office</a>
                </div>
                <div class="row">
                        <a class="cuiServiceButton" target="_self"
href="http://maps.google.com/maps?saddr=Holden+MA&daddr=1000+Massachusetts+Ave,
+Boston,+MA">Directions To Office</a>
                </div>
            </fieldset>
            <fieldset>
                <div class="row">
                        <a   class="cuiServiceButton" target="_self" onclick="return
(navigator.userAgent.indexOf('iPhone') != -1)"href="mailto:jack@ibmcorp.com?subject
=Meeting&body=Dear Jack,<br/>I look forward to our upcoming meeting together
<strong>this Friday at 8am.</strong><br/>Sincerely,<br/>Jason Malone&cc=jason@
iphogcorp.com">Email Reminder</a>
                </div>
            </fieldset>
    </div>
            <!-- iUI Search form -->
        <form id="searchForm" class="dialog" action="search.php">
            <fieldset>
                <h1>Contact Search</h1>
                <a class="button leftButton" type="cancel">Cancel</a>
                <a class="button blueButton" type="submit">Search</a>
                <label>Name:</label>
                <input type="text" name="name"/>
                <label>Company:</label>
                <input type="text" name="company"/>
            </fieldset>
        </form>
</body>
</html>
```

Listing 7-2: cui.css

```css
/* cui Contacts Extension to Joe Hewitt's iUI */
/* Contact Header */
.panel h1.cui {
    margin: 5px 0 0px 80px;
    font-size: 20px;
    font-weight: bold;
```

(continued)

Listing 7-2 *(continued)*

```
        color: black;
        text-shadow: rgba(255, 255, 255, 0.75) 2px 2px 0;
         top: 5px;
         clear: none;
    }
.panel h2.cui {
        margin: 0 0 30px 80px;
        font-size: 14px;
        font-weight: normal;
        color: black;
        text-shadow: rgba(255, 255, 255, 0.75) 2px 2px 0;
         top: 43px;
         clear: none;
    }
.panel img.cui {
        margin: 0px 15px 5px 0px;
        border: 1px solid #666666;
        float: left;
        -webkit-border-radius: 5px;
    }
.panel > div.cuiHeader {
        position: relative;
        margin-bottom: 0px 0px 10px 14px;
    }
/* Contact Fields */
.row > label.cui, .rowCuiAddressBox > label.cui  {
        position: absolute;
        margin: 0 0 0 14px;
        line-height: 42px;
        font-weight: bold;
        color: #7388a5;
    }
.cuiServiceLink {
        display: block;
        margin: 0;
        border: none;
        padding: 12px 10px 0 80px;
          text-align: left;
        font-weight: bold;
        text-decoration: inherit;
        height: 42px;
        color: inherit;
         box-sizing: border-box;
    }
.cuiServiceButton {
        display: block;
        margin: 0;
        border: none;
        padding: 12px 10px 0 0px;
          text-align: center;
        font-weight: bold;
        text-decoration: inherit;
```

```css
    height: 42px;
    color: #7388a5;
     box-sizing: border-box;
}
a[cuiSelected], a:active {
    background-color: #194fdb !important;
    color: #FFFFFF !important;
}
.row[cuiSelected]  {
    position: relative;
    min-height: 42px;
    border-bottom: 1px solid #999999;
    -webkit-border-radius: 0;
    text-align: right;
    background-color: #194fdb !important;
    color: #FFFFFF !important;
}
.row[cuiSelected] > label.cui  {
    position: absolute;
    margin: 0 0 0 14px;
    line-height: 42px;
    font-weight: bold;
    color: #FFFFFF;
}
fieldset > .row[cuiSelected]:last-child  {
    border-bottom: none !important;
}
/* Contact Address Box (Display-only)  */
.rowCuiAddressBox    {
    position: relative;
    min-height: 24px;
    border-bottom: 1px solid #999999;
    -webkit-border-radius: 0;
    text-align: left;
}
.rowCuiAddressBox > p.cui {
    box-sizing: border-box;
    margin: 0;
    border: none;
    text-align: left;
    padding: 2px 10px 0 80px;
    height: 30px;
    background: none;
    font-weight: bold;
}
fieldset > .rowCuiAddressBox:first-child  {
     padding-top: 12px;
    border-bottom: none !important;
}
fieldset > .rowCuiAddressBox:last-child  {
    min-height: 25px;
    text-align: left;
    border-bottom: none !important;
}
```

Listing 7-3: Modified portion of iui.js

```
addEventListener("click", function(event)
{
    var link = findParent(event.target, "a");
    if (link)
    {
        function unselect() { link.removeAttribute("selected"); }
        if (link.href && link.hash && link.hash != "#")
        {
            link.setAttribute("selected", "true");
            iui.showPage($(link.hash.substr(1)));
            setTimeout(unselect, 500);
        }
        // Begin cui insertion
        else if ( (link.getAttribute("class") == "cuiServiceLink" )  ||  ( link
.getAttribute("class") == "cuiServiceButton") )
         {
             var curRow = findParent( link, "div" );
             curRow.setAttribute("cuiSelected", "true");
                            setTimeout(function() {
                                curRow.removeAttribute("cuiSelected");
                 }, 500);
                 return;
         }
         // End cui insertion
        else if (link == $("backButton"))
            history.back();
        else if (link.getAttribute("type") == "submit")
            submitForm(findParent(link, "form"));
        else if (link.getAttribute("type") == "cancel")
            cancelDialog(findParent(link, "form"));
        else if (link.target == "_replace")
        {
            link.setAttribute("selected", "progress");
            iui.showPageByHref(link.href, null, null, link, unselect);
        }
        else if (!link.target)
        {
            link.setAttribute("selected", "progress");
            iui.showPageByHref(link.href, null, null, null, unselect);
        }
        else
            return;
    }
}, true);
```

8

Enabling and Optimizing Web Sites for iPhone and iPod touch

Oh, the irony. On the same day that I began writing a chapter on enabling Web sites for iPhone and iPod touch, I would realize firsthand the frustration of browsing sites that just don't work with my iPhone. My boys and I were watching the third quarter of a Monday Night Football game when the electricity suddenly went out because of a town-wide outage. Because my son's favorite team was playing, he was frantic. *What's happening in the game? Are the Titans still winning?* I immediately pulled out my iPhone and confidently launched Mobile Safari in search of answers. But upon going to NFL.com, I discovered that its live updating scoreboard is Flash only. I was left with a gray box with a Lego-like block in its place. I then pointed the browser to the official Tennessee Titans site, only to discover useless Lego blocks scattered across its front page as well. We then spent the rest of the outage scouring the Web, looking for a site to help us.

If you manage a Web site, Apple's release of iPhone and iPod touch introduce a whole new way of thinking in the design and development of a site. In the past, you could design a minimalist, text-only style sheet for mobile users — fully expecting your normal Web site to be viewed only by desktop browsers. However, expectations of iPhone and iPod touch users are not so modest. They are expecting to view the *full Web* in the palm of their hands. Therefore, as you design and develop your Web site, you will want to consider the level of support you wish to provide for these Apple devices — whether to offer mere compatibility, device friendliness, or even a design specifically targeting them. This chapter goes over the four tiers of enabling your Web site for Mobile Safari:

- ❑ Tier 1: Compatibility
- ❑ Tier 2: Navigation friendliness
- ❑ Tier 3: Device-specific style sheets
- ❑ Tier 4: Dedicated alternative site

Tier 1: iPhone/iPod touch Compatibility

The first tier of support for iPhone and iPod touch is simply making your Web site work for iPhone and iPod touch. Fortunately, because Mobile Safari is a sophisticated browser, far closer in capability to a desktop than a mobile browser, this is usually not problematic. However, there are some gotchas that you need to avoid. These include:

❑ Flash media

❑ Java applets

❑ Scalable vector graphics (SVG)

❑ Plug-ins

❑ CSS property `position:fixed`

❑ JavaScript functions `showModalDialog()` and `print()` and several mouse events (see Chapter 5)

❑ HTML element `input type="file"`

Given its widespread popularity and desktop install base, Flash is the thorniest incompatibility for many Web designers and developers. Until the iPhone's release, Flash support was typically considered a given except for a relatively small percentage of users. In fact, many designers could take it for granted that if a user was coming to their site without Flash support, then they probably were not a target visitor anyway and so they could either ignore them or simply refer them to the Adobe download page. However, with the release of iPhone and iPod touch, those assumptions are now invalid. Web designers are thus forced to rethink their reliance on a technology that they had become dependent upon. Figures 8-1

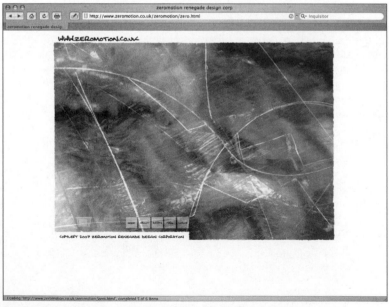

Figure 8-1: Flash-based site that attracts desktop users . . .

and 8-2 demonstrate the harsh reality, in which a state-of-the-art Web site that looks amazing in Safari for Mac OS X never accounts for iPhone and iPod touch users.

Figure 8-2: . . . leaves iPhone/iPod touch users out in the cold.

Therefore, if you plan on using Flash for an interactive portion of a page, then you should plan to degrade gracefully to a static graphic or alternative content. At a minimum, you should at least do what Adobe does (see Figure 8-3) in placing a disclaimer over Flash content. It's not ideal, but it is better than the Lego block. Or, if you have a Flash-driven site (such as the one shown in Figure 8-1), then you should consider an alternative HTML site or, if warranted, even an iPhone/iPod touch–specific site.

In order to detect Flash support, one solution is to use SWFObject, an open source JavaScript library that is used for detecting and embedding Flash content (available at `blog.deconcept.com/swfobject`). SWFObject is not iPhone/iPod–touch specific, but encapsulates the Flash Player detection logic, making it easy for you to degrade gracefully for Mobile Safari. For example, the following code will display a

Figure 8-3: Adobe homepage

Flash file for Flash-enabled desktop browsers, but will display a splash .png graphic for non-Flash visitors, including iPhone and iPod touch users:

```
<!DOCTYPE html PUBLIC "-//W3C//DTD XHTML 1.0 Strict//EN"
          "http://www.w3.org/TR/xhtml1/DTD/xhtml1-strict.dtd">
<html xmlns="http://www.w3.org/1999/xhtml">
<head>
<title>Company XY Home Page</title>
<meta name="viewport" content="width=780">
<script type="text/javascript" src="swfobject.js"></script>
</head>
<body>
<div id="splashintro">
  <a href="more.html"><img src="splash_noflash.png"/></a>
</div>
```

```
<script type="text/javascript">
   var so = new SWFObject("csplash.swf", "company_intro", "300", "240", "8",
"#338899");
   so.write("splashintro");
</script>
</body>
</html>
```

As you can see, the swfobject.js library file is added to the homepage. When Flash is available, the script replaces the content of the splashintro div with Flash media. But, when Flash is not supported, then appropriate content is substituted inside the splashintro div.

Therefore, at a minimum, you should seek to make your Web site fully aware and compatible for Mobile Safari users.

Tier 2: Navigation-Friendly Web Sites

Once your Web site degrades gracefully for iPhone and iPod touch users, you have achieved a base level of support for these mobile devices. However, while a user may be able to see all of the content on a Web site, that does not mean that it is easy for Mobile Safari users to navigate and read. A wide section of text, for example, becomes a stumbling block for iPhone and iPod touch users to read because horizontal scrolling is required when the user zooms in to read it. With this in mind, the second tier of support is to structure the site in a manner that is easy for Mobile Safari to zoom and navigate.

Working with the Viewport

As mentioned in Chapter 2, a *viewport* is a rectangular area of screen space within which a Web page is displayed. It determines how content is displayed and scaled to fit onto the iPhone and iPod touch. Using the viewport is analogous to looking at a panoramic scenic view of a mountain range through a camera zoom lens. If you want to see the entire mountainside, then you zoom out using the wide angle zoom. As you do so, you see everything, but the particulars of each individual mountain becomes smaller and harder to discern. Or, if you want to see a close-up picture of one of the peaks, then you zoom in with the Telephoto lens. Inside of the camera's viewfinder, you can no longer see the range as a whole, but the individual mountain is shown in terrific detail. The viewport meta tag in Mobile Safari works much the same way, allowing you to determine how much of the page to display, its zoom factor, and whether you want the user to zoom in and out or whether they need to browse using one scale factor.

The way in which Mobile Safari renders the page is largely based on the width (and/or initial-scale) property of the viewport meta tag. With no viewport tag present, Mobile Safari will consider the Web page it is loading as being 980 pixels in width, and then shrinks the page scaling so that the entire page width can fit inside of the 320-pixel viewport (see Figure 8-4). Here is the default declaration:

```
<meta name="viewport" content="width=980;user-scalable=1;"/>
```

Figure 8-4: A 980px–wide Web page scaled to fit in iPhone

Suppose your Web site is only 880 pixels wide. If you let Mobile Safari stick with its default 980-pixel setting, then the page is scaling more than it needs to. Therefore, to adjust the viewport magnification, you can specify a width optimized for your site:

```
<meta name="viewport" content="width=880"/>
```

Figures 8-5 and 8-6 show the noticeable difference between a 980- and an 880-width viewport for an 880-pixel width site.

With this declaration, instead of trying to fit 980 pixels into the 320 pixels of width, it only needs to shrink 880 pixels. Less scaling of content is needed (.363 scale instead of .326), making the site easier to use for iPhone and iPod touch users. Note that the `viewport` meta tag will not affect the rendering of the page in a normal desktop browser.

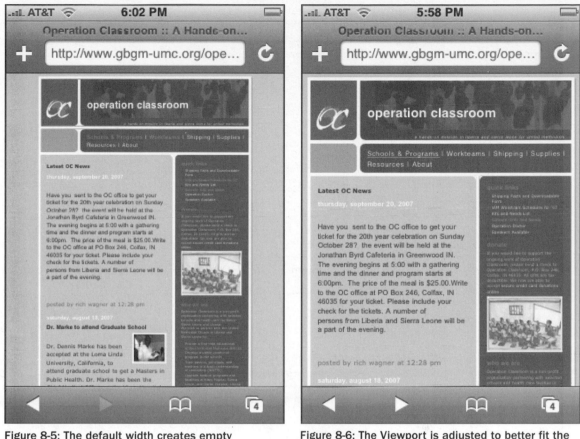

Figure 8-5: The default width creates empty space on the right side.

Figure 8-6: The Viewport is adjusted to better fit the Web page.

In addition to the `width` property, you can also programmatically control the scale of the viewport when the page initially loads through the `initial-scale` parameter. For example, if you wanted to set the initial scale to be .90, the declaration would be:

```
<meta name="viewport" content="initial-scale=.9;user-scalable=1;"/>
```

Once the page loads, however, the user is able to change the scale factor as they want using pinch and double-tap gestures as long as the `user-scalable` property is set to true (the default). If you want to limit the scale range, you can use the `minimum-scale` and `maximum-scale` properties:

```
<meta name="viewport" content="initial-scale=.9;maximum-scale=1.0;minimum-scale=.8;user-scalable=1;"/>
```

In this way, the user has the ability to pinch and zoom, but only to the extent that you want to allow.

If you develop a site or application specifically for iPhone/iPod touch, you want to size the page to the viewport (as discussed in Chapters 2 and 3) by setting the width=device-width (device-width is a constant) and initial-scale=1.0. Because the scale is 1.0, you don't want the user to be able to rescale the application interface, so the user-scalable property should be disabled. Here's the declaration:

```
<meta name="viewport" content="width=device-width; initial-scale=1.0; maximum-
scale=1.0; user-scalable=0;">
```

Table 8-1 lists the viewport properties. You don't need to set every property. Mobile Safari will infer values based on the properties you have set.

Keep in mind that the width attribute does not refer to the size of the Mobile Safari browser window, but instead the perceived size of the page in which Mobile Safari shrinks down to be displayed properly on the mobile device.

Table 8-1: viewport Meta Tag Properties

Property	Default Value	Minimum Value	Maximum Value	Description
width	980	200	10000	Width of viewport
height	based on aspect ratio	223	10000	Height of viewport
initial-scale	fit to screen	minimum-scale	maximum-scale	Scale to render when page loads
user-scalable	1 (yes)	0 (no)	1 (yes)	If yes, user can change scale through pinch and double-tap
minimum-scale	0.25	>0	10	Use to set the lower end for scaling
maximum-scale	1.6	>0	10	Use to set the higher end for scaling

Although it's not generally recommended, you can specify the width of the content to be greater than the viewport width, but that will require the user to scroll horizontally.

Note that iPhone 1.1.1 and above support two new width and height constants: device-width (width of device in pixels or 320) and device-height (height of device in pixels or 480).

Turning Your Page into Blocks

One of the most important ways to make your Web site friendly for iPhone and iPod touch users is turn your Web page into a series of columns and blocks. Columns make your page readable like a newspaper and help you avoid wide blocks of text that cause users to horizontally scroll left and right to read.

When an element is double-tapped, iPhone looks at element that is double-tapped and finds its closest block (div, ol, ul, table, and so on.) or image ancestor. If a block is found, then Safari zooms the content to fit the block's content based on the viewport tag's width property value and then centers it. If an image is tapped, then Mobile Safari zooms to fit the image and centers it. If already zoomed, then zoom out occurs.

Figure 8-7 shows a sample page with a relatively simple structure, but one that makes it difficult for the iPhone/iPod touch to zoom in on. The table is defined at a fixed width of 1000px, and the first column takes up 875px of that space. The text above the table spans the full document width, but because it is outside of any block, Mobile Safari can do no zooming when the text is double-tapped. The user is forced to go to landscape mode and pinch to get readable text, but it still scrolls off the right of the screen (see Figure 8-8).

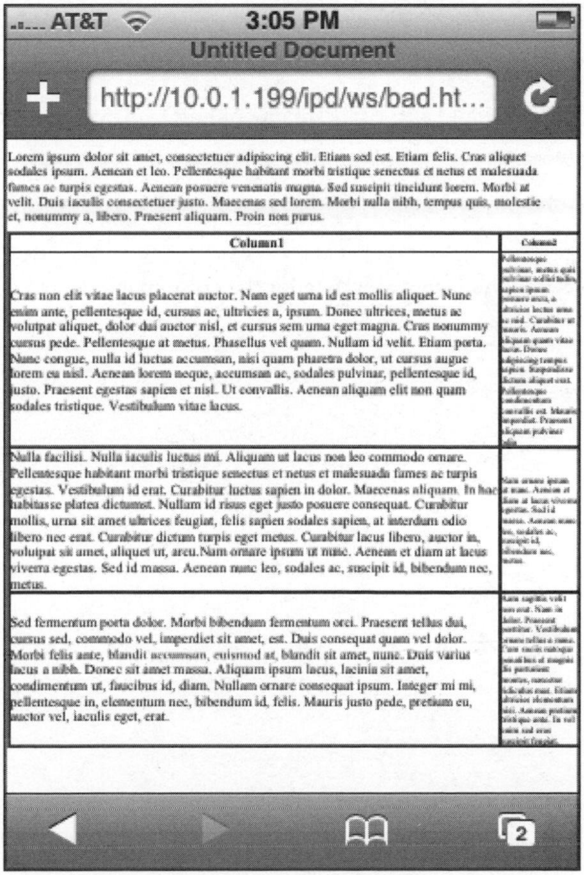

Figure 8-7: Unfriendly page on page load

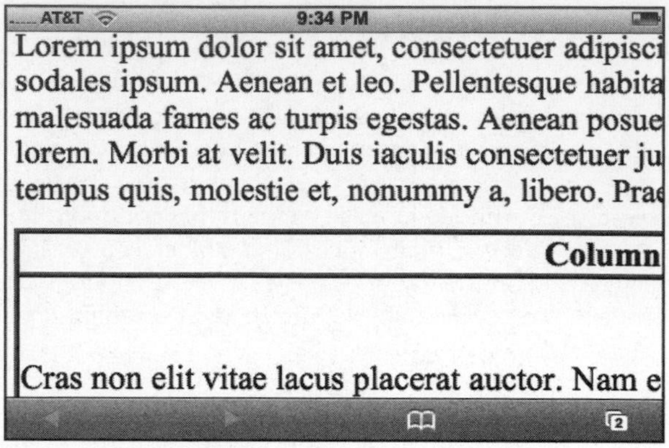

Figure 8-8: Zooming to a cell

However, with a few simple tweaks, you can transform the page into something far easier for iPhone and iPod touch to work with. First, you can add a `viewport` meta tag to gain greater control over the width:

```
<meta name="viewport" content="width=950"/>
```

Next, you enclose the paragraph into a `div` block element and transform it into a column (say 50 percent of page):

```
<div style="width:50%">
</div>
```

In the real world, you would obviously want to tailor the entire page design around a more column-based approach.

Third, you make the table to be sized by percentage (90 percent of width) rather than the fixed width of 1000px:

```
<table width="90%" border="1" cellspacing="1" cellpadding="1">
  <tr>
    <th width="75%" valign="top" scope="col"><div align="center">Column1</div></th>
    <th width="25%" valign="top" scope="col">Column2</th>
  </tr>
  <tr>
...
</table>
```

Even with these rudimentary changes, the page becomes easier to browse when you double-tap the page, as shown in Figure 8-9.

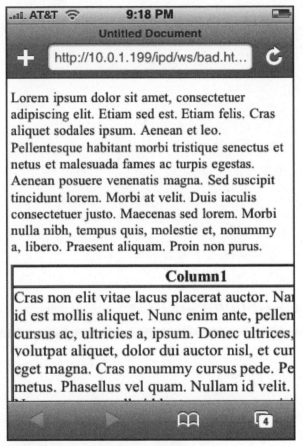

Figure 8-9: The text block is now readable.

Figure 8-10 shows the model block-based Web page that is easily navigated with double-tap and pinch gestures of iPhone and iPod touch.

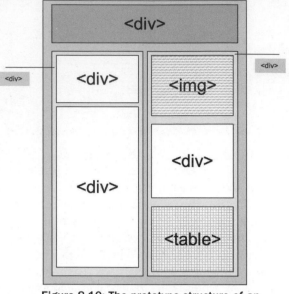

Figure 8-10: The prototype structure of an easy-to-browse page

Defining Multiple Columns (Future Use)

Safari 3 and Mozilla-based browsers provide support for new CSS3 properties that enable you to create newspaper-like, multicolumn layouts. For a content block, you can specify the number of columns, width of the columns, and the gap between them. Because Internet Explorer does not currently support multiple columns, these style properties are prefixed with -webkit and -moz:

```
-webkit-column-count: 2;
-moz-column-count: 2;
-webkit-column-width: 200px;
-moz-column-width: 200px;
-webkit-column-gap: 13px;
-moz-column-gap: 13px;
```

Unfortunately, the current version of Mobile Safari does not support these properties. However, be watching for their future support. When Mobile Safari does support multicolumns, it can offer an easy way to transform existing content into the columnar structure that iPhone and iPod touch users love.

Tier 3: Custom iPhone/iPod touch Styles

An iPhone and iPod touch user can navigate a Tier 2 Web site with double-tap, pinch, and flick gestures, but that does not necessarily mean that it is easy or enjoyable to do so. Panning and scrolling across the screen can become quickly tiresome after the excitement over the "full Web" wears off. Users will quickly find themselves returning to sites that provide a richer, more tailored experience for Mobile Safari. The easiest way to do this is to create custom styles specifically for iPhone and iPod touch.

Media Queries

If you wish to specify a style sheet for iPhone and iPod touch usage, you can use a CSS3 media query. iPhone and iPod touch do not support the dumbed down handheld or print media types. Instead, iPhone and iPod touch look for the screen media type. You can then use the link element to set specific styles for iPhone and iPod touch by looking only for devices that support screen and have a maximum width of 480px:

```
<link media="only screen and (max-device-width: 480px)"
  rel="stylesheet" type="text/css" href="iphone-ipod.css"/>
```

Or, to set iPhone/iPod touch–specific styles inside a particular CSS style sheet, you could use:

```
@media only screen and (max-device-width: 480px) {
  /* Add styles here */
}
```

The link element and the CSS rule would apply only to devices that have a maximum width of 480 pixels. And, for browsers that do not support the only keyword, they will ignore the rule anyway. However, the problem is that, under certain situations, Internet Explorer 6 and 7 fail to ignore this rule and will render the page anyway using the iPhone/iPod touch–specific style sheet. As a result, you need to guard against this possibility by using IE's conditional comments:

```
<!--[if !IE]>-->
<link media="only screen and (max-device-width: 480px)"
  rel="stylesheet" type="text/css" href="iphone-ipod.css"/>
<!--<![endif]-->
```

Internet Explorer will now ignore this link element, because the [if !IE] indicates that the enclosed code should only be executed outside of IE.

Therefore, if you would like to have a default style sheet for normal browsers and a custom style sheet for iPhone and iPod touch users, you would use the following combination:

```
<link media="screen and (min-device-width: 481px)"
  rel="stylesheet" type="text/css" href="default.css"/>
<!--[if !IE]>-->
<link media="only screen and (max-device-width: 480px)"
  rel="stylesheet" type="text/css" href="iphone-ipod.css"/>
<!--<![endif]-->
```

Text Size Adjustment

Normally, the font size of a Web page adjusts automatically when the viewport is adjusted. For instance, after a double-tap gesture, Mobile Safari looks at the zoomed width of the content block and adjusts the text to zoom in proportion. This behavior makes the text easier to read for typical uses, though it can affect absolute positioning and fixed layouts. However, if you would like to prevent the text from resizing, then use the following CSS rule:

```
-webkit-text-size-adjust: none;
```

In general, for most Web site viewing, you will want to keep this property enabled. For iPhone/iPod touch–specific applications in which you want more control over scaling and sizing, you will want to disable this option.

Case Study

Consider a case study example, the Web site of Operation Classroom, a nonprofit organization doing educational work in Africa. Keep in mind that the style sheet of each Web site will need to be optimized in a unique manner, but this case study will demonstrate some of the common issues that will crop up.

Figure 8-11 displays a page from the site with a basic `viewport` meta tag set at `width=780`, which gives it the best scale factor for the existing page structure. However, even when the viewport setting is optimized, a user will still need to double-tap in order to read any of the text on the page. What's more, the top-level links are difficult to tap unless you pinch and zoom first.

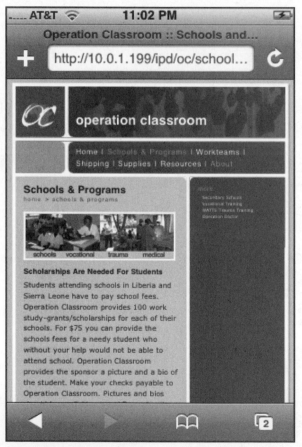

Figure 8-11: The prototype structure of an easy-to-browse page

However, by creating an iPhone and iPod touch–specific style sheet, you can transform the usability site for Mobile Safari users without impacting any of the HTML code. Looking at the page (see Figure 8-12), you'll notice that several transformations need to occur:

❑ Shrink the page width.

❑ Shrink the Operation Classroom logo at the top of the page.

❑ Increase the font size for the menu links, page header, rabbit trail links, and body text.

❑ Move the sidebar to appear below body text.

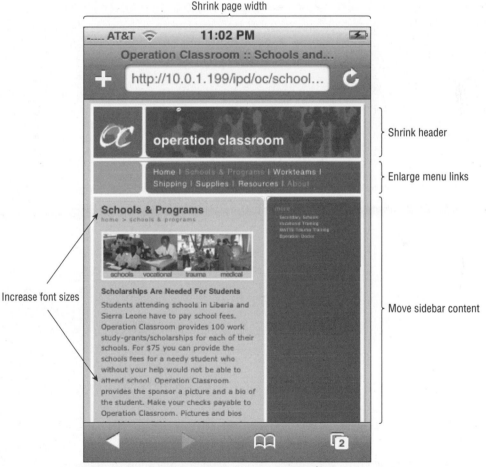

Figure 8-12: Transforming the structure using CSS

As a first step, add a media query to the document head of each page in the site:

```
<link media="screen and (min-device-width: 481px)"
  rel="stylesheet" type="text/css" href="css/oc-normal.css"/>
<!--[if !IE]>-->
<link media="only screen and (max-device-width: 480px)"
  rel="stylesheet" type="text/css" href="css/oc-iphone-ipod.css"/>
<!--<![endif]-->
```

Next, inside of the HTML files, change the `viewport` meta tag to a smaller width:

```
<meta name="viewport" content="width=490"/>
```

The 490px width is wide enough to be compatible with the existing site structure, but small enough to minimize the scaling.

That's all of the work that you need to do to the HTML files.

To create the new custom style sheet, you will begin with the default style sheet already being used and then save as a new name — oc-iphone-ipod.css. Your first task is to change the width of the document from 744px to 490px. Here's the updated style:

```
@media all {
  #wrap {
    position:relative;
    top:4px;
    left:4px;
    background:#ab8;
    width:490px;
    margin:0 auto;
    text-align:left;
  }
```

Next, you change the original `font-size:small` property defined in `body` to a more specific pixel size:

```
body {
  background:#cdb;
  margin:0;
  padding:10px 0 14px;
  font-family: Verdana,Sans-serif;
  text-align:center;
  color:#333;
  font-size: 15px;
  }
```

While this size is not as large as what an iPhone/iPod touch application would use, it is the largest font size that works with the current structure of the Operation Classroom Web site. Fortunately, the *rabbit trail* (pathway) and page header fonts are relative to the body font:

```
#pathway {
  margin-top:3px;
  margin-bottom: 25px;
  letter-spacing   : .18em;
  color: #666666;
  font-size: .8em;

}
#pageheader {
  font-family:Helvetica,Arial,Verdana,Sans-serif;
  font-weight: bold;
  font-size: 2.2em;
  margin-bottom: 1px;
  margin-top: 3px;
}
```

The next issue is to shrink the size of the banner at the top of the page. Here's the style for the banner text:

```
#banner-text{
  background:url("../images/bg_header.jpg") no-repeat left top;
  margin:0;
  padding:40px 0 0;
  font:bold 275%/97px Helvetica,Arial,Verdana,Sans-serif;
  text-transform:lowercase;
  }
```

The two properties you need to try and shrink are the padding and the font size. Here's a workable solution:

```
#banner-title {
  background:url("../images/bg_header.jpg") no-repeat left top;
  margin:0;
  padding:10px 0 10px;
  font: Bold 35px Helvetica,Arial,Verdana,Sans-serif;
  text-transform:lowercase;
  }
```

The final and perhaps most important change is to enable the sidebar to follow the main text rather than float along side of it. Here's the original definition:

```
#sidebar {
  background:#565 url("..images/corner_sidebar.gif") no-repeat left top;
  width: 254px;
  float: right;
  padding:0;
  color:#cdb;
  }
```

To move the sidebar content below the main body text, you remove the float property and add a clear: both declaration to prevent the sidebar from any side wrapping. You also change the small width of 254px to 100 percent, which enables it to take up the entire contents of the content div. Here's the code:

```
#sidebar {
   background:#565 url("../images/corner_sidebar.gif") no-repeat left top;
   width:100%;
   clear: both;
   padding:0;
   color:#cdb;
}
```

Figures 8-13, 8-14, and 8-15 show the results of the transformation.

Figure 8-13: The top banner is smaller, but the link sizes are larger.

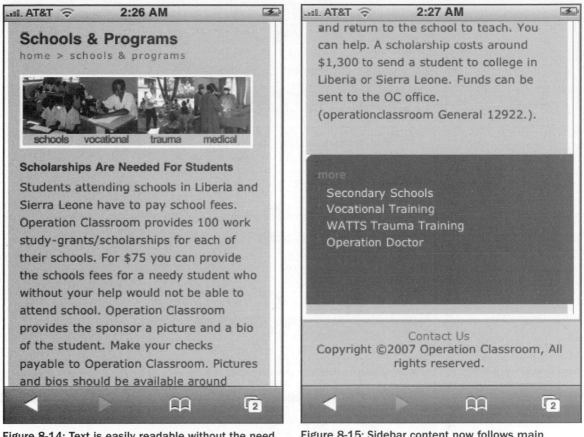

Figure 8-14: Text is easily readable without the need for double-tap or pinch gestures.

Figure 8-15: Sidebar content now follows main body text.

Tier 4: Parallel Sites

Unless you are creating an iPhone or iPod touch application, developing for Tier 2 or 3 support will provide sufficient support for most sites. However, you might find a compelling need to actually develop a site specifically written for iPhone/iPod touch. The content may be the same, but it needs to be structured in a manner discussed in Chapters 2 and 3.

Avoid Handcuffs, Offer Freedom

If you are going to offer an iPhone/iPod touch version of your site, you want to offer your users the freedom to choose between the customized site and your normal site. Don't auto-redirect based on user agent. Because Mobile Safari can navigate a normal Web site, you should always allow users to make the decision themselves. Amazon.com provides a good model. As Figure 8-16 shows, when you access their homepage on your iPhone, it clearly notifies you of the alternative site, but does not handcuff you into using it.

Figure 8-16: Amazon offers freedom to use the normal site or an iPhone-specific version.

To add a similar functionality to a Web site, begin by adding an empty `div` element at the top of your content, just below the top menu:

```
<div id="iphone-ipod-notify"></div>
```

This element will serve as the placeholder for the message that you will display to iPhone and iPod touch users.

Next, add the following script:

```
<script type="application/x-javascript">
function isAppleMobile() {
  result ((navigator.platform.indexOf("iPhone") != -1) ||
          (navigator.userAgent.indexOf('iPod') != -1))
}
function init() {
```

```
    if ( isAppleMobile ) {
       var o = document.getElementById( 'iphone-ipod-notify' );
       o.innerHTML = "<h1 style='text-align:center;border: 1px solid #a23e14; -
webkit-border-radius: 10px;'><a href='iphone-ipod-index.html'>Tap here to go to
our<br/>iPhone/iPod touch web site.</a></h1>";
    }
}
</script>
```

The init() function calls isAppleMobile() function to determine whether the user agent is an Apple mobile device. If so, then HTML content is added to the placeholder div element. If not, then nothing is added. The init() function is then called from the onload handler of the body. Figure 8-17 shows the results when viewed from an iPhone or iPod touch.

Figure 8-17: Offering a freedom of choice to your users

Transform a Site to an iPhone/iPod touch Design

Once you decide to create a companion site specifically for Mobile Safari users, you have to decide how existing content best fits inside of an iPhone and iPod touch UI design. You need to determine whether you want to create your own custom design or model after the standard edge-to-edge navigation. (See Chapters 2 and 3 for more on UI design.) The edge-to-edge design scheme works well for many Web sites, as you'll see here.

As a case study, you'll turn once again to the Operation Classroom Web site, the homepage of which is shown in Figure 8-18. Several aspects of this site lend itself to using the edge-to-edge navigation UI. First, the site hierarchy could be easily converted to a series of nested list items. Second, the news entries and quick links entries also work great as lists.

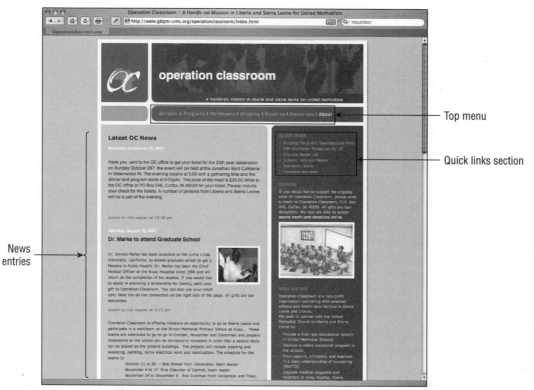

Figure 8-18: Operation Classroom homepage

Using the iUI framework and the cUI extension (see Chapter 7), you'll create a new HTML page containing the top-level menu. Here's the initial code:

```
<body>
    <!-- Top iUI toolbar -->
    <div class="toolbar">
        <h1 id="pageTitle"></h1>
```

```
        <a id="backButton" class="button" href="#"></a>
    </div>
    <!-- Top-level menu -->
    <ul id="home" title="OC for iPhone" selected="true">
        <li><a href="#news">News</a></li>
        <li><a href="#quick-links">Quick Links</a></li>
        <li><a href="#schools-programs">Schools and Programs</a></li>
        <li><a href="#workteams">Workteams</a></li>
        <li><a href="#shipping">Shipping</a></li>
        <li><a href="#supplies">Supplies</a></li>
        <li><a href="#resources">Resources</a></li>
        <li><a href="#about">About OC</a></li>
        <li><a href="index.html" target="_self">Return to Regular Web Site</a></li>
    </ul>
</body>
```

The top list items include both the top-level links from the regular site, along with news entries, quick links, as well as a link back to the regular Web site. Figure 8-19 shows the top-level menu when displayed on the iPhone.

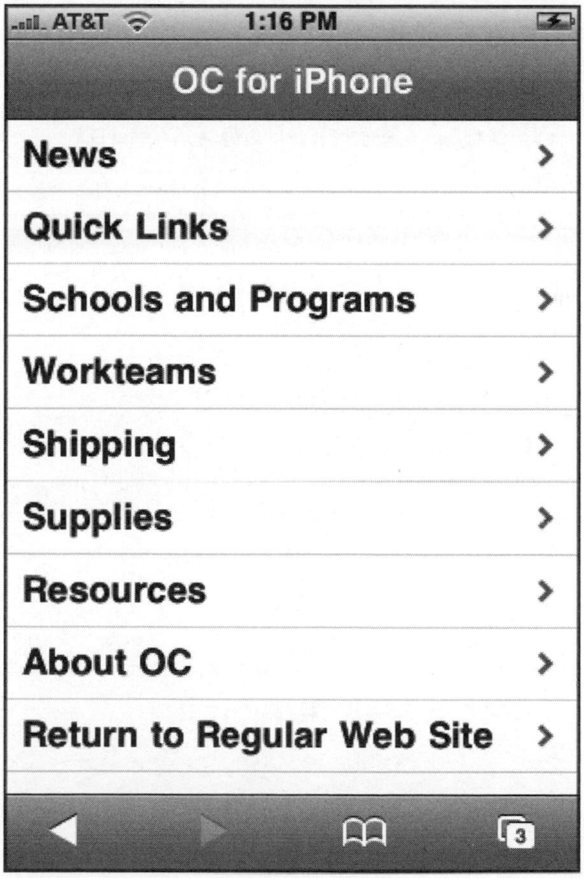

Figure 8-19: OC for iPhone/iPod touch

The news entries from the regular homepage are converted to their own list of new articles. Notice that the entries are organized by date (see Figure 8-20) using the iUI class group:

```
<!-- News menu -->
<ul id="news" title="Latest News">
    <li class="group">Sept. 20, 2007</li>
    <li><a href="#news1">20 Year Celebration Coming Soon</a></li>
    <li class="group">Aug. 18, 2007</li>
    <li><a href="#news2">Dr. Marke To Attend Graduate School</a></li>
    <li><a href="#news3">Workteam Scheduled for Kissy Clinic</a></li>
    <li class="group">June 23, 2007</li>
    <li><a href="#news4">Special Speakers Coming to Indiana in October</a></li>
    <li class="group">May 24, 2007</li>
    <li><a href="#Bill_Drake">Combat Malnutrition in Sierra Leone</a></li>
</ul>
```

Figure 8-20: News entries by date

Each of these links is connected with a destination page:

```
<div id="news1" class="panel" title="OC News">
<h2>20 Year Celebration Coming Soon</h2>
<p>Have you sent to the OC office to get your ticket for the 20th year celebration
on Sunday October 28? The event will be held at JB's Cafeteria in Greeley, IN. The
evening begins at 5:00pm with a gathering time and the dinner and program starts at
6:00pm. The price of the meal is $25.00. Email the OC office for your ticket.
Please include your check for the tickets. A number of persons from Liberia and
Sierra Leone will be a part of the evening.</p>
</div>
```

Figure 8-21 displays the results of this page.

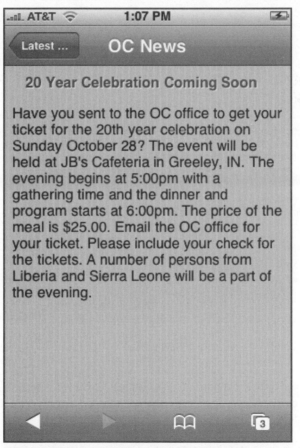

Figure 8-21: News article as a destination page

iPhone services integration offers you some special things with Contact Us pages. For example, when displaying contact information for the organization, you use a cUI destination page, which is discussed in Chapter 7:

```
            <!-- Contact panel -->
       <div id="about" title="About Us" class="panel">
             <div class="cuiHeader">
                  <img class="cui" src="images/iclass.png"/>
             <h1 class="cui">Operation Classroom</h1>
             <h2 class="cui">Partnering in Sierra Leone and Liberia</h2>
          </div>
          <fieldset>
             <div class="row">
                 <label class="cui">office</label>
                 <a class="cuiServiceLink" target="_self" href="tel:(765) 555-1212"
onclick="return (navigator.userAgent.indexOf('iPhone') != -1)">(765) 555-1212</a>
                 </div>
             <div class="row">
                 <label class="cui">mobile</label>
                 <a class="cuiServiceLink" target="_self" href="tel:(765) 545-1211"
onclick="return (navigator.userAgent.indexOf('iPhone') != -1)">(765) 545-1211</a>
                 </div>
             <div class="row">
                 <label class="cui">email</label>
                 <a class="cuiServiceLink" target="_self"
href="mailto:info@operationclassroom.org" onclick="return
(navigator.userAgent.indexOf('iPhone') != -1)">info@oc.org</a>
                 </div>
          </fieldset>
          <fieldset>
             <div class="rowCuiAddressBox">
                    <label class="cui">office</label>
                    <p class="cui">P.O. Box 120208.N</p>
                    <p class="cui">Colfax, IN 46035</p>
                 </div>
          </fieldset>
          <fieldset>
             <div class="row">
                 <a   class="cuiServiceButton" target="_self"
href="http://maps.google.com/maps?q=2012+Main,+Lapel,+IN">Map To Warehouse</a>
                 </div>
          </fieldset>
       </div>
```

The top div contains a thumbnail image and a place for company name and tagline. The next fieldset provides telephone and email links (see Figure 8-22). iPod touch users will not be able to link to Phone or Mail applications, so an onclick handler is added to each link to enable the link only if it is running on an iPhone. (That's also why the text label for the email link displays the actual address instead of "Email Us.") The middle `fieldset` provides static address information, while the bottom `fieldset` contains a Google Maps link to the Operation Classroom warehouse (see Figure 8-23). If running on an iPhone, the Maps application will open. If running on an iPod touch, the Google Maps Web site is displayed.

Figure 8-22: iPhone service integration

Figure 8-23: The link to Google Maps works in both iPhone and iPod touch.

The following code shows the full source code for the sample OC for iPhone/iPod touch site. Note that many sections are not shown for this example that would need to be implemented for a live site.

```
<!DOCTYPE html PUBLIC "-//W3C//DTD XHTML 1.0 Strict//EN"
         "http://www.w3.org/TR/xhtml1/DTD/xhtml1-strict.dtd">
<html xmlns="http://www.w3.org/1999/xhtml">
<head>
<title>Operation Classroom</title>
<meta name="viewport" content="width=320; initial-scale=1.0; maximum-scale=1.0;
user-scalable=0;"/>
```

(continued)

(continued)

```
<style type="text/css" media="screen">@import "../iui/iui.css";</style>
<style type="text/css" media="screen">@import "../iui/cui.css";</style>
<script type="application/x-javascript" src="../iui/iui.js"></script>
</head>
<body>
        <!-- Top iUI toolbar -->
    <div class="toolbar">
        <h1 id="pageTitle"></h1>
        <a id="backButton" class="button" href="#"></a>
    </div>
    <!-- Top-level menu -->
    <ul id="home" title="OC for iPhone" selected="true">
        <li><a href="#news">News</a></li>
        <li><a href="#quick-links">Quick Links</a></li>
        <li><a href="#schools-programs">Schools and Programs</a></li>
        <li><a href="#workteams">Workteams</a></li>
        <li><a href="#shipping">Shipping</a></li>
        <li><a href="#supplies">Supplies</a></li>
        <li><a href="#resources">Resources</a></li>
        <li><a href="#about">About OC</a></li>
        <li><a href="index.html" target="_self">Return to Regular Web Site</a></li>
    </ul>
    <!-- News menu -->
    <ul id="news" title="Latest News">
        <li class="group">Sept. 20, 2007</li>
        <li><a href="#news1">20 Year Celebration Coming Soon</a></li>
        <li class="group">Aug. 18, 2007</li>
        <li><a href="#news2">Dr. Marke To Attend Graduate School</a></li>
        <li><a href="#news3">Workteam Scheduled for Kissy Clinic</a></li>
        <li class="group">June 23, 2007</li>
        <li><a href="#news4">Special Speakers Coming to Indiana in October</a></li>
        <li class="group">May 24, 2007</li>
        <li><a href="#Bill_Drake">Combat Malnutrition in Sierra Leone</a></li>
    </ul>
    <div id="news1" class="panel" title="OC News">
      <h2>20 Year Celebration Coming Soon</h2>
      <p>
Have you sent to the OC office to get your ticket for the 20th year celebration on
Sunday October 28? The event will be held at JB's Cafeteria in Greeley, IN. The
evening begins at 5:00pm with a gathering time and the dinner and program starts at
6:00pm. The price of the meal is $25.00. Email the OC office for your ticket.
Please include your check for the tickets. A number of persons from Liberia and
Sierra Leone will be a part of the evening.          </p>
    </div>
    <!-- More content would appear here -->
      <!-- About Us panel -->
     <div id="about" title="About Us" class="panel">
            <div class="cuiHeader">
                <img class="cui" src="images/iclass.png"/>
            <h1 class="cui">Operation Classroom</h1>
            <h2 class="cui">Partnering in Sierra Leone and Liberia</h2>
        </div>
```

```
            <fieldset>
                <div class="row">
                    <label class="cui">office</label>
                    <a class="cuiServiceLink" target="_self" href="tel:(765) 555-1212"
onclick="return (navigator.userAgent.indexOf('iPhone') != -1)">(765) 555-1212</a>
                </div>
                <div class="row">
                    <label class="cui">mobile</label>
                    <a class="cuiServiceLink" target="_self" href="tel:(765) 545-1211"
onclick="return (navigator.userAgent.indexOf('iPhone') != -1)">(765) 545-1211</a>
                </div>
                <div class="row">
                    <label class="cui">email</label>
                    <a class="cuiServiceLink" target="_self"
href="mailto:info@operationclassroom.org" onclick="return
(navigator.userAgent.indexOf('iPhone') != -1)">info@oc.org</a>
                </div>
            </fieldset>
            <fieldset>
                <div class="rowCuiAddressBox">
                    <label class="cui">office</label>
                    <p class="cui">P.O. Box 120208.N</p>
                    <p class="cui">Colfax, IN 46035</p>
                </div>
            </fieldset>
            <fieldset>
                <div class="row">
                    <a  class="cuiServiceButton" target="_self"
href="http://maps.google.com/maps?q=2012+Main,+Lapel,+IN">Map To Warehouse</a>
                </div>
            </fieldset>
        </div>
    </body>
    </html>
```

9

Bandwidth and Performance Optimizations

Once Apple made the strategic decision to support Web-based applications for iPhone and iPod touch rather than native applications, optimization emerged as a *front burner* issue for application developers. With native applications, programmers can code in their personal style, efficient or not, because the actual performance hit is negligible, even on a mobile device like iPhone. What's more, in a decade where broadband is now the norm, many Web developers have fallen into those same tendencies and allow their sites and applications to be composed of ill-formed HTML, massive JavaScript libraries, and multiple CSS style sheets.

However, when you are developing applications for iPhone and iPod touch, you need to refocus your programming and development efforts toward optimization and efficiency. What makes it different from normal Web 2.0 apps is that the developer can no longer rely on the fact that the user is accessing the application from a broadband connection. iPhone users may be coming to your application using Wi-Fi or a much slower EDGE connection.

Therefore, as you develop your applications, you will want to formulate an optimization strategy that makes the most sense for your context. You'll want to think about both bandwidth and code performance optimizations.

Your Optimization Strategy

If you spend much time at all researching optimization strategy and techniques, you quickly discover that there are two main schools of thought. The first camp is referred to as *hyper-optimizers* in this book. A hyper-optimizer will do almost anything to save a byte or an unneeded call to the Web server. They are far more concerned with saving milliseconds than they are about the readability of the code that they are optimizing. The second camp, perhaps best described as *relaxed optimizers*, are interested in optimizing their applications. But, they are not interested in sacrificing code readability and manageability in an effort to save a nanosecond here or there.

Decide which camp you fall into. But at the same time, don't go through complex optimization hoops unless you prove that your steps are going to make a substantive difference in the usability of your application. Many optimization techniques you'll find people advocating may merely make your code harder to work with and don't offer any notable performance boost.

Best Practices to Minimize Bandwidth

Arguably the greatest bottleneck of any iPhone and iPod touch application is the time it takes to transport data from the Web server to Mobile Safari, especially if your application is running over EDGE. Therefore, consider the following techniques as you assemble your Web application.

General

❑　Separate your page content into separate .css, .js, and .html files so that each file can be cached by Mobile Safari.

❑　Reduce white space (tabs and spaces) wherever possible. Although this might seem like a nominal issue, the amount of excess white space can add up, particularly on a larger-scale Web application with dozens of files.

❑　Remove useless tags, and unused styles and JavaScript functions in your HTML, CSS style sheets, and JavaScript library files.

❑　Remove unnecessary comments. However, keep in mind the following caveat: Removing comments can reduce file size, but it can make it harder to manage your code in the future.

❑　Use shorter filenames. For example, it is much more efficient to reference tb2.png than TopBannerAlternate2_980.png.

❑　Minimize the total number of external style sheets and JavaScript library files you include with your page. Because browsers typically make just two requests at a given time, every additional file that a browser has to wait on for the request to complete will create latency.

❑　Write well-formed and standard XHTML code. While not a bandwidth issue, well-formed XHTML requires less passes and parsing by Mobile Safari before it renders the page. As a result, the time from initial request to final display can be improved through this coding practice.

❑　Consider using gzip compression when you serve your application. (See the following section for more on compression options.)

❑　Consider using a JavaScript compressor on your JavaScript libraries. You could then work with a normal, un-optimized JavaScript library for development (mylibrary.js) and then output a compressed version for runtime purposes (mylibrary-c.js). (See the following section for more on compression options.)

Images

❑　Large image sizes are a traditional bottleneck to always target for your applications. Be meticulous in optimizing the file size of your images. Shaving off 5kb or so from several images in your application can make a notable performance increase.

❑ Make sure your images are sized appropriately for display on the iPhone and iPod touch viewport. Never ever rely on browser scaling. Instead, match image size to image presentation.

❑ Image data is more expensive than text data. Therefore, consider using canvas drawing in certain cases.

❑ Instead of using image borders, consider using CSS borders instead, particularly with the enhanced `-webkit-border-radius` property.

❑ Instead of using one large background image, consider using a small image and tiling it.

CSS and JavaScript

❑ Combine rules to create more efficient style declarations. For example, the second declaration is much more space efficient than the first one is:

```
// Less efficient
div #content {
                font-family: Helvetica, Arial, sans-serif;
                font-size: 12px; /* Randy: do we want this as px or pt? */
                line-height: 1.2em; /* Let's try this for now...*/
                font-weight: bold;
}
// More efficient
div #content {font: bold 12px/1.2em Helvetica, Arial, sans-serif};
```

❑ Consider using shorter CSS style names and JavaScript variable and function names. After all, the longer your identifiers are, the more space your files will take. But, at the same time, do not make your identifiers so short that they become hard to work with. For example, consider the trade-offs with the following three declarations:

```
/* Inefficient */
#homepage-blog-subtitle-alternate-version{letter-spacing:.1em;}
/* Efficient, but cryptic */
#hbsa{letter-spacing:.1em;}
/* Happy medium */
#blog-subtitle-alt{letter-spacing:.1em;}
```

As you work through these various strategies and test results, a good way to check the total page size is to save the page as a Web archive in a desktop version of Safari. The file size of the archive file indicates the HTML page size with all of the external resources (images, style sheets, and script libraries) associated with it.

Compressing Your Application

Normally, an iPhone/iPod touch Web application will be launched when a user types the URL in their Mobile Safari browser. The Web server will respond to the HTTP request and serve the HTML file and each of the many supporting files that are used in the display and execution of the Web app. While image files may have been optimized as much as possible to minimize bandwidth, each uncompressed HTML file, CSS style sheet, and JavaScript library file requested will always take up much more space than if it were compressed. Therefore, with that idea in mind, several options are available to compress files and/or JavaScript code on the fly on the server.

Gzip File Compression

Mobile Safari provides support for gzip compression, a compression option offered by many Web servers. Using gzip compression, you can reduce the size of HTML, CSS, and JavaScript files and reduce the total download size by up to 4 to 5 times. However, because Mobile Safari must uncompress the resources when it receives them, be sure to test to ensure that this overhead does not eliminate the benefits gained.

To turn on gzip compression in PHP, use the following code:

```
<?php
ob_start("ob_gzhandler");
?>
<html>
<body>
<p>This page has been compressed.</p>
</body>
</html>
```

JavaScript Code Compression

In addition to reducing the total file size of your Web site, another technique is to focus on JavaScript code. These compression strategies go far beyond the manual coding techniques described in this chapter and seek to compress and *minify* — remove all unnecessary characters — your JavaScript code. In fact, using these automated solutions, you can potentially reduce the size of your scripts by 30–40 percent.

There are a variety of open source solutions that you turn to that tend to take two different approaches. The safe optimizers remove whitespace and comments from code, but do not seek to actually change naming inside of your source code. The aggressive optimizers go a step further and seek to crunch variable and function names. While the aggressive optimizers achieve greater compression ratios, they are not as safe to use in certain situations. For example, if you have eval() or with in your code (not recommended anyway), these routines will be broken during the compression process. What's more, some of the optimizers, such as Packer, use an eval-based approach to compress and uncompress. However, there is a performance hit in the uncompression process and it could actually slow down your script under certain conditions.

Here are some of the options available (ranked in order of conservatism employed in their algorithms):

❑ JSMin (JavaScript Minifier; www.crockford.com/javascript/jsmin.html) is perhaps the best-known JavaScript optimizer. It is the most conservative of the optimizers, focusing on simply removing whitespace and comments from JavaScript code.

❑ YUI Compressor (www.julienlecomte.net/blog/2007/08/13/introducing-the-yui-compressor) is a recently introduced optimizer that claims to offer a happy medium between the conservative JSMin and the more aggressive ShrinkSafe and Packer listed next.

❏ Dojo ShrinkSafe (`alex.dojotoolkit.org/shrinksafe`) optimizes and crunches local variable names to achieve greater compression ratios.

❏ Dean Edwards's Packer (`dean.edwards.name/packer`) is an aggressive optimizer that achieves high compression ratios.

Deciding which of these options to use should depend on your specific needs and the nature of your source code. I recommend starting on the safe side and moving up as needed.

If you decide to use one of these optimizers, make sure you use semicolons to end your lines in your source code. Besides being good programming practice, most optimizers need them to accurately remove excess whitespace.

Additionally, while Packer requires semicolons, Dojo ShrinkSafe does not require them and will actually insert missing semicolons for you. So you can pre-process a JavaScript file through ShrinkSafe before using it in a semicolon requiring compressor like Packer.

To demonstrate the compression ratios that you can achieve, I ran the iUI.js JavaScript library file through several of these optimizing tools. Table 9-1 displays the results.

Table 9-1: Benchmark of Compression of iUI.js File

Compressor	JavaScript compression (bytes)	With gzip compression (bytes)
No compression	100% (11284)	26% (2879)
JSMin	65% (7326)	21% (2403)
Dojo ShrinkSafe	58% (6594)	21% (2349)
YUI Compressor	64% (7211)	21% (2377)
YUI Compressor (w/Munged)	46% (5199)	18% (2012)
YUI Compressor (w/Preserve All Semicolons)	64% (7277)	21% (2389)
YUI Compressor (w/Munged and Preserve All Semicolons)	47% (5265)	18% (2020)

One final option worth considering is a PHP-based open source project called Minify. Minify combines, minifies, and caches JavaScript and CSS files to decrease the number of page requests that a page has to make. To do so, it combines multiple style sheets and script libraries into a single download (`code.google.com/p/minify`).

JavaScript Performance Optimizations

The performance of JavaScript on iPhone and iPod touch is much slower than on the Safari desktop counterparts. For example, consider the following simple DOM-access performance test:

```
<!DOCTYPE html PUBLIC "-//W3C//DTD XHTML 1.0 Strict//EN"
        "http://www.w3.org/TR/xhtml1/DTD/xhtml1-strict.dtd">
<html xmlns="http://www.w3.org/1999/xhtml">
<head>
<title>Performance Test</title>
</head>
<body>
<form id="form1">
<input id="i1" value="zero" type="text">
</form>
<div id="output"></div>
</body>
<script type="application/x-javascript">
var i = 0;
var start1 = new Date().getTime();
divs = document.getElementsByTagName('div');
for(i = 0; i < 80000; i++)
{
        var d = divs[0];
}
var start2 = new Date().getTime();
var delta1 = start2 - start1;
document.getElementById("output").innerHTML = "Time: " + delta1;
</script>
</html>
```

Safari for Mac OS X executes this script in 529 milliseconds, while Safari for iPhone takes 13,922 milliseconds. That's over 26 times longer! Therefore, in addition to the optimizations that can be made in shrinking the overall file size of your application, you should also give priority to making performance gains in execution based on your coding techniques. Here several best practices to consider.

Smart DOM Access

When working with client-side JavaScript, accessing the DOM can be at the heart of almost anything you do. However, as essential as these DOM calls may be, it is important to remember that DOM access is expensive from a performance standpoint and so should be done with forethought.

Cache DOM References

Cache references that you make to avoid multiple lookups on the same object or property. For example, compare the following inefficient and efficient routines:

```
// Ineffecient
var str = document.createTextNode("Farther up, further in");
document.getElementById("para1").appendChild(str);
document.getElementById("para1").className="special";
// More efficient
```

```
var str = document.createTextNode("Farther up, further in");
var p = document.getElementById("para1");
p.appendChild(str);
p.className="special";
```

What's more, if you make a sizeable number of references to a document or another common DOM object, cache them, too. For example, compare the following:

```
// Less efficient
var l1=document.createTextNode('Line 1');
var l2=document.createTextNode('Line 2');
// More efficient
var d=document;
var l1=d.createTextNode('Line 1');
var l2=d.createTextNode('Line 2');
```

If you reference `document` a handful of times, then it is probably not practical to go through this trouble. But if you find yourself writing `document` a thousand times in your code, the efficiency gains make this practice a definite consideration.

Offline DOM Manipulation

When you are writing to the DOM, assemble your subtree of nodes outside of the actual DOM, and then insert the subtree once at the end of the process. For example, consider the following:

```
var comments=customBlog.getComments('index');
var c=comments.count;
var entry;
var commentDiv = document.createElement('div');
document.body.appendChild(commentDiv);
for (var i=0;i<c;i++) {
  entry=document.createElement('p');
  entry.appendChild( document.createTextNode(comments[i]);
  commentDiv.appendChild( entry );
}
```

Consider the placement of the grayed, highlighted line. Because you add the new `div` element to the DOM before you add children to it, the document must be updated for each new paragraph added. However, you can speed up the routine considerably by moving the offending line to the end:

```
var comments=customBlog.getComments('index');
var c=comments.count;
var entry;
var commentDiv = document.createElement('div');
for (var i=0;i<c;i++) {
  entry=document.createElement('p');
  entry.appendChild( document.createTextNode(comments[i]);
  commentDiv.appendChild( entry );
}
document.body.appendChild(commentDiv);
```

With the restructured code, the document display only needs to be updated once instead of multiple times.

Combining document.write() calls

Along the same line, you should avoid excessive `document.write()` calls. Each call is a performance hit. Therefore, a much better practice is to assemble a concatenated string variable first. For example, compare the following:

```
// Inefficient
document.write('<div class="row">');
document.write('<label class="cui">office</label>');
document.write('<a class="cuiServiceLink" target="_self" href="tel:(765) 555-
1212">(765) 555-1212</a>');
document.write('</div>');
// More efficient
var s = '<div class="row">' + '<label class="cui">office</label>' +
'<a class="cuiServiceLink" target="_self" href="tel:(765) 555-1212">(765) 555-
1212</a>' + '</div>';
document.write(s);
```

Using the Window Object

The window object is faster to use because Mobile Safari does not have to navigate the DOM to respond to your call. The following window reference is more efficient than the top three:

```
// Inefficient
var h=document.location.href;
var h=document.URL;
var h=location.href;
// More efficient
var h=window.location.href
```

Local and Global Variables

One of the most important practices JavaScript coders should implement in their code is to use local variables and avoid global variables. When Mobile Safari processes a script, local variables are always looked for first in the local scope. If it can't find a match, then it moves up the next level, then next, until it hits the global scope. So global variables are the slowest in a lookup. For example, defining variable a at the global level in the following code is much more expensive than defining it as a local variable inside of the `for` routine:

```
// Inefficient
var a=1;
function myFunction(){
  for(var i=0;i<10;i++) {
    var t = a+i;
    // do something with t
  }
}
//More efficient
function myFunction(){
  for(var i=0,a=1;i<10;i++) {
    var t = a+i;
    // do something with t
  }
}
```

Dot Notation and Property Lookups

Accessing objects and properties by dot notation is never efficient. Therefore, consider some alternatives.

Avoiding Nested Properties

Aim to keep the levels of dot hierarchy small. Nested properties, such as `document.property` `.property.property`, cause the biggest performance problems and should be avoided or accessed as few times as possible.

```
// Inefficient
m.n.o.p.doThis();
m.n.o.p.doThat();
// More efficient
var d = m.n.o.p;
d.doThis();
d.doThat();
```

Accessing a Named Object

If you access a named object, it is more efficient to use `getElementById()` rather than access it via dot notation. For example, compare the following:

```
// Inefficient
document.form1.addressLine1.value
// More efficient
document.getElementById( 'addressLine1' ).value;
```

Property Lookups Inside Loops

When accessing a property inside of a loop, it is much better practice to cache the property reference first, and then access the variable inside of the loop. For example, compare the following:

```
// Inefficient
for(i = 0; i <10; i++) {
var v = document.object.property(i);
var y = myCustomObject.property(i);
// do something
}
// More efficient
var p = document.object.property;
var cp = myCustomObject.property(i);
for(i = 0; i <10; i++) {
var v= p(i);
var y=cp(i);
// do something
}
```

Here's another example of using the `length` property of an object in the condition of a `for` loop:

```
// Inefficient
for (i=0;i<myObject.length;i++) {
  // Do something
}
// More efficient
for (i=0,var j=myObject.length;i<j;i++) {
  // Do something
}
```

Similarly, if you are using arrays inside of loops and using its `length` as a conditional, you want to assign its length to a variable rather than evaluating at each pass. Check this out:

```
// Inefficient
myArray = new Array();
for (i=0;i<myArray.length;i++) {
  // Do something
}
// More efficient
myArray = new Array();
len = myArray.length;
for (i=0;i<len;i++) {
  // Do something
}
```

String Concatenation

Another traditional problem area in JavaScript is string concatenation. In general, you should try to avoid an excessive number of concatenations and an excessively large string that you are appending to. For example, suppose you are trying to construct a table in code and then write out the code to the document once you are finished. The `stringTable()` function in the following code is less efficient than the second function `intermStringTable()`, because the latter uses an intermediate string variable `row` as a buffer in the `for` loop.

```
<html>
<script type="text/javascript" language="javascript">
function stringTable() {
  var start = new Date().getTime();
  var buf = "<table>";
  for (var i=0; i<10000;i++){
    buf += "<tr>";
    for (var j=0;j<40;j++){
      buf += "<td><i>" + "content" + "</i></td>";
    }
    buf += "</tr>";
  }
  buf += "</table>";
  var duration = new Date().getTime() - start;
  document.write( 'String concat method: ' + duration + '</br>');
}
```

```
function intermStringTable(){
  var start = new Date().getTime();
  var buf = "<table>";
  for (var i=0; i<10000;i++){
    var row = "<tr>";
    for (var j=0;j<40;j++){
      row += "<td><i>" + "content" + "</i></td>";
    }
    row += "</tr>";
    buf += row
  }
  buf += "</table>";
  var duration = new Date().getTime() - start;
  document.write('Intermediate concat method: ' + duration + '</br>');
}
</script>
<body>
</body>
<script type="text/javascript" language="javascript">
stringTable();
intermStringTable();
</script>
</html>
```

What to Do and Not to Do

You will want to be sure to avoid `with` statements, which slow down the processing of the related code block. In addition to the fact that `with` is inefficient, it has also been depreciated in the JavaScript standard. Second, avoid using `eval()` in your scripts. It is very expensive from a performance standpoint. Besides, you should be able to develop a more efficient solution rather than resorting to `eval()`.

Comments add to readability and manageability, but be wise in their usage. For example, minimize their use inside of loop routines, functions, and arrays. If possible, place before or after to ensure greater efficiency.

```
// Inefficient
var a=0,c=100;
for (var i=0;i<c;i++) {
  // Assign d the value of the next div in the current document
  var d = document.getElementByTagName('div')[i];
  // Perform some math for a
  a=i*1.2;
  // Perform some math for b
  b=(a+i)/3;
}
// More efficient
// Assign val of d to 100 divs and perform y on them
// based on val of a and b.
var a=0,c=100;
for (var i=0;i<c;i++) {
  var d = document.getElementByTagName('div')[i];
  a-i*1.2;
  b=(a+i)/3;
}
```

10

Packaging Apps as Bookmarks: Bookmarklets and Data URLs

Because iPhone and iPod touch applications function inside of the Mobile Safari environment, there are two seemingly obvious restrictions for the Web developer: You must live with the built-in capabilities of the Mobile Safari browser; and you need a constant Wi-Fi (or, for iPhone, EDGE) connection in order to run any application.

The truth is that you can get around these limitations by taking advantage of two lesser-known technologies — bookmarklets and data URLs. These technologies have actually been around for years, but they have tended to exist on the periphery of mainstream Web development. However, developers are now reexamining these two developer tools to maximize the potential of the iPhone application platform.

Bookmarklets (short for *bookmark applets*) are mini JavaScript "applets" that can be stored as a bookmark inside of Safari. A data URL is a technique for storing an entire Web page or application (pages, styles, images, data, and scripts) inside of a single URL, which can then be saved as an iPhone/iPod touch Bookmark. This application-in-a-bookmark can then be accessed in offline mode.

Bookmarklets

A *bookmarklet* is JavaScript stored as a URL and saved as a bookmark in the browser. It is typically used as a one-click applet that performs a very specific task or performs an action on the current Web page. A bookmarklet uses the `javascript:` protocol followed by script code. For instance, here's the simplest of examples:

```
javascript:alert('iPhone')
```

Because the scripting code for a bookmarklet is housed inside of a URL, the script must be condensed into one long string of code. Therefore, to enter multiple statements, separate each line with a semicolon:

```
javascript:alert('Bookmarklet 1');alert('Bookmarklet 2')
```

As you can see, there are spaces inside each of the strings. You can either substitute %20 for a blank space or let Safari do the conversion for you.

If the script returns a value, then it should be enclosed inside of void() to ensure that the JavaScript code runs as expected. For example, the following Search Wikipedia bookmarklet displays a JavaScript prompt dialog box (see Figure 10-1), and then calls a Wikipedia search URL using the user's value as the search term:

```
javascript:t=prompt('Search
Wikipedia:',getSelection());if(t)void(location.href='http://en.wikipedia.org/w/wiki
.phtml?search='+escape(t))
```

Figure 10-1: Search Wikipedia bookmarklet

Here's a second example that provides a front-end onto Google's define service:

```
javascript:d=prompt('Define:',getSelection());if(d)void(location.href='http://
www.google.com/search?q=define:'+escape(d))
```

Adding a Bookmarklet to Mobile Safari

Bookmarklets are normally added in a standard browser through a drag-and-drop action. However, because that user input is not available in Mobile Safari, you need to add the bookmarklet through the following process:

1. On your main computer, create your bookmarklet script and test it by pasting it into the URL box of Safari.

2. Once the functionality works as expected, drag the `javascript:` URL onto your Bookmarks bar in Safari. If you are going to have a set of bookmarklets, you may wish to create a special Bookmarklets folder to store these scripts.

   Or, if your bookmarklet is contained within the `href` of an a link, then drag the link onto the Bookmarks bar instead.

3. Synch the bookmarks of your iPhone and main computer through iTunes.

4. Access the bookmarklet in the Bookmarks inside Mobile Safari (see Figure 10-2).

Figure 10-2: Accessing a bookmarklet from iPhone

Alternatively, you can add a bookmarklet directly into Mobile Safari's Bookmarks by creating a link to any normal Web page, and then editing the URL of the bookmark.

Exploring How Bookmarklets Can Be Used

While bookmarklets can be used for these sorts of general purposes, their real usefulness to the iPhone application developer is turning JavaScript into a macro language for Mobile Safari to extend the functionality of the browser. For example, Mobile Safari always opens normal links in the existing window, replacing the existing page. Richard Herrera from doctyper.com wrote a bookmarklet that transforms the links of a page and forces them to open in a new tab. Here is the script, which is tricky to read because it is contained within a one-line, encoded URL:

```
javascript:(function(){var%20a=document.getElementsByTagName('a');for(var%20i=0,j=a
.length;i%3Cj;i++){a[i].setAttribute('target','_blank');var%20img=document.createEl
ement('img');img.setAttribute('class',%20'new-
window');img.setAttribute('src','data:image/gif;base64,'+'R0lGOD1hEAAMALMLAL66tBISE
jExMdTQyBoaGjs7OyUlJWZmZgAAAMzMzP//////wAAAAAAAAAAAAA'+'ACH5BAEAAAsALAAAAAAQAAwAA
AQ/cMlZqr2Tps13yVJBjOT4gYairqohCTDMsu4iHHgwr7UA/LqdopZS'+'DBBIpGG51BQH0GgtU9xNJ9XZ1
cnsNicRADs=');img.setAttribute('style','width:16px!important;height:12px!important;
border:none!important;');a[i].appendChild(img);}})();
```

At the time of this writing, Windows Safari has several issues working with bookmarklets. In order for this bookmarklet to work on an iPhone synched with Windows Safari, it must be completely URI encoded:

```
javascript:(function()%7Bvar%20a%3Ddocument.getElementsByTagName('a')%3Bfor(var%20i
%3D0%2Cj%3Da.length%3Bi%3Cj%3Bi%2B%2B)%7Ba%5Bi%5D.setAttribute('target'%2C'_blank')
%3Bvar%20img%3Ddocument.createElement('img')%3Bimg.setAttribute('class'%2C'new-
window')%3Bimg.setAttribute('src'%2C'data%3Aimage%2Fgif%3Bbase64%2C'%2B'R0lGOD1hEAA
MALMLAL66tBISEjExMdTQyBoaGjs7OyUlJWZmZgAAAMzMzP%2F%2F%2F%2F%2F%2F%2FwAAAAAAAAAAAAA
'%2B'ACH5BAEAAAsALAAAAAAQAAwAAAQ%2FcMlZqr2Tps13yVJBjOT4gYairqohCTDMsu4iHHgwr7UA%2FL
qdopZS'%2B'DBBIpGG51BQH0GgtU9xNJ9XZ1cnsNicRADs%3D')%3Bimg.setAttribute('style'%2C'w
idth%3A16px!important%3Bheight%3A12px!important%3Bborder%3Anone!important%3B')%3Ba%
5Bi%5D.appendChild(img)%3B%7D%7D)()%3B
```

Note that while this URI encoded script works on iPhone, it (along with other iPhone-specific bookmarklets in this chapter) still will not work on Windows Safari. Additionally, when you synch with Windows Safari, iPhone bookmarklets can occasionally behave unexpectedly.

An iPhone user can then use this self-contained "applet" on any page in which they wish to transform the links. Notice that the image itself is encoded in a data URL, so that the script is not dependent on any external files.

While the entire script needs to be condensed into a single string of commands, Safari is actually smart enough to convert the hard breaks for you when a multilined script is pasted into the URL box. Just make sure each statement is separated by a semicolon. Therefore, the following code, which is much easier to work with and debug, would still execute properly when pasted directly into the URL box:

```
javascript:(
 function(){
        var a=document.getElementsByTagName('a');
        for(var i=0,j=a.length;i%3Cj;i++) {
                a[i].setAttribute('target','_blank');
                var img=document.createElement('img');
                img.setAttribute('class','new-window');
  img.setAttribute('src','data:image/gif;base64,'+'R0lGOD1hEAAMALMLAL66tBISEjExMdTQy
BoaGjs7OyUlJWZmZgAAAMzMzP///////wAAAAAAAAAAAA'+'ACH5BAEAAAsALAAAAAAQAAwAAAQ/cM1Zq
r2Tps13yVJBjOT4gYairqohCTDMsu4iHHgwr7UA/LqdopZS'+'DBBIpGG51BQH0GgtU9xNJ9XZ1cnsNicRA
Ds=');
                img.setAttribute('style','width:16px!important;
                height:12px!important;
                border:none!important;');
                a[i].appendChild(img);
        }
 })();
```

Bookmarklets can be handy developer tools to assist in testing and debugging on iPhone. For example, the following bookmarklet, based on a script created at iPhoneWebDev.com, gives you View Source functionality (see Figure 10-3) on iPhone itself:

```
javascript:
var sourceWindow = window.open("about:blank");
var newDoc = sourceWindow.document;
newDoc.open();
newDoc.write(
"<html><head><title>Source of " + document.location.href +
"</title><meta name=\"viewport\" id=\"viewport\" content=\"initial-scale=1.0;" +
"user-scalable=0;maximum-scale=0.6667;width=480\"/><script>function do_onload()" +
"{setTimeout(function(){window.scrollTo(0,1);},100);}if(navigator.userAgent.indexOf
" + "(\"iPhone\")!=-
1)window.onload=do_onload;</script></head><body></body></html>");
newDoc.close();
var pre = newDoc.body.appendChild(newDoc.createElement("pre")); pre.
appendChild(newDoc.createTextNode(document.documentElement.innerHTML));
```

If your iPhone is synching with Windows, you would want to fully URI encode the script:

```
javascript:var%20sourceWindow%3Dwindow.open%28%27about%3Ablank%27%29%3B%0Avar%20new
Doc%3DsourceWindow.document%3B%0AnewDoc.open%28%29%3B%0AnewDoc.write%28%27%3Chtml%3
E%3Chead%3E%3Ctitle%3ESource%20of%20%27%2Bdocument.location.href%2B%27%3C/title%3E%
3Cmeta%20name%3D%22viewport%22%20id%3D%22viewport%22%20content%3D%22initial-
scale%3D1.0%3B%20user-scalable%3D0%3B%20maximum-
scale%3D0.6667%3B%20width%3D480%22/%3E%3Cscript%3Efunction%20do_onload%28%29%7BsetT
imeout%28function%28%29%7Bwindow.scrollTo%280,1%29%3B%7D,100%29%3B%7Dif%28navigator
.userAgent.indexOf%28%22iPhone%22%29!%3D-
1%29window.onload%3Ddo_onload%3B%3C/script%3E%3C/head%3E%3Cbody%3E%3C/body%3E%3C/ht
ml%3E%27%29%3B%0AnewDoc.close%28%29%3B%0Avar%20pre%3DnewDoc.body.appendChild%28newD
oc.createElement%28%22pre%22%29%29%3B%0Apre.appendChild%28newDoc.createTextNode%28d
ocument.documentElement.innerHTML%29%29%3B
```

Figure 10-3: Viewing a page's source on iPhone

Go to www.wrox.com for a useful set of bookmarklets that you can use.

Storing an Application in a Data URL

In addition to JavaScript functionality, you can also store a Web page or even a complete application inside of a bookmark. The data: protocol allows you to encode an entire page's content — HTML, CSS, JavaScript, and images — inside a single URL. To be clear, data URLs store, not a simple link to a remote page, but the actual contents of the page. This data URL can then be saved as a bookmark. When users access this bookmark, they can interact with the page whether or not they have Internet access. The implications are significant — you can use data URLs to package certain types of Web applications and get around the live Internet connection requirement.

Constraints and Issues with Using Data URLs

While the potential of data URLs is exciting for the developer, make sure you keep the following constraints and issues in mind before working with them:

❑ You can store client-side technologies — such as HTML, CSS, JavaScript, and XML — inside a data URL. However, you *cannot* package PHP, MYSQL, or any server-side applications in a bookmark.

❑ Any Web application that requires server access for data or application functionality will need to have a way to pack and go: (1) use client-side JavaScript for application functionality, and (2) package up a snapshot of the data and put it in a form accessible from a client script.

❑ The application must be *entirely* self-contained. Therefore, every external resource the application needs, such as images, style sheets, and .js libraries, must be encoded inside of the main HTML file.

❑ External resources that are referenced multiple times cannot be cached. Therefore, each separate reference must be encoded and embedded in the file.

❑ Images must be encoded as base64, though the conversion will increase their size by approximately 33 percent.

❑ The maximum size of a data URL in Mobile Safari is technically 128KB, though in actual practice, you can work with URLs much larger, at least up to several megabytes. However, performance of the Mobile Safari Bookmark manager suffers significantly when large amounts of data are stored inside of a bookmark. Therefore, think thin for data URL–based applications.

❑ Mobile Safari has issues working with complex JavaScript routines embedded in a data URL application. For example, at the time of this writing, certain parts of the iUI framework are not functional inside of a data URL, thus greatly limiting the potential for Web developers to take advantage of offline storage.

Creating an Offline iPhone/iPod touch Application

After examining these constraints, it is clear that the best candidates for offline iPhone/iPod touch applications are those that are relatively small in both scope and overall code base. A tip calculator, for example, is a good example applet because its UI would be simple and its programming logic would be straightforward and not require accessing complex JavaScript libraries. I'll walk you through the steps needed to create an offline application.

After reviewing the constraints and making sure that your application will likely work in an offline mode, you will want to begin by designing and programming as if it were a normal iPhone/iPod touch application. For this sample applet, the interface of the tip calculator is based on a subset of the iUI framework. (Because the functionality inside iui.js is not compatible with data URLs, I am not including any references to this external file.) Figure 10-4 shows the Tipster application interface that you will be constructing.

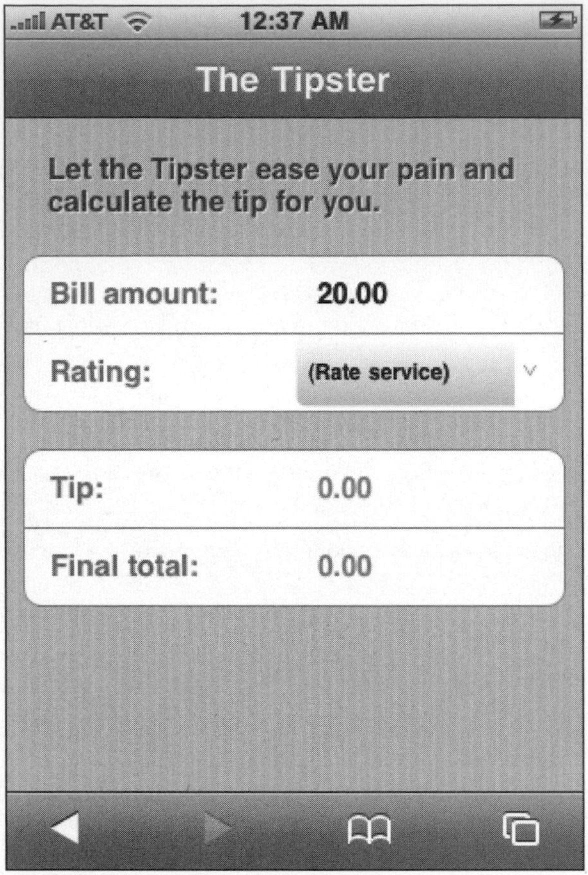

Figure 10-4: Tipster application design

The following source file shows the core HTML and JavaScript code:

```
<!DOCTYPE html PUBLIC "-//W3C//DTD XHTML 1.0 Strict//EN"
         "http://www.w3.org/TR/xhtml1/DTD/xhtml1-strict.dtd">
<html xmlns="http://www.w3.org/1999/xhtml">
<head>
<title>Tipster</title>
<meta name="viewport" content="width=320; initial-scale=1.0; maximum-scale=1.0;
user-scalable=0;"/>
<style type="text/css" media="screen">@import "../iui/iui.css";</style>
<script type="application/x-javascript">
addEventListener('load', function() {
  setTimeout(function() {
      window.scrollTo(0, 1);
  }, 100);
}, false);
function checkTotal(fld) {
```

```
        var x=fld.value;
        var n=/(^\d+$)|(^\d+\.\d+$)/;
        if (n.test(x)) {
            if (fldTipPercent.selectedIndex != 0) getRec();
        }
        else {
            alert('Please enter a valid total')
            clearTotal(fld);
        }
}
function clearTotal(fld) {
  fld.value = '';
}
function getRec() {
    if (fldTipPercent.selectedIndex == 0) { alert('Please rate the service first.');
return; }
    var selPercent = Number( eval( fldTipPercent.
        var billAmount = Number( eval( fldBillTotal.value));
      var tipAmount = (selPercent*billAmount);
      var finalP = tipAmount + billAmount;
    fldTipRec.value = '$' + tipAmount.toFixed(2);
    fldFinalTotal.value = '$' + finalP.toFixed(2);
}
</script>
</head>
<body>
    <div class="toolbar">
        <h1 id="pageTitle">The Tipster</h1>
        <a id="backButton" class="button" href="#"></a>
    </div>
     <div id="main" title="Tipster" class="panel" selected="true">
        <h2 class="tip">Let the Tipster ease your pain and calculate the tip for
you.</h2>
        <fieldset>
            <div class="row">
                <label>Bill amount:</label>
                <input type-"text" id="fldBillTotal" value="20.00" tabindex="1"
onfocus="clearTotal(this)" onchange="checkTotal(this)"/>
            </div>
            <div class="row">
                <label>Rating:</label>
                            <select id="fldTipPercent" onchange="getRec()"
                                    tabindex="2">
                        <option value="0">(Rate service)</option>
                        <option value="10">Very poor</option>
                            <option value="12.5">Poor</option>
                            <option value="15">Just as
                                    expected</option>
                            <option value="17.5">Above
                                    average</option>
                        <option value="20">Exceptional</option>
                        <option value="25">Wow!</option>
                    </select>
            </div>
        </fieldset>
```

(continued)

(continued)

```
            <fieldset>
                <div class="row">
                    <label>Tip: </label>
                    <input type="text" id="fldTipRec" value="0.00" readonly="true"
disabled="true"/>
                </div>
                <div class="row">
                    <label>Final total:</label>
                    <input type="text" id="fldFinalTotal" value="0.00" readonly="true"
disabled="true"/>
                </div>
            </fieldset>
        </div>
    </body>
</html>
```

The `fldBillTotal` input field captures the total before the tip. The `fldTipPercent` select list displays a set of ratings for the service, each corresponding with a percentage value (see Figure 10-5). These two factors are then calculated together to generate the output values in the `fldTipRec` and `fldFinalTotal` input fields.

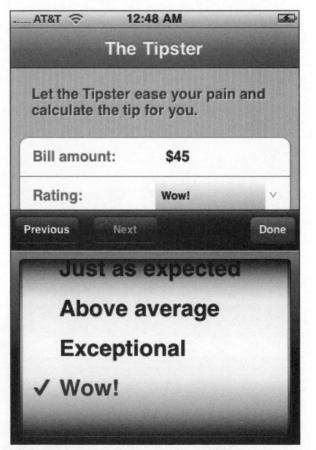

Figure 10-5: Scrolling through the select list

Because iUI does not provide all of the styles you need for the control layout you are using, `tip` classes are defined for the `h2`, `label`, `input`, `select` elements. A `style` element is added to the document head to contain these styles:

```css
<style type="text/css" media="screen">
h2.tip {
    margin-top: 10px;
    margin-bottom: 20px;
}
.row > label.tip {
    position: absolute;
    margin: 0 0 0 14px;
    line-height: 42px;
    font-weight: bold;
    color: #7388a5;
}
.row > input.tip {
    display: block;
    margin: 0;
    border: none;
    padding: 12px 10px 0 160px;
    text-align: left;
    font-weight: bold;
    text-decoration: inherit;
    height: 42px;
    color: inherit;
    box-sizing: border-box;
}
.row > select.tip {
    display: inline;
    text-align: left;
    font-weight: bold;
    font-size: 12px;
    text-decoration: inherit;
    height: 36px;
    color: inherit;
    border: none;
    padding: 12px 0 0 10px;
    float: none;
    position: absolute;
    left: 150px;
    top: 3px;
    width: 140px;
}
</style>
```

Embedding External Styles and Scripts

The UI and functionality of the Tipster application is now complete. However, it will not run in offline mode. Given that, the next step is to turn it into a standalone offline application. To begin, change the `@import` reference of iui.css into an embedded style sheet. At the same time, to minimize the size of the encoded styles, keep only the iUI styles that you are using for this mini application. Here is the new style element that replaces the iui.css reference:

```css
<style type="text/css" media="screen">
body {
    margin: 0;
    font-family: Helvetica;
    background: #FFFFFF;
    color: #000000;
    overflow-x: hidden;
    -webkit-user-select: none;
    -webkit-text-size-adjust: none;
}
body > .toolbar {
    box-sizing: border-box;
    -moz-box-sizing: border-box;
    border-bottom: 1px solid #2d3642;
    border-top: 1px solid #6d84a2;
    padding: 10px;
    height: 45px;
    background: url(toolbar.png) #6d84a2 repeat-x;
}
.toolbar > h1 {
    position: absolute;
    overflow: hidden;
    left: 50%;
    margin: 1px 0 0 -75px;
    height: 45px;
    font-size: 20px;
    width: 150px;
    font-weight: bold;
    text-shadow: rgba(0, 0, 0, 0.4) 0px -1px 0;
    text-align: center;
    text-overflow: ellipsis;
    white-space: nowrap;
    color: #FFFFFF;
}
input {
    box-sizing: border-box;
    width: 100%;
    margin: 8px 0 0 0;
    padding: 6px 6px 6px 44px;
    font-size: 16px;
    font-weight: normal;
}
body > .panel {
    box-sizing: border-box;
    padding: 10px;
    background: #c8c8c8 url(pinstripes.png);
}
.panel > fieldset {
    position: relative;
    margin: 0 0 20px 0;
    padding: 0;
```

```
        background: #FFFFFF;
        -webkit-border-radius: 10px;
        border: 1px solid #999999;
        text-align: right;
        font-size: 16px;
    }
    .row  {
        position: relative;
        min-height: 42px;
        border-bottom: 1px solid #999999;
        -webkit-border-radius: 0;
        text-align: right;
    }
    fieldset > .row:last-child  {
        border-bottom: none !important;
    }
    .row > input {
        box-sizing: border-box;
        margin: 0;
        border: none;
        padding: 12px 10px 0 110px;
        height: 42px;
        background: none;
    }
    .row > label {
        position: absolute;
        margin: 0 0 0 14px;
        line-height: 42px;
        font-weight: bold;
     }
    .panel > h2 {
        margin: 0 0 8px 14px;
        font-size: inherit;
        font-weight: bold;
        color: #4d4d70;
        text-shadow: rgba(255, 255, 255, 0.75) 2px 2px 0;
    }
    </style>
```

Encoding Images

While you now have all of the styles and scripting code inside of the HTML document, there is one last issue. Two of the styles reference external images for backgrounds. Therefore, in order to use them, you need to encode these images first. The easiest way to do this is to use an online converter, such as the data: URI Image Encoder available at www.scalora.org/projects/uriencoder. This service performs a base64 encoding of a local file or a URL. You can then replace the image file reference with the attached encoded string:

```
body > .toolbar {
    box-sizing: border-box;
    -moz-box-sizing: border-box;
    border-bottom: 1px solid #2d3642;
    border-top: 1px solid #6d84a2;
```

(continued)

(continued)

```
        padding: 10px;
        height: 45px;
        background: url(
"data:image/png;base64,iVBORw0KGgoAAAANSUhEUgAAAAEAAAArCAIAAAA2QHWOAAAAGXRFWHRTb2Z0
d2FyZQBBZG9iZSBJbWFnZVJlYWR5ccllPAAAAE1JREFUCNddjDEOgEAQAgn//5qltYWFnb1GB4vdSy4WBAY
StKyb9+O0FJMYyjMyMWCC35lJM71r6vF1P07/lFSfPx6ZxNLcy1HtihzpA/RWcOj0zlDhAAAAAElFTkSuQm
CC"
        ) #6d84a2 repeat-x;
}
body > .panel {
    box-sizing: border-box;
    padding: 10px;
    background: #c8c8c8
url('data:image/png;base64,iVBORw0KGgoAAAANSUhEUgAAAcAAAABCAIAAACdaSOZAAAAGXRFWHRT
b2Z0d2FyZQBBZG9iZSBJbWFnZVJlYWR5ccllPAAAABdJREFUeNpiPHrmCgMC/GNjYwNSAAEGADdNA3dnzP1
QAAAAAElFTkSuQmCC');
}
```

Now that all external resources are embedded, the application is fully standalone. However, you are not there yet. You now need to get it into a form that is accessible when the browser is offline.

Converting Your Application to a Data URL

You are now ready to convert your Web application into an encoded URL. Fortunately, several free tools can automate this process for you:

❑   *The data: URI Kitchen* (`software.hixie.ch/utilities/cgi/data/data`). This is probably the best-known encoder on the Web (see Figure 10-6). It will convert source code, URL, or a local file to a data URL.

❑   *Url2iphone* (`www.somewhere.com/url2iphone.html`). This enables you to convert a URL into a bookmark. The most powerful aspect of this tool is that it will look for images, style sheets, and other files that are referenced are encode these as well.

❑   *data: URI image encoder* (`www.scalora.org/projects/uriencoder`). This tool is great for encoding images into base64 format. You can specify a URL or upload a local file.

❑   *Filemark Maker* (`www.insanelygreattees.com/news/?p=51`). This is a free Mac-based utility that is oriented toward storing Word, Excel, and PDF documents as data URLs. However, it can also be used for HTML pages.

❑   *Encoding bookmarklet.* Developer David Lindquist developed a handy bookmarklet that grabs the current page's source, generates a data: URL, and loads the URL. You can then drag the generated URL onto your Bookmarks bar. Here's the JavaScript code:

```
javascript:x=new
XMLHttpRequest();x.onreadystatechange=function(){if(x.readyState==4)location='data:
text/html;charset=utf-
8;base64,'+btoa(x.responseText)};x.open('GET',location);x.send('');
```

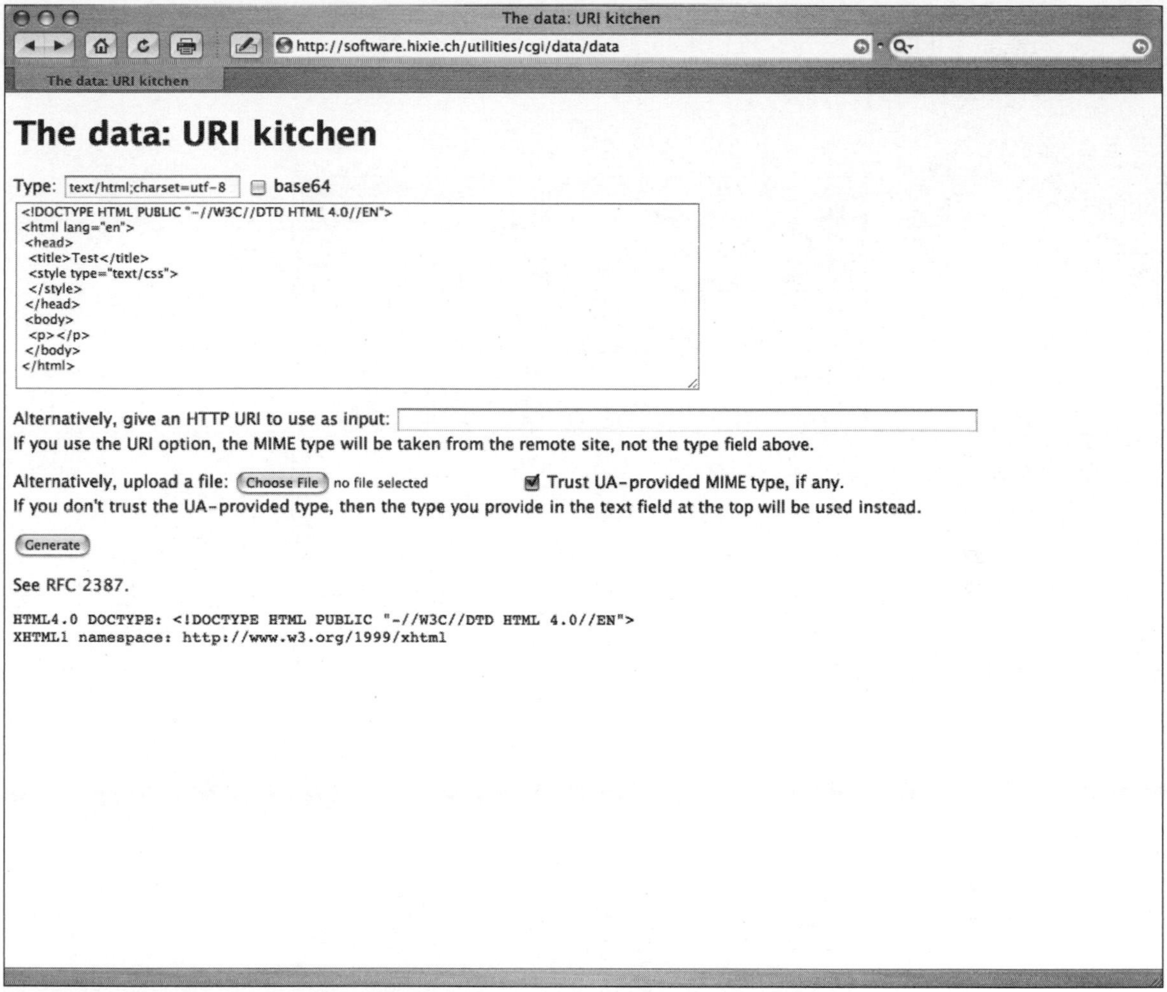

Figure 10-6: Encoding a Web application

❑   **Perl.** The following Perl syntax turns HTML into a data URL:

```
perl -0777 -e 'use MIME::Base64; $text = <>; $text = encode_base64($text); $text =~
s/\s+//g; print "data:text/html;charset=utf-8;base64,$text\n";'
```

❑   **PHP.** In PHP, you could create a function to do the same thing:

```
<?php
function data_url($file)
{
  $contents = file_get_contents($file);
  $base64   = base64_encode($contents);
  return ('data:text/html;charset=utf-8;base64,' . $base64);
}
?>
```

Once you have used one of these tools to create a data URL, make sure it is in the URL bar of Safari. Then, drag the URL onto your Bookmarks bar. Synch up with your iPhone and your application is now ready to run in offline mode. Figure 10-7 shows a fully functional Tipster.

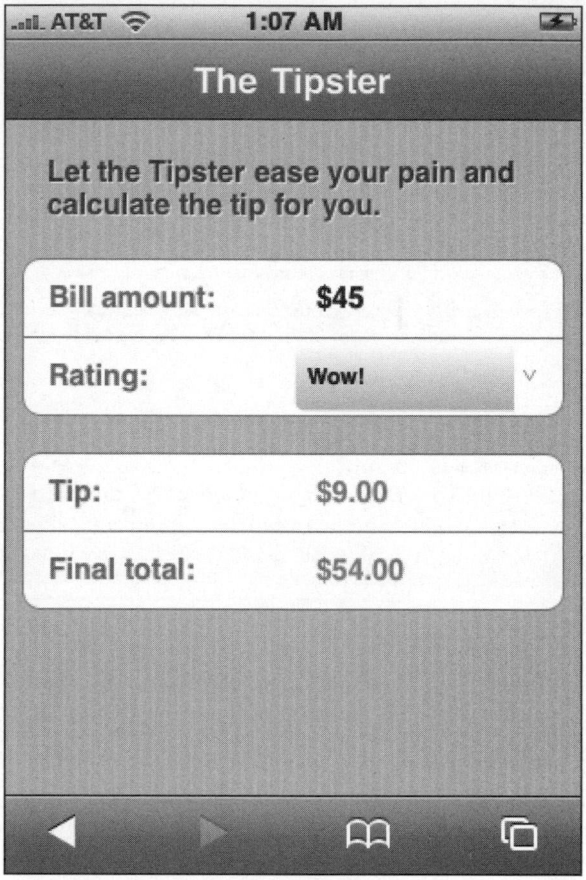

Figure 10-7: The Tipster application

11

Case Studies: Beyond Edge-to-Edge Design

Throughout this book, you've focused on building iPhone and iPod touch applications that generally adhere to the edge-to-edge navigation UI model. For example, Chapter 3 used the standard UI model for iRealtor, a home buyers application. Chapter 7 did the same for iProspector, a contact manager. However, not all applications that you wish to create lend themselves to standard navigation lists and destination pages. Just a quick scan of built-in applications on iPhone and iPod touch shows a variety of different UI design models.

This chapter walks you through two case study applications that offer new takes on extending the normal application models. The first application extends iRealtor to provide an iPhone-like photo viewer to display home photos. The second application, WYFFL Online, demonstrates more techniques on converting a standard Web site into an iPhone/iPod touch application. Both of these case studies show you how to extend the iUI application framework for your own custom needs.

Case Study: iRealtor 2.0

Chapter 3 showcased iRealtor as a mobile application for home buyers. Perhaps its greatest limitation was only providing a single picture of the house on its listings page. To overcome that limitation, you wanted to add a photo viewer inside of iRealtor. Though there are limitations because of the Mobile Safari environment, you want to emulate the basic look of the built-in Photo application (see Figure 11-1) with its black background and toolbar and Next and Previous buttons. However, you want to do this customization without leaving the basic iUI framework of the application.

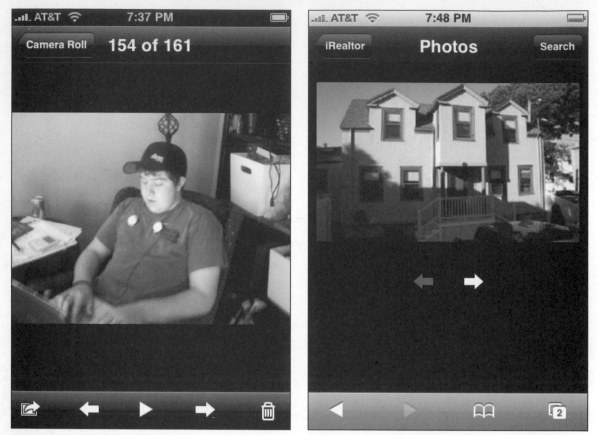

Figure 11 -1: Photos application   Figure 11-2: Emulating Photos inside of Mobile Safari

Figure 11-2 shows the final look of the page that the case study is building.

The first step is to create a new style sheet called photo.css and add a link to the style from the main Web page:

```
<style type="text/css" media="screen">@import "../iui/photo.css";</style>
```

Next, the following div element is added to the irealtor.html file to serve as the Photos page, assigning a class of photoPanel:

```
<div id="photos" class="photoPanel" title="Photos">
</div>
```

Customizing the Application Toolbar

Once those preliminary tasks are completed, you are ready to create the graphics and style rules necessary for displaying a black toolbar rather than the default blue one. The standard iUI toolbar uses the blue-colored backButton.png and toolButton.png for the background of the back and search buttons. Using Photoshop, you recreated those buttons in black and called them blackButton.png and blackToolButton.png. You also created a black background image for the entire toolbar called blackToolbar.png.

Rather than creating a second black toolbar, it is much easier to customize the look of the standard toolbar when the application enters a photo state (a photo attribute on the body element). Here's the new rule for the new toolbar class selector:

```
body[photo="true"]  > .toolbar {
    background: url(blackToolbar.png) #000000 repeat-x !important;
    border-bottom: 1px solid #000000 !important;
}
```

Next, the button class selector and backButton id selector are customized for the photo state:

```
body[photo="true"]  .button {
    -webkit-border-image: url(blackToolButton.png)  0 5 0 5;
}
body[photo="true"]  #backButton {
    -webkit-border-image: url(blackButton.png) 0 8 0 14;
}
```

In order for the application to change into photo state, it is necessary to customize the showPage function inside of iui.js:

```
showPage: function(page, backwards)
{
    if (page)
    {
        if (currentDialog)
        {
            currentDialog.removeAttribute("selected");
            currentDialog = null;
        }
        if (hasClass(page, "dialog"))
            showDialog(page);
        else
        {
            var fromPage = currentPage;
            currentPage = page;
            if (hasClass(page, "photoPanel"))
              document.body.setAttribute("photo", "true");
            else
              document.body.removeAttribute("photo");
            if (fromPage)
                setTimeout(slidePages, 0, fromPage, page, backwards);
            else
                updatePage(page, fromPage);
        }
    }
},
```

Using the support function `hasClass()`, the function checks to see whether the `page` element (a `div`) is assigned the `photoPanel` class. If so, then `photo` attribute is added to body. The `else` statement removes the photo attribute from body for all other pages.

No more changes are needed to enable iui.js for this new application state.

Creating and Styling the Photos Page

The next step is to create a rule for the `photoPanel` class in photo.css:

```css
body > .photoPanel {
    box-sizing: border-box;
    padding: 10px;
    background: #000000;
    width: 100%;
    min-height: 417px;
}
```

The Photos page contains an image element and buttons for moving between photos. Because a links are heavily controlled by iUI (`onclick` events and styles), `input elements` are used for the Next and Previous buttons to eliminate potential conflicts. Here's the HTML code:

```html
<div id="photos" class="photoPanel" title="Photos">
    <img id="photoImage"/>
    <div class="controlbar">
      <input class="previousControlButton" type="button" id="prevButton">
      <input class="nextControlButton" type="button" id="nextButton">
    </div>
</div>
```

The two `input` buttons are each assigned specific styles, which are housed in a `div` element assigned to a `controlbar` class.

Returning to photo.css, styles are added for each of these elements:

```css
.photoPanel img {
  display: block;
  margin: 10px auto 0px auto;
  width:300px;
}
.photoPanel .controlbar {
  display: block;
  margin-top:30px;
  width: 100%;
  height: 40px;
  text-align: center;
}
.previousControlButton {
  display: inline-block;
  height: 40px;
  width: 36px;
  margin: 0 20px;
```

```
    background: url(prev.png) no-repeat;
    border-style: none;
}
.nextControlButton {
    display: inline-block;
    margin: 0 auto;
    height: 40px;
    width: 36px;
    background:  url(next.png) no-repeat;
    border-style: none;
}
```

Each of the images has a physical width of 300px. The image rule is assigned a width of 300px and is centered in the viewport.

Because developers cannot hide the bottom toolbar in Mobile Safari, the positioning of the div controlbar is better suited to be displayed higher inside the application than in the built-in Photo app. The style rule sets the controlbar to display 30px below the image. The buttons are positioned inside of the controlbar.

Listing 11-1 displays the entire source of the photo.css style sheet.

Listing 11-1: photo.css

```
body[photo="true"]  > .toolbar {
    background: url(blackToolbar.png) #000000 repeat-x !important;
    border-bottom: 1px solid #000000 !important;
}
body[photo="true"]  .button {
    -webkit-border-image: url(blackToolButton.png)  0 5 0 5;
}
body[photo="true"]  #backButton {
    -webkit-border-image: url(blackButton.png) 0 8 0 14;
}
body > .photoPanel {
  box-sizing: border-box;
  padding: 10px;
  background: black;
  width: 100%;
  min-height: 417px;
}
.photoPanel img {
  display: block;
  margin: 10px auto 0px auto;
   width:300px;
}
.photoPanel .controlbar {
  display: block;
  margin-top:30px;
  width: 100%;
  height: 40px;
  text-align: center;
}
```

(continued)

Listing 11-1 *(continued)*

```
.previousControlButton {
  display: inline-block;
  height: 40px;
  width: 36px;
  margin: 0 20px;
  background: url(prev.png) no-repeat;
  border-style: none;
}
.nextControlButton {
  display: inline-block;
  margin: 0 auto;
  height: 40px;
  width: 36px;
  background:  url(next.png) no-repeat;
  border-style: none;
}
```

Programming the Photos Page

With the HTML and CSS code ready to go, the photo page needs to be scripted to display pictures. However, because bandwidth is a critical issue, you want to implement a scheme that preloads photos to minimize delay, but only does one image ahead of time to minimize bandwidth.

In the document head of irealtor.html, you begin by adding a link to the JavaScript library that you will be constructing:

```
<script type="application/x-javascript" src="../iui/photo.js"></script>
```

The next step is to create a photo.js file and enter the code shown in Listing 11-2. To save time, you can download the photo.js from this book's Web site.

Listing 11-2: photo.js

```
(function() {
  var photoEnabled = false;
  var current = -1;
  var nextPhoto;
  var photoFiles = new Array(
    'images/3202-001.jpg',
    'images/3202-002.jpg',
    'images/3202-003.jpg',
    'images/3202-004.jpg',
    'images/3202-005.jpg',
    'images/3202-006.jpg',
    'images/3202-007.jpg',
    'images/3202-008.jpg');
  function showPhoto(direction) {
    if (photoEnabled) {
        nextPhoto=current+direction;
        document.getElementById('prevButton').disabled = (nextPhoto == 0);
```

```
            document.getElementById('nextButton').disabled = (nextPhoto ==
(photoFiles.length-1));
            if ((nextPhoto>=0) && (nextPhoto<photoFiles.length)) {
              document.getElementById('photoImage').src = photoFiles[nextPhoto].src;
              current=nextPhoto++;
              if (direction==1) fetchNext();
            }
            return true;
          }
        }
    function pollStatus() {
      if (photoFiles[nextPhoto].complete)
          photoEnabled = true;
      else
          setTimeout(pollStatus, 200);
      return true;
    }
    function fetchNext() {
      if ((nextPhoto<photoFiles.length) && (typeof photoFiles[nextPhoto] == 'string'))
{
          photoEnabled = false;
          convertSrcToImage(nextPhoto);
          pollStatus();
        }
        return true;
    }
  function convertSrcToImage(idx) {
      var i = new Image();
      i.src = photoFiles[idx];
      photoFiles[idx] = i;
    }
    addEventListener("load", function(event) {
        convertSrcToImage(0);
        photoEnabled = true;
        showPhoto(1);
      }, false);
    addEventListener("click", function(event) {
        var input = findParent(event.target, "input");
        if (input) {
          if (input.id=='nextButton')
            showPhoto(1);
          else if (input.id=='prevButton')
            showPhoto(-1);
        }
      }, false);
    function findParent(node, localName) {
        while (node && (node.nodeType != 1 || node.localName.toLowerCase() !=
localName))
            node = node.parentNode;
        return node;
    }
})();
```

There are several aspects of this code to touch upon. To begin, notice that all of the code is contained within an anonymous function to keep the variables private to this .js file. Next, the photos for this example are contained within a JavaScript array. However, for real world use, you could modify this to be stored in an XML file and loaded using AJAX. Also, there are two event listeners — one for document load and the other to listen for click events by the input elements.

When the load event listener is triggered when the page opens, it calls the support function `convertSrcToImg()` that converts the first item in the `photoFiles` array from a string into an `Image` object. The `photoEnabled` variable is set to `true` and then `showPhoto()` is called initially to display the first photo.

The `showPhoto()` function is the controller of which photo is displayed inside of the Photos page. It disables the Previous button if there are no images that appear before it. It disables the Next button if the last image in the `photoFiles` array is already displayed. Once this has been completed, it attempts to load the image file for the next image in the array. If the Next button was clicked, then the `fetchNext()` support function is called to attempt to download the next image in the array.

The `fetchNext()` function evaluates whether the item in the `photoFiles` array is a `string` or not. If it is a `string`, then it attempts to download and cache the image by calling `convertSrcToImage()`. If not, then it knows that the image is already cached. The `pollStatus()` function is called, which monitors the download. Once the download is completed, then the `photoEnabled` variable is set to `true`.

The `click` event listener captures the click event of the input elements on the Photos page. If `nextButton` is the source, then `showPhoto(1)` is called. If `prevButton` is the source, then `showPhoto(-1)` is called. Note that the click event handler uses an `if-else-if` conditional so that the handler only calls `showPhoto()` when the `id` of the button is matched.

The Photos page of iRealtor is now enabled and ready for use.

Attaching the Photos Page to iRealtor

There are a variety of locations in which the Photos page feature could be integrated into the iRealtor application. However, perhaps the most natural is to simply add a link from the image displayed on an MLS listing page (likely a document fragment integrated using AJAX). Here's the MLS listing page with the new a link added:

```
<div title="20 May Lane" class="panel">
  <div>
    <a href="#photos"><img src="images/406509171.png"/></a>
  </div>
  <h2>Details</h2>
  <fieldset>
    <div class="row">
      <label>mls #</label>
      <p>406509171</p>
    </div>
    <div class="row">
      <label>address</label>
      <p>20 May Lane</p>
    </div>
```

```
        <div class="row">
          <label>city</label>
          <p>Acton</p>
        </div>
        <div class="row">
          <label>price</label>
          <p>$318,000</p>
        </div>
        <div class="row">
          <label>type</label>
          <p>Single Family</p>
        </div>
        <div class="row">
          <label>acres</label>
          <p>0.27</p>
        </div>
        <div class="row">
          <label>rooms</label>
          <p>6</p>
        </div>
        <div class="row">
          <label>bath (f)</label>
          <p>1</p>
        </div>
        <div class="row">
          <label>bath (h)</label>
          <p>0</p>
        </div>
    </fieldset>
    <fieldset>
        <div class="row">
            <a   class="serviceButton" target="_self"
href="http://maps.google.com/maps?q=20+May+Lane,+Acton,+MA">Map To House</a>
        </div>
        <div class="row">
            <a   class="serviceButton" target="_self"
href="http://www.mass.gov/?pageID=mg2localgovccpage&L=3&L0=Home&L1=State%20
Government&L2=Local%20Government&sid=massgov2&selectCity=Acton">View Town Info</a>
        </div>
    </fieldset>
</div>
```

Therefore, once this functionality is enabled, users can click an MLS house image to invoke the Photos page viewer. When they are finished, then they can tap the Back button to return to the main iRealtor application.

Case Study: Mobile WYFFL

A second case study demonstrates how you can turn a plain vanilla Web site with minimal functionality into a useful mobile Web application. For this example, you'll venture out of the corporate world to transform a community sports Web site, as shown in Figure 11-3. The use for this mobile app is that parents and coaches of the sports league will have fingertip access to the league schedule, game results, league news, and the rule book — either at the games or else en route to them.

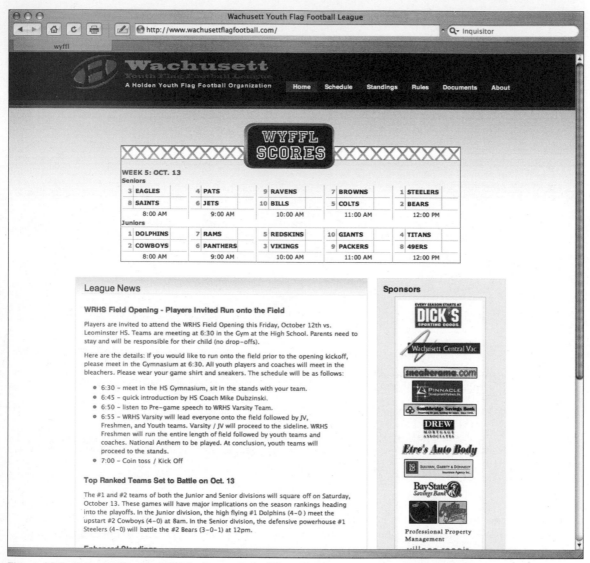

Figure 11-3: Community sports Web site ready for *iPhonification*

The screenshots displayed in this section were captured on Safari for Mac OS X, not on iPhone or iPod touch. The results are not fully identical to the optimized UI when viewed under Mobile Safari.

Given the traditional site structure of the site, an edge-to-edge navigation scheme is an ideal design model for the entry-level page. The iUI framework will be used in the implementation. However, as you'll see later on, Mobile WYFFL will employ some design ideas not included with iUI to give parts of the application a fresh look, but one that remains consistent with Apple's built-in applications.

Each of the links on the top-level menu will be translated to a menu item on the Mobile WYFFL application. However, note the scoreboard at the top of the homepage. It serves a double purpose. Before games, it provides a game schedule for the current week. Then, after the games are completed each Saturday, the scoreboard is then used to display the scoring results. To display this information in Mobile WYFFL, you'll add a menu item called Gameday.

Not all of the content on the main Web site makes sense to include in the mobile version of the application. For example, the Documents page containing downloadable forms is not useful in iPhone or iPod touch. Therefore, in these cases, you will simply refer them to the main Web site by adding a final link to it in the initial list. Here is the initial code for the primary HTML page of the application:

```
!DOCTYPE html PUBLIC "-//W3C//DTD XHTML 1.0 Strict//EN"
         "http://www.w3.org/TR/xhtml1/DTD/xhtml1-strict.dtd">
<html xmlns="http://www.w3.org/1999/xhtml">
<head>
<title>WYFFL Mobile</title>
<meta name="viewport" content="width=300; initial-scale=1.0; maximum-scale=1.0;
user-scalable=0;"/>
<style type="text/css" media="screen">@import "../iui/iui.css";</style>
<style type="text/css" media="screen">@import "../iui/iuiadd.css";</style>
<script type="application/x-javascript" src="../iui/iui.js"></script>
</head>
<body>
    <div class="toolbar">
        <h1 id="pageTitle"></h1>
        <a id="backButton" class="button" href="#"></a>
    </div>
    <ul id="home" title="WYFFL Mobile" selected="true">
        <li><a href="news.html">Latest News</a></li>
        <li><a href="gameday.html">Game Day</a></li>
        <li><a href="standings.html">Standings</a></li>
        <li><a href="#schedule">Schedule</a></li>
        <li><a href="#rules">Rules</a></li>
        <li><a href="about.html">About WYFFL</a></li>
        <li><a href="http://www.wachusettflagfootball.com" target="_self">Visit Web
Site</a></li>
    </ul>
</body>
</html>
```

Note the link to the iuiadd.css style sheet, which will be used to extend the default iUI style rules. Figure 11-4 displays the opening page of the application.

Figure 11-4: Mobile WYFFL (as shown in Safari for Mac)

There are three types of links represented in the navigation list: AJAX links (Latest News, Game Day, Standings, and About); Page links (Schedule and Rules); and External links (Visit Web Site). The Standings and Schedule pages on the regular Web site are lengthy. Therefore, for the mobile version, these pages are broken into small readable sections. These sections are displayed as second tier menus:

```
<ul id="schedule" title="Schedules">
    <li><a href="seniors.html">Seniors</a></li>
    <li><a href="juniors.html">Juniors</a></li>
    <li><a href="freshman.html">Freshman</a></li>
    <li><a href="instructional.html">Instructional</a></li>
</ul>
<ul id="rules" title="Rules">
    <li><a href="field.html">Fields and Players</a></li>
    <li><a href="game.html">Game</a></li>
    <li><a href="time.html">Time</a></li>
    <li><a href="penalties.html">Penalties</a></li>
    <li><a href="enforce.html">Enforcement of Penalties</a></li>
</ul>
```

Figures 11-5 and 11-6 show these two submenus.

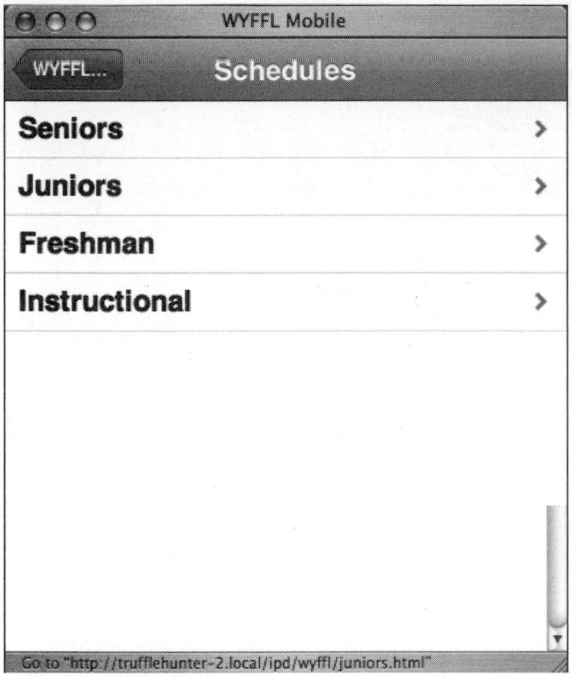

Figure 11-5: Schedule submenu (as shown In Safari for Mac)

Figure 11-6: Rules submenu (as shown in Safari for Mac)

Text-Based Destination Pages

The Latest News page is a destination page that is designed for readability of short, bite-sized articles. Here's the document fragment used for this purpose:

```
<div id="news" class="panel" title="News">
<fieldset>
<h3>Top Ranked Teams Set to Battle on Oct. 13</h3>
<p>The #1 and #2 teams of both the Junior and Senior divisions will square off on
Saturday, October 13. These games will have major implications on the season
rankings heading into the playoffs. In the Junior division, the high flying #1
Dolphins (4-0 ) meet the upstart #2 Cowboys (4 0) at 8am. In the Senior division,
the defensive powerhouse #1 Steelers (4-0) will battle the #2 Bears (3-0-1) at
12pm.</p>
<h3>No Games on Columbus Day Weekend</h3>
<p>Just a reminder that there will be no games this week due to the holiday
weekend. Have a great weekend.</p>
<h3>Open Practices for Junior and Senior Divisions</h3>
<p>Open Practices are on Wednesday evenings from 5:30-7:00pm for both Junior and
Senior Divisions, but not Freshman Division. The Open Practices will be held at the
Jefferson School Fields in Holden.</p>
<h3>Wachusettflagfootball.com - Your Best Source for Weather Info</h3>
```

(continued)

(continued)

```
<p>Be sure to come to this web site throughout the year in case it looks rainy
outside on a Saturday morning. Throughout the season, the league will post any rain
postponement or cancellation announcements here by 7:00am on gameday.</p>
<h3>Dick's Sporting Goods as Community Partner</h3>
<p>Wachusett Youth Flag Football would like to thank and recognize Dick's Sporting
Goods as a sponsor and community partner.</p>
</fieldset>
</div>
```

As is standard for iUI apps, a `div` with `class="panel"` is used to contain this type of destination page. A `fieldset` is used as a container for the rest of the content to take advantage of the iUI styles. Custom styles are set inside of iuiadd.css for the h3, p, and a styles:

```
.panel p, .panel a {
  text-align: left;
  padding: 0 10px 0 10px;
}
.panel h3 {
  margin: 3px 0 10px 10px;
  text-align: left;
  font-size: 1.2em;
}
```

Figure 11-7 shows the page displayed in Safari.

Figure 11-7: Latest News (as shown in Safari for Mac)

The text-based Rules page and About page employ the same div element structure and the same style rules.

Table-Based Destination Pages

Because of the tabular nature of the information they present, the Standings and Schedule pages are implemented as table-based destination pages. Here is a portion of the document fragment for the Standings page:

```
<div id="standings" class="panel" title="Standings">
<table border="1" cellpadding="0" cellspacing="0">
 <tr class="first" >
  <th >Seniors</td>
  <th >W</td>
  <th>L</td>
  <th>T</td>
  <th>PS</td>
  <th>PA</td>
 </tr>
<tr class="row-a" >
  <td>Steelers</td>
  <td >4</td>
  <td >0</td>
  <td >0</td>
  <td >74</td>
  <td >6</td>
 </tr>
<tr class="row-b" >
  <td>Bears</td>
  <td >3</td>
  <td >0</td>
  <td >1</td>
  <td >92</td>
  <td >36</td>
 </tr>
<tr class="row-a" >
  <td>Eagles</td>
  <td >3</td>
  <td >1</td>
  <td >0</td>
  <td >104</td>
  <td >54</td>
 </tr>
 <tr class="row-b" >
  <td>Pats</td>
  <td >2</td>
  <td >1</td>
  <td >1</td>
  <td >81</td>
  <td >61</td>
 </tr>
```

(continued)

(continued)

```
    <tr class="row-a" >
      <td>Colts</td>
      <td >2</td>
      <td >1</td>
      <td >1</td>
      <td >51</td>
      <td >36</td>
    </tr>
    <tr class="row-a" >
      <td>Jets</td>
      <td >2</td>
      <td >2</td>
      <td >0</td>
      <td >74</td>
      <td >100</td>
    </tr>
    <tr class="row-b" >
      <td>Browns</td>
      <td >1</td>
      <td >3</td>
      <td >0</td>
      <td >53</td>
      <td >93</td>
    </tr>
    <tr class="row-a" >
      <td>Saints</td>
      <td >1</td>
      <td >3</td>
      <td >0</td>
      <td >62</td>
      <td >81</td>
    </tr>
    <tr class="row-b" >
      <td>Ravens</td>
      <td >0</td>
      <td >3</td>
      <td >1</td>
      <td >43</td>
      <td >97</td>
    </tr>
    <tr class="row-a" >
      <td>Bills</td>
      <td >0</td>
      <td >4</td>
      <td >0</td>
      <td >38</td>
      <td >108</td>
    </tr>
  </table>
  </div>
```

Style rules need to be added to iuiadd.css in order to effectively display this information inside of a Mobile Safari viewport:

```
table {
  width: 100%;
  font-size: 14px;
  border-collapse: collapse;
  color: #305A6D;
  text-align: left;
}
th {
  height: 29px;
  padding-left: 11px;
  padding-right: 11px;
  color: #FFFFFF;
  text-align: left;
  margin: 0 0 8px 14px;
  font-size: inherit;
  font-weight: bold;
  color: #4d4d70;
  text-shadow: rgba(255, 255, 255, 0.75) 2px 2px 0;
  padding-left: 2px;
}
td {
  height: 2em;
  padding: 1px;
  padding-left: 2px;
}
tr.row-a {
  background: #F8F8F8;
}
tr.row-b {
  background: #EFEFEF;
}
```

The table is set to 100 percent of the div container. The remaining rules set basic formatting properties for the th, td, and tr elements. You will notice that the font size is smaller (14px) than is normal for Mobile Safari applications. The reason is twofold. First, no links are added to these tables, so users will never need to tap onto the smaller text. Second, the 14px size is large enough for easy reading, but small enough to display several columns of tabular information. Figure 11-8 shows the Standings page under Safari.

The four Schedule pages use the identical styles, except that the HTML table declaration specifies a border="0" attribute to display a slightly different look (see Figure 11-9).

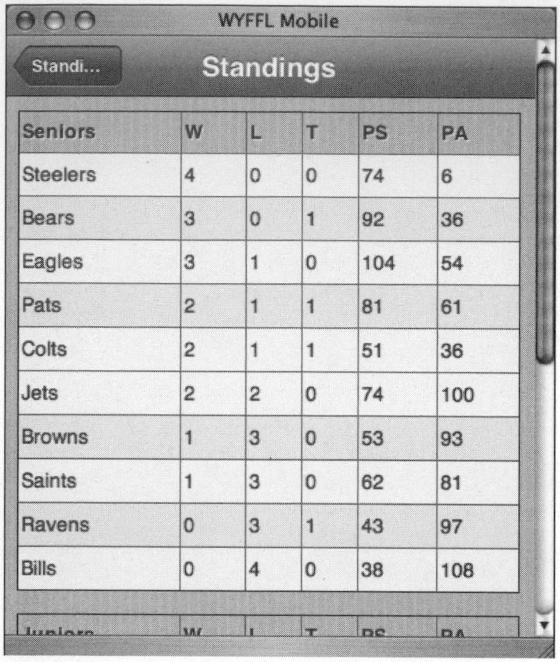

Figure 11-8: Standings page (as shown in Safari for Mac)

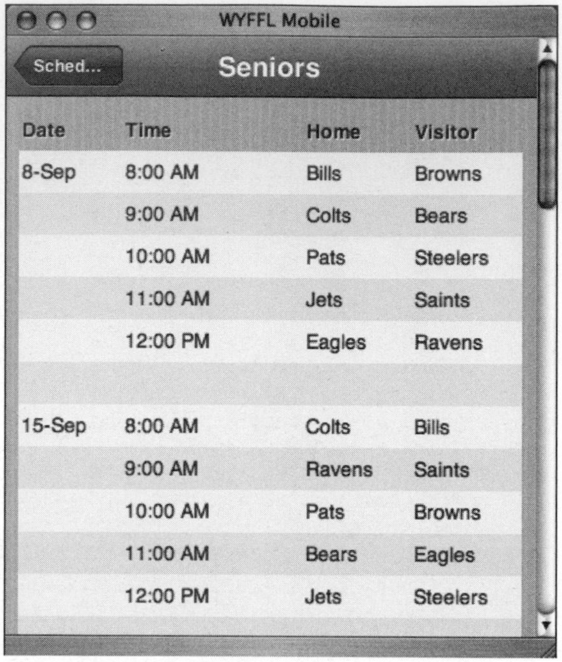

Figure 11-9: Schedule page without a border (as shown in Safari for Mac)

Game Day Navigation List Page

While the Game Day content could be displayed in a table structure much like the Schedule pages, a much more attractive solution would be to consider an alternative UI design for this destination page. The three pieces of information that need to be displayed for a given game are the game time, teams, and their scores. In considering alternatives, I looked around at the native Apple applications and was intrigued with the idea of using the World Clock app as an inspiration with its large clocks displayed in a list. Figure 11-10 shows the end result of what you are going to build under Safari for Mac.

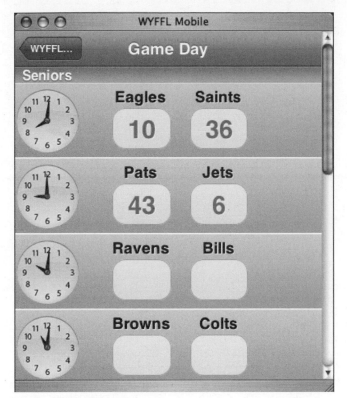

Figure 11-10: Game Day page (as shown in Safari for Mac)

The HTML document fragment used to display this page is as follows:

```html
<ul id="gameday" title="Game Day">
 <li class="group">Seniors</li>
 <li class="grayrow">
   <a class-"clock clock8"></a>
   <p class="team team-visitor">Eagles</p>
    <p class="team team-home">Saints</p>
   <p class="score score-visitor">10</p>
   <p class="score score-home">36</p>
 </li>
 <li class="grayrow">
    <a class="clock clock9"></a>
     <p class="team team-visitor">Pats</p>
    <p class="team team-home">Jets</p>
   <p class="score score-visitor">43</p>
   <p class="score score-home">6</p>
 </li>
 <li class="grayrow">
   <a class="clock clock10"></a>
      <p class="team team-visitor">Ravens</p>
```

(continued)

(continued)

```
        <p class="team team-home">Bills</p>
      <p class="score score-visitor"></p>
      <p class="score score-home"></p>
    </li>
    <li class="grayrow">
      <a class="clock clock11"></a>
      <p class="team team-visitor">Browns</p>
       <p class="team team-home">Colts</p>
      <p class="score score-visitor"></p>
      <p class="score score-home"></p>
    </li>
    <li class="grayrow">
      <a class="clock clock12"></a>
      <p class="team team-visitor">Steelers</p>
       <p class="team team-home">Browns</p>
      <p class="score score-visitor"></p>
      <p class="score score-home"></p>
    </li>
  <li class="group">Juniors</li>
  <li class="grayrow">
      <a class="clock clock8"></a>
      <p class="team team-visitor">Dolphins</p>
       <p class="team team-home">Cowboys</p>
      <p class="score score-visitor">20</p>
      <p class="score score-home">32</p>
    </li>
    <li class="grayrow">
        <a class="clock clock9"></a>
          <p class="team team-visitor">Rams</p>
       <p class="team team-home">Panthers</p>
      <p class="score score-visitor"></p>
      <p class="score score-home"></p>
    </li>
    <li class="grayrow">
      <a class="clock clock10"></a>
          <p class="team team-visitor">Redskins</p>
       <p class="team team-home">Vikings</p>
      <p class="score score-visitor"></p>
      <p class="score score-home"></p>
    </li>
    <li class="grayrow">
      <a class="clock clock11"></a>
      <p class="team team-visitor">Giants</p>
       <p class="team team-home">Packers</p>
      <p class="score score-visitor"></p>
      <p class="score score-home"></p>
    </li>
    <li class="grayrow">
      <a class="clock clock12"></a>
      <p class="team team-visitor">Titans</p>
```

```
        <p class="team team-home">49ers</p>
        <p class="score score-visitor"></p>
        <p class="score score-home"></p>
    </li>
</ul>
```

Instead of a div element, a ul element is used given the list-based nature of the content. You assign the id="gameday". The Senior and Junior league games are divided by the group list item (<liclass="group">), which is a style that is a standard part of the iui.css style sheet. The remaining list items are assigned the grayrow class. The grayrow class provides the sizing and formatting needed for this 90px high item:

```
body > ul > li.grayrow {
    position: relative;
    top: -1px;
    margin-bottom: -2px;
    border-top: 1px solid #eeeeef;
    border-bottom: 1px solid #9c9ea5;
    padding: 1px 10px;
    background: url(grayrow.png) repeat-x;
    font-size: 17px;
    font-weight: bold;
    text-shadow: rgba(255, 255, 255, 0.75) 2px 2px 0;
    color: #000000;
    line-height: 90px;
    height:  90px;
}
body > ul > li.grayRow:first-child {
    top: 0;
    border-top: none;
}
```

Each list item contains an a link to display the clock and p elements to display the teams and scores. Several styles are used for positioning and formatting these elements. The following style rules are used for displaying the clock image at the left side of the item:

```
li .clock {
  display: block;
  position: absolute;
  margin: 0;
  left: 3px;
  top: 0px;
  width: 76px;
  height: 90px;
}
.clock8 {
    background: url(clock8.png) no-repeat;
}
.clock9 {
    background: url(clock9.png) no-repeat;
}
```

(continued)

(continued)

```css
.clock10 {
    background: url(clock10.png) no-repeat;
}
.clock11 {
    background: url(clock11.png) no-repeat;
}
.clock12 {
    background: url(clock12.png) no-repeat;
}
```

The base `clock` class formats and positions the element, while the remaining styles customize the background image. Each item then calls the base class plus one of the others. For example:

```html
<a class="clock clock9"></a>
```

While images are being used to display the clock, you could also use the `canvas` object to render the clocks. Canvas drawing would not only allow greater flexibility for displaying times, but also cut down on bandwidth needed to render the page.

Next, the rules for the team name text are shown in the following code:

```css
li .team {
  display: block;
  position: absolute;
  top: 1px;
  margin-top: 5px;
  line-height: 20px;
  font-size: 19px;
  width:  70px;
  text-overflow: clip;
  text-align: center;
}
.team-visitor {
  left: 120px;
}
.team-home {
  left: 215px;
}
```

The `team` class sets most of the properties, while the `team-visitor` and `team-home` styles are used to horizontally position the two paragraphs.

Finally, the `score`, `score-visitor`, and `score-home` classes follow the same pattern for the score boxes:

```css
li .score {
    display: block;
    top: 28px;
    position: absolute;
    margin: 0;
    margin-top: 2px;
```

```
        text-align: center;
        font-size: 1.8em;
        color: #6d84a2;
        font-weight: bold;
        text-decoration: none;
        width: 70px;
        height: 48px;
        line-height: 50px;
        background-color:rgba( 255, 255, 255, 0.7 );
        -webkit-border-radius: 16px;
        border: 1px solid #b4b4b4;
}
.score-visitor {
        left: 120px;
}
.score-home {
        left: 215px;
}
```

Testing and Debugging

Get in, get out. That's the attitude that most developers have in testing and debugging their applications. Few developers look forward to these tasks during the development cycle, and so they want to efficiently get into the code, figure out what's working and what's not, fix any problems, and then move on.

Given the heterogeneous nature of Web applications, debugging has always been challenging, particularly when trying to work with client-side JavaScript. To address this need, fairly sophisticated debugging tools have emerged over the past few years among the developer community, most notably Firebug and other add-ons to Firefox. However, the problem is that most of these testing tools that Web developers have come to rely on for desktop browsers are not yet compatible with the iPhone and iPod touch platform.

Many iPhone developers, unsure of where else to turn, end up resorting to `alert()` debugging — you know, adding `alert()` throughout the body of the script code to determine programmatic flow and variable values. However, not only is this type of debugging painful, but it can also throw off the timing of your script, making it difficult or impossible to simulate real world results. While the number of debugging and testing tools are indeed limited right now for Mobile Safari, you still have options that either work directly inside Mobile Safari or emulate Mobile Safari on your desktop. You will probably want to incorporate aspects of both as part of your regular debugging and testing process.

iPhone and iPod touch Debug Console

The 1.1.1 update of iPhone and the initial release of iPod touch introduced a Debug Console inside of Mobile Safari. If active, the Debug Console displays below the URL bar when a scripting error occurs. You can click the right arrow to display a list of console messages. The errors can be filtered by JavaScript, HTML, or CSS. You can enable the Debug Console from Settings ➪ Safari ➪ Developer and turn toggling on the Debug Console option.

Working with Desktop Safari Debugging Tools

Firefox has often been considered the browser of choice for Web application developers because of its support for third-party tools and add-ons, such as Firebug. However, when creating an application specifically for iPhone or iPod touch, you will usually want to work with Safari-specific tools. Fortunately, because Mobile Safari is so closely related to the newer desktop versions of Safari, you can take advantage of the debugging tools that are provided with Safari for Windows and Mac. Because you are working with a close relative to Mobile Safari, you will still need to perform a second round of testing and debugging on an iPhone and iPod touch, but these tools will help you during initial Safari testing.

Enabling the Debug Menu

The Safari debug tools are accessible through a Debug menu, which is hidden by default when you install Safari. If you are running on a Mac, you can type the following command in a terminal window (when Safari is closed):

```
% defaults write com.apple.Safari IncludeDebugMenu 1
```

Or, if you are working with Safari for Windows, you will want to edit the Preferences.plist file when Safari is closed. This .plist file is found in the following locations. For Windows Vista:

```
C:\Users\[Your Name]\AppData\Roaming\Apple Computer\Safari
```

For Windows XP:

```
C:\Documents and Settings\[Your Username]\Application Data\Apple Computer\Safari
```

The file itself is an XML document, so use Notepad or another text editor to open it. When you open it, modify the following key element at the end of the document, just before the final </dict> and </plist> closing tags:

```
<key>IncludeDebugMenu</key>
<true/>
```

Alternatively, in Safari for Windows, you can also enable or disable the Debug menu through command-line arguments: /enableDebugMenu displays the menu and /disableDebugMenu hides it. (These arguments are case sensitive.) Once you define this switch, Safari will remember the setting until you change it back.

Open the browser and the new menu appears, as shown in Figure 12-1. Many of these menu items are not relevant to Mobile Safari development, but a few are worth mentioning (see Table 12-1).

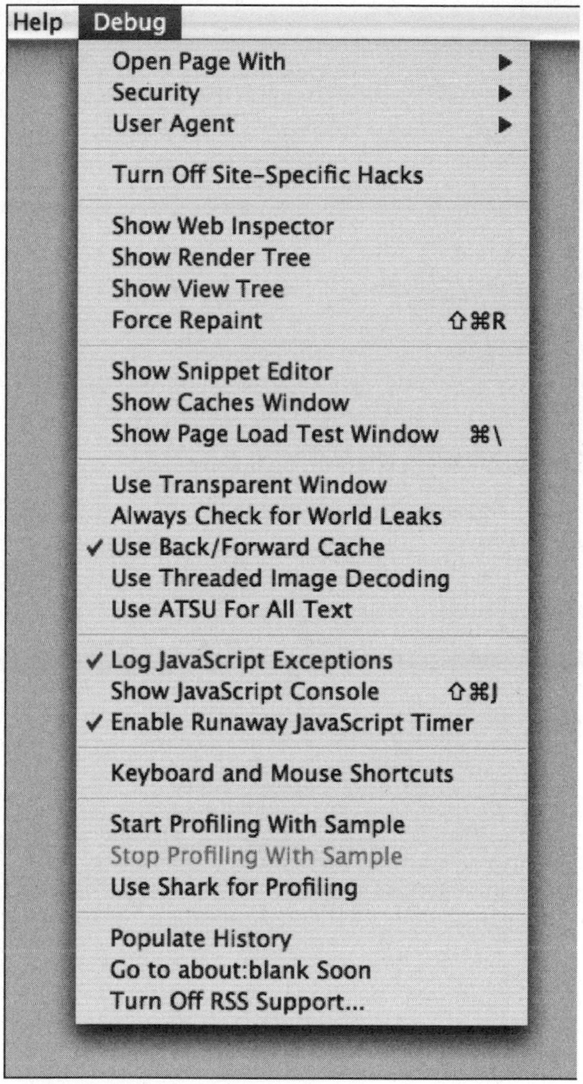

Help	Debug	
	Open Page With	▶
	Security	▶
	User Agent	▶
	Turn Off Site-Specific Hacks	
	Show Web Inspector	
	Show Render Tree	
	Show View Tree	
	Force Repaint	⇧⌘R
	Show Snippet Editor	
	Show Caches Window	
	Show Page Load Test Window	⌘\
	Use Transparent Window	
	Always Check for World Leaks	
✓	Use Back/Forward Cache	
	Use Threaded Image Decoding	
	Use ATSU For All Text	
✓	Log JavaScript Exceptions	
	Show JavaScript Console	⇧⌘J
✓	Enable Runaway JavaScript Timer	
	Keyboard and Mouse Shortcuts	
	Start Profiling With Sample	
	Stop Profiling With Sample	
	Use Shark for Profiling	
	Populate History	
	Go to about:blank Soon	
	Turn Off RSS Support...	

Figure 12-1: Safari's Debug menu

Table 12-1: Useful Safari Debug Commands for the iPhone Developer

Name	Description
User Agent	Spoof another browser (though current version does not include a Mobile Safari user agent string).
Show Web Inspector	View and search the DOM (currently Mac OS X only).
Show Snippet Editor	Get instant rendering of an HTML snippet.
Log JavaScript Exceptions	Turn on to log exceptions.
Show JavaScript Console	View JavaScript errors occurring on a page.
Enable Runaway JavaScript Timer	Toggle the timer that halts long-running scripts.

The two Safari debug features worth special attention are the Web Inspector and JavaScript Console.

Working with the Safari Web Inspector

The best debugging feature available in Safari is certainly the Web Inspector. The Web Inspector, shown in Figure 12-2, enables you to browse and inspect the DOM of the current Web page. You can access this feature through the Debug menu. However, the handiest way to use it is to right-click an element in your document and choose the Inspect Element menu item. The Web Inspector is displayed, showing the element in the context that you selected in the browser window.

> *At the time of this writing, the Web Inspector is only available on Mac OS X. However, expectations are that a cross-platform version of this developer tool will be available in the future.*

Here are the basic functions of the Web Inspector:

❑ *Selecting a node to view:* When you click on a node in the inspector pane, two things happen. First, the bottom pane displays node and attribute details, style hierarchy, style metrics, and property values. Second, if the selected node is a visible element in the browser window, the selected block is highlighted with a red border in Safari.

❑ *Changing the root:* To avoid messing with a massive nested DOM hierarchy, you can change the context of the Web Inspector. Double-clicking a node makes it the hierarchical "root" in the inspector pane. Later, if you want to move back up the document hierarchy, use the up arrow or the drop-down combo box above.

❑ *Searching the DOM:* You can use the Search box to look for any node of the DOM — element names, node attributes, even content. Results of the search are shown in the inspector pane, displaying the line on which a match was found. If you want to get a better idea at the exact node you are working with, select it and then look for the red outlined box in the Safari window.

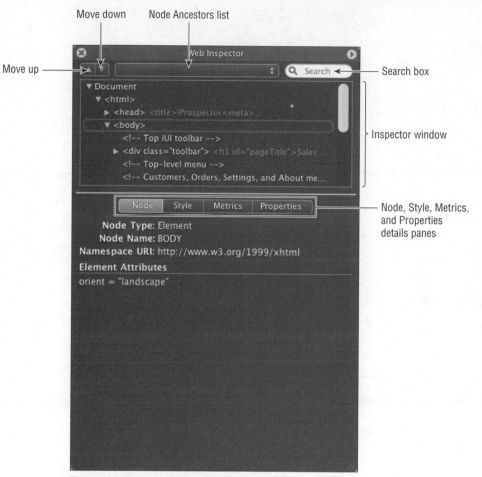

Figure 12-2: Web Inspector in Safari

❑   *Viewing node details:* The Node pane provides basic node information, including type, name, namespace, and attribute details.

❑   *Viewing CSS properties:* The Style pane displays CSS rules that are applied to the selected node (see Figure 12-3). It shows the computed style of the selected element by showing you all of the declarations that are used in determining the final style rendering. The rules are lists in cascade order. Any properties that have been overridden are displayed with strikethrough text.

Figure 12-3: Style rules for the selected node

❑   *Viewing style metrics:* The Metrics pane displays the current element as a rectangular block displaying the width x height dimensions, as well as the padding and margin settings (see Figure 12-4).

❑   *Viewing all properties:* The Properties pane displays all of the DOM properties (such as `id` and `innerHTML`) for the selected node. Because you cannot drill down on object types, this pane is less useful than the others.

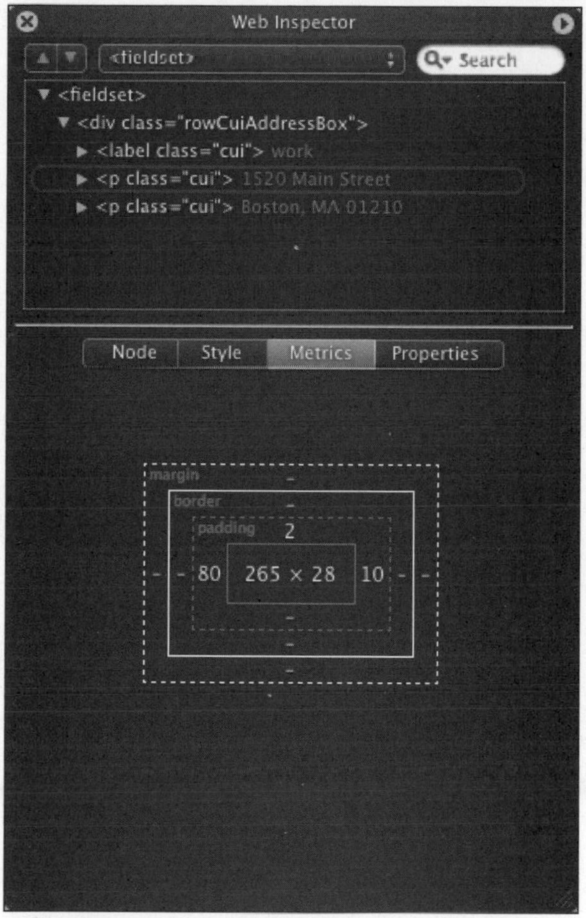

Figure 12-4: An element's metrics are easily seen in the Metrics pane.

Working with the JavaScript Console

Safari also sports a JavaScript Console, as shown in Figure 12-5; you can use it to display exceptions as you test your iPhone application on your desktop. However, the actual usefulness of the console is fairly modest. It does allow you to find the basic details of an error (type, file, line number), but other than that, you are on your own. But if you plan on doing anything more than looking for the occasional syntax error, I recommend using Drosera, which is discussed in the next section.

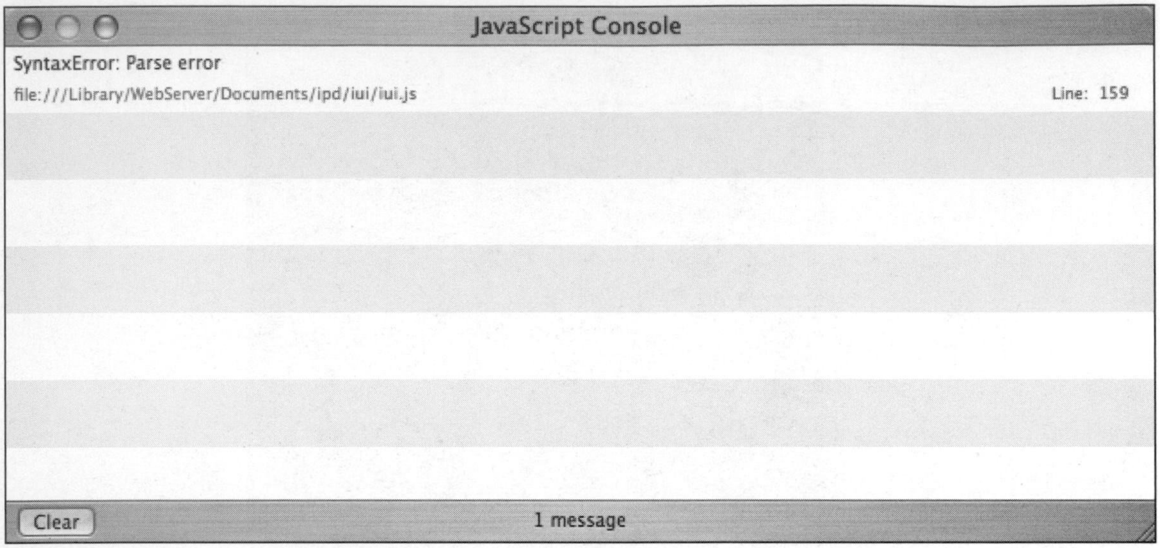

Figure 12-5: Safari's JavaScript Console

Industrial Strength Debugging with Drosera

If you recall from Chapter 1, Safari is built on top of the open source WebKit browser engine. Drosera is a high-powered JavaScript debugger that is included with the WebKit nightly builds, but is not part of Safari itself. However, if you are running Mac OS X, you can download the latest nightly build of WebKit at www.webkit.org and take advantage of using Drosera. At the time of this writing, Drosera is not available on Microsoft Windows platforms. Refer to www.webkit.org for the latest compatibility information.

As you would expect from a full-fledged debugger, Drosera enables you to set breakpoints, step into/out/over functions, and view variable state at a point of execution.

Preparing Drosera for Safari

After downloading the latest nightly WebKit build and installing it to your Applications folder, you first need to prepare your environment. Drosera works by attaching itself to a running WebKit browser. However, by default, it does not recognize Safari. Therefore, follow these instructions to enable it:

1. Be sure Safari, WebKit, and Drosera are all closed.

2. Enter the following into a terminal window:

```
defaults write com.apple.Safari WebKitScriptDebuggerEnabled -bool true
```

3. Launch Safari and navigate to your application URL.

4. Launch Drosera.

5. In the Attach dialog box, select Safari from the list and click Attach.

The Drosera debugger is shown in Figure 12-6.

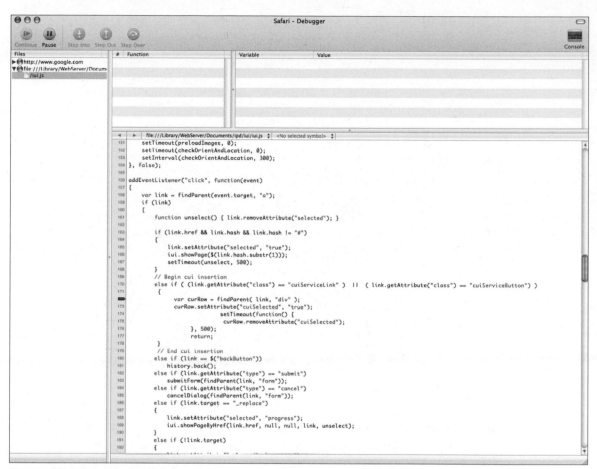

Figure 12-6: Drosera debugger

Working with Drosera

When you open your application URL, the source files will be automatically loaded into the Drosera window. You can then view the JavaScript source code in the code window.

❑   *Setting breakpoints and stepping through code:* You can set a breakpoint in your code by clicking the line number on the left margin of the code window. As Figure 12-7 shows, an arrow is displayed on the breakpoint line. When the line code is executed, then the breakpoint is triggered. You can then step through the script as desired by clicking the Step into, Step Out, and Step Over buttons. As you step through the code, Drosera will update its state for each line executed.

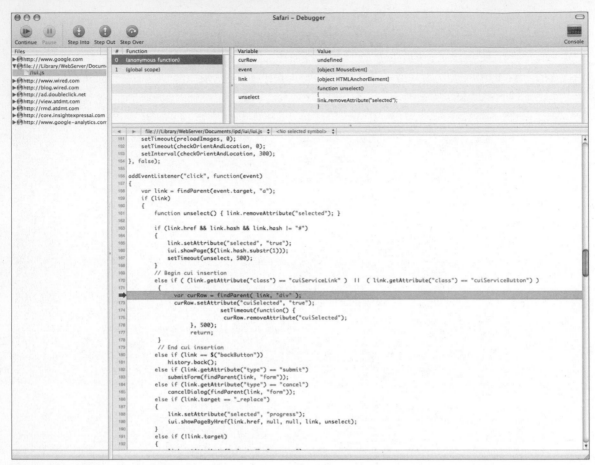

Figure 12-7: Setting a breakpoint

❑ *Inspecting variables:* The variable box at the top of the Drosera window displays the variables in scope. You can inspect these variables by right-clicking them and choosing Inspect Element. The WebKit version of the Web Inspector is displayed on top of the Drosera window, as shown in Figure 12-8. The features of the Web Inspector are equivalent to the Safari Web Inspector discussed earlier in viewing a node in its hierarchy along with style, metric, and property details. Close the Web Inspector to return to the debugging session.

While Drosera does not work directly with Mobile Safari, it does serve as the most powerful debugging option that the iPhone and iPod touch application developers have in their toolkit.

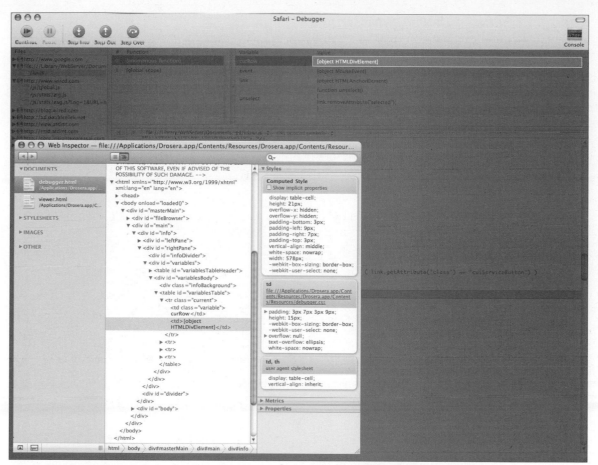

Figure 12-8: Inspecting the current state of an element in a debugging session

Simulating Mobile Safari on Your Desktop

In addition to using the debugging tools available for Safari for Mac and Safari for Windows, you can also simulate running Mobile Safari on your desktop. This will enable you to look at the UI as it will look in Mobile Safari as well as test to see how a Web application or site responds when it identifies the browser as Mobile Safari. You can either customize the desktop version of Safari or you can use a free tool named iPhoney.

Using Safari for Mac or Windows

Because Mobile Safari is closely related to its Mac and Windows desktop counterparts, you can perform initial testing and debugging right on your desktop. However, before doing so, you will want to turn Safari into an iPhone simulator by performing two actions — change the user agent string and resize the browser window.

Changing Safari's User Agent String

Safari allows you to set the user agent provided by the browser through the Debug ⇨ User Agent list. At the time of this writing, Safari 3.0 does not display Mobile Safari on its preset user agent list. However, you can specify a `CustomUserAgent` in Safari's preferences file to provide this custom string.

To do so on a Mac, navigate to the `com.apple.Safari.plist` in your `/Users/[Username]/Library/Preferences` folder. Double-click it to open the Properties List editor.

Next, add a new `CustomUserAgent` property in these files and give it the following value:

```
Mozilla/5.0 (iPhone; U; CPU like Mac OS X; en) AppleWebKit/420+ (KHTML, like Gecko)
Version/3.0 Mobile/1A538b Safari/419.3
```

Alternatively, if you are using a Mac, you can type the following in the terminal window when Safari is closed:

```
defaults write com.apple.Safari 'CustomUserAgent' '"Mozilla/5.0 (iPhone; U; CPU
like Mac OS X; en) AppleWebKit/420+ (KHTML, like Gecko) Version/3.0 Mobile/1A538b
Safari/419.3"'
```

You can then keep this as your default user agent setting until you change it back to normal through the Debug ⇨ User Agent menu.

To delete the custom user agent on a Mac system, you can enter the following as a command line:

```
defaults delete com.apple.Safari 'CustomUserAgent'
```

Changing the Window Size

To get the same viewport dimensions in Safari, you will want to create a bookmarklet (see Chapter 10), and then add it to your Bookmarks bar. The code for the bookmarklet is as follows:

```
javascript:window.resizeTo(320,480)
```

Using iPhoney

Rather than messing around with the settings of your desktop browser, however, you can use iPhoney, a free open source iPhone web simulator created by Marketcircle (www.marketcircle.com/iphoney). iPhoney (see Figure 12-9) is a great tool to use when you are initially designing an iPhone or iPod touch UI as well as when you are performing early testing. One of the handy features of iPhoney is that you can easily change orientations between portrait and landscape (see Figure 12-10). iPhoney also allows you to spoof with the iPhone user agent, hide the URL bar, and turn off Flash and other add-ins.

Figure 12-9: iPhoney simulates the iPhone on your Mac desktop.

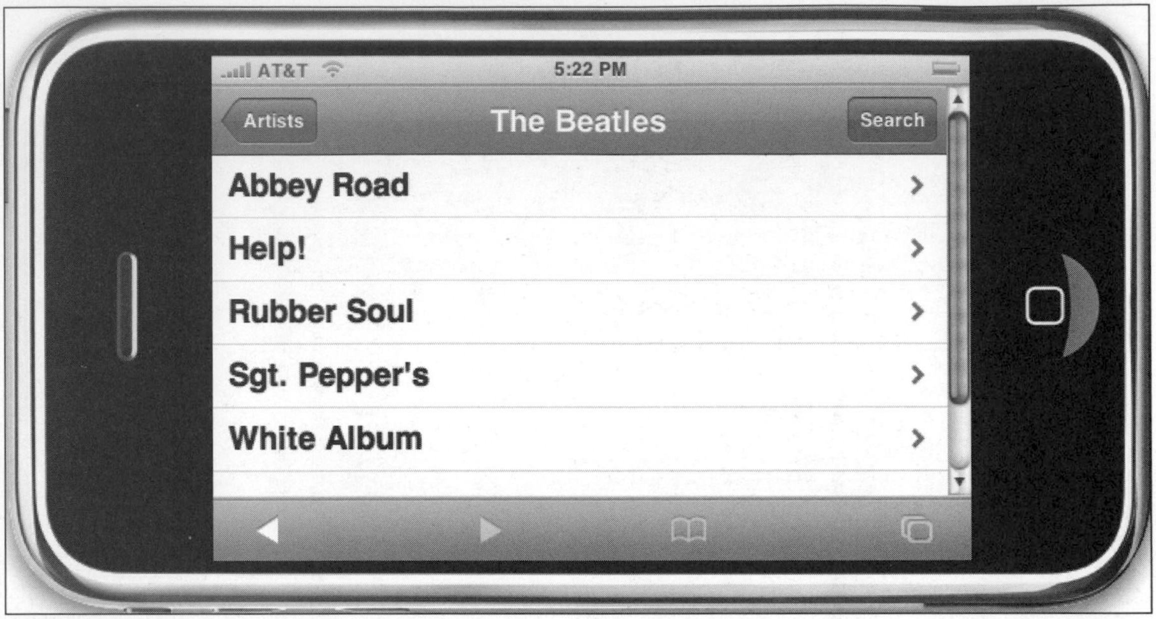

Figure 12-10: Rotating iPhoney to landscape mode

Debugging Inside Mobile Safari

So far, you've seen how to test and debug your iPhone and iPod touch applications on your desktop using desktop-based solutions. While those tools are good for general testing or specific problem solving, you will want to spend a good part of your time debugging directly on the iPhone or iPod touch devices themselves. Unfortunately, no robust debugging tools such as Drosera are available, but there are several community-based debugging tools that should be a standard part of your Mobile Safari development toolkit.

Firebug for iPhone

Joe Hewitt — developer of the popular Firefox debugger, Firebug — has developed a debugger for iPhone and iPod touch called Firebug for iPhone. This debugger is a Python-based Web server running on your desktop computer. It connects Mobile Safari on your iPhone to a Firebug console running on your desktop. When code is executed inside of the Mobile Safari browser, Firebug for iPhone logs the details directly to the Firebug console.

> *At the time of this writing, the Firebug console was not functional inside Safari 3.0 for Mac beta. Therefore, if you experience problems, be sure to run it inside of Firefox on your desktop machine.*

Before beginning, you will need to download the free, open source file at www.joehewitt.com/blog/firebug_for_iph.php. You will also need to make sure you have Python installed on your computer. Mac systems already have it. If you are running Windows, you can download it at www.python.org/download.

Launching Firebug for iPhone

Once you have downloaded the zip file and unzipped it into a folder on your computer, open a terminal window in Mac or a command window in Windows. Change to the directory into which you placed the files. Then, enter the following command line:

```
python ibug.py launch
```

Your browser will load with the Firebug for iPhone page displayed. (If the console is opened in Safari, simply copy and paste the URL in Firefox and then continue.) See Figure 12-11.

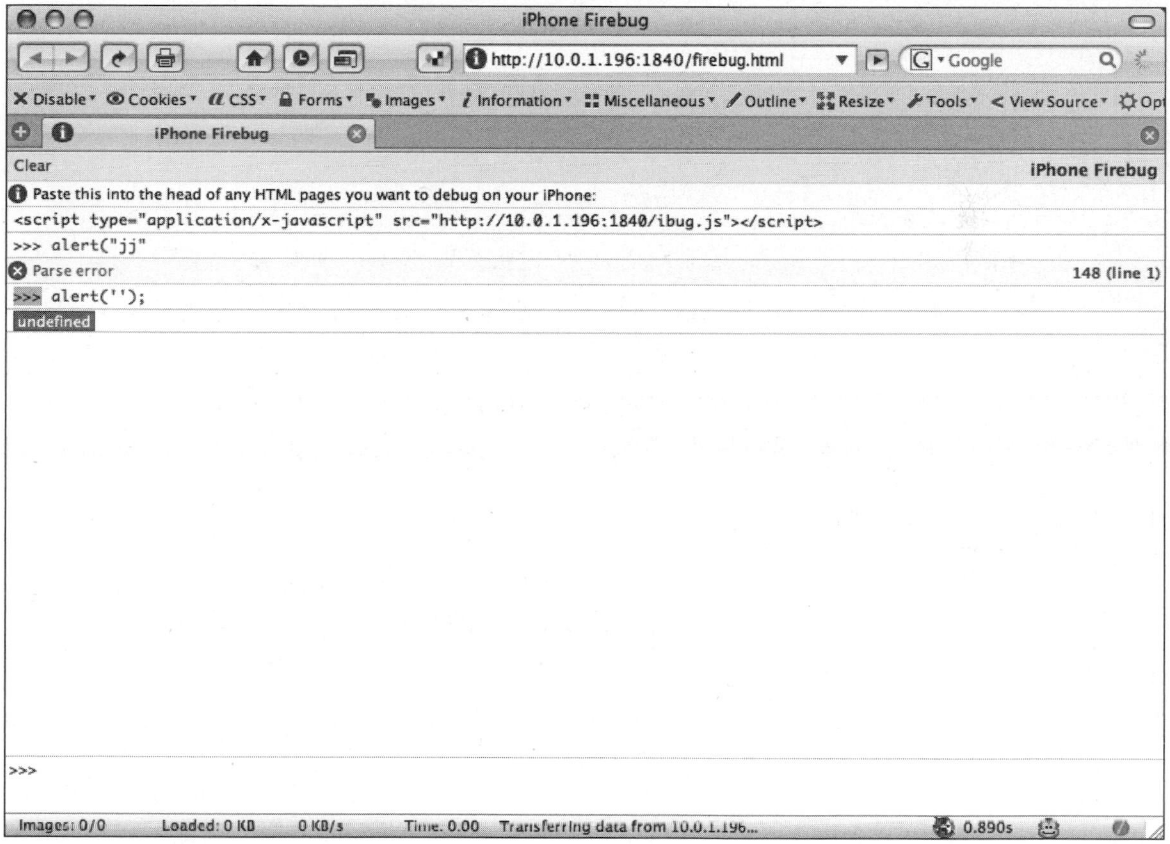

Figure 12-11: Firebug for iPhone

Adding a Script Tag to Your Page

The Firebug console provides a script tag that you need to copy and paste into the head of each page of your iPhone application. The tag will look something like this:

```
<script type="application/x-javascript"
src="http://10.0.1.196:1840/ibug.js"></script>
```

Note that if you are running a firewall, you may need to open the port (specified after the colon in the script tag) that Firebug uses. In the previous example, Firebug is using the 1840 port.

Debugging with Firebug for iPhone

Once you have the Firebug console running, you are ready to begin testing. To test, simply interact with your application on your iPhone or iPod touch. Firebug will log any exceptions or errors on your desktop.

Firebug for iPhone also provides a command line in which you can enter JavaScript code and have it execute on the iPhone. As a simple example, enter `alert("Hello world")` into the command line and the alert box is displayed on the iPhone.

Terminating the Debug Session

When you are done, close the running instance of Python by pressing Ctrl+C in the Terminal window.

DOM Viewer

The DOM Viewer, available from Brainjar.com, is a Web-based DOM viewer that you can work with directly inside of Mobile Safari. The DOM Viewer provides an expandable tree structure that lists all of the properties of a given node. When a property of a node is another node, then you can view its properties by clicking its name. The tree expands to show these details. The DOM Viewer is housed in a separate HTML page that is launched in a separate window from the original page.

While DOM Viewer does not have the robust capabilities of the desktop Safari's Web Inspector, it does have the assurance that all of the information you are looking at comes directly from Mobile Safari itself, not its desktop cousins.

Starting the DOM Viewer

To use DOM Viewer, follow these steps:

1. Download the source file at `brainjar.com/dhtml/domviewer/domviewer.html`. Save the file in the same folder as your application.

2. Add a test link to your page to launch the viewer:

   ```
   <a href="domviewer.html" target="_blank">View in DOM Viewer</a>
   ```

   Alternatively, you can add a script to the end of your HTML page in which you wish to inspect:

   ```
   <script type="application/x-javascript">
   window.open('domviewer.html');
   </script>
   ```

   The problem with this solution, however, is that iUI gets in the way of the default open action if you are using an iUI-based application.

3. Save the file.

4. Open the page inside of Mobile Safari. If needed, click the View in DOM Viewer link.

The DOM Viewer is displayed in a new pane inside of Mobile Safari (see Figure 12-12). Interact with it as desired.

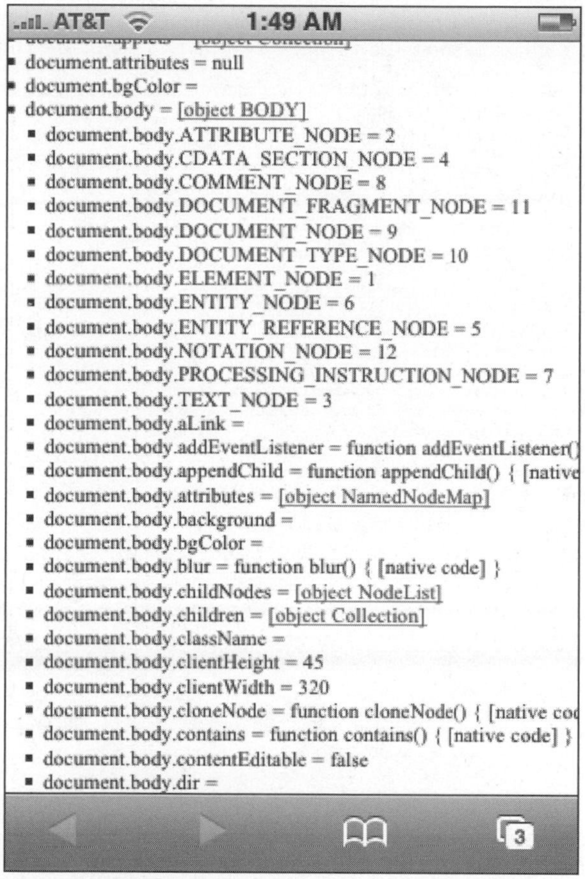

Figure 12-12: DOM Viewer

Specifying a Root Node

One of the things you will immediately notice when working with the DOM Viewer inside of the small iPhone viewport is the sheer amount of information you have to scroll through to find what you are looking for. To address this issue, DOM Viewer allows you to specify a particular node (identified by `id`) as the document root (see Figure 12-13). Here's the code to add, specifying the desired element as the `getElementById()` parameter:

```
<script type="application/x-javascript">
  var DOMViewerObj = document.getElementById("Jack_Armitage")
  var DOMViewerName = null;
</script>
```

277

Figure 12-13: Specifying a root node for the DOM Viewer

Because it will reference the desired element directly by `getElementById()`, you can add this code in your HTML page *after* the element you wish to examine in the body but not before it.

Go to `brainjar.com/dhtml/domviewer` for full details on the DOM Viewer.

Index